MILITARIZED MODERNITY AND

GENDERED CITIZENSHIP IN SOUTH KOREA

POLITICS, HISTORY, AND CULTURE

A series from the International Institute
at the University of Michigan

Series Editors: George Steinmetz and Julia Adams

Series Editorial Advisory Board: Fernando Coronil,
Mamadou Diouf, Michael Dutton, Geoff Eley, Fatma
Müge Göcek, Nancy Rose Hunt, Andreas Kalyvas Webb
Keane, David Laitin, Lydia Liu, Julie Skurski, Margaret
Somers, Ann Laura Stoler, Katherine Verdery, Elizabeth
Wingrove

Sponsored by the International Institute at the University
of Michigan and published by Duke University Press, this
series is centered around cultural and historical studies of
power, politics, and the state—a field that cuts across the
disciplines of history, sociology, anthropology, political
science, and cultural studies. The focus on the relationship between state and culture refers both to a method-
ological approach—the study of politics and the state
using culturalist methods—and to a substantive one that
treats signifying practices as an essential dimension of
politics. The dialectic of politics, culture, and history figures prominently in all the books selected for the series.

MILITARIZED MODERNITY AND

GENDERED CITIZENSHIP IN SOUTH KOREA

Seungsook Moon

Duke University Press *Durham and London* 2005

© 2005 Duke University Press

All rights reserved

Printed in the United States of

America on acid-free paper ∞

Designed by Amy Ruth Buchanan

Typeset in Minion by Tseng

Information Systems, Inc.

Library of Congress Cataloging-in-

Publication Data appear on the last

printed page of this book.

To Farzin, Dosŏn, and Mahin

CONTENTS

ACKNOWLEDGMENTS

In the process of doing research and writing this book, I have benefited from the support of numerous individuals. Graciously sharing their time and thoughts, many people turned the seemingly solitary endeavor into intersubjective engagements. I would like to thank Roger Janelli, Laurel Kendall, and Uma Narayan for reading an earlier version of this book. I would also like to thank Nancy Abelmann, Cynthia Enloe, and John Lie for their interests in my work and reading all or parts of a later version. Their comments were very helpful for sharpening my ideas. I also owe thanks to Martha Kaplan and Eileen Leonard for their intellectual support. I gained substantially from my conversations with Joo-hyun Cho, Hyaeweol Choi, Chŏng-hŭi Kim, Seung Kyung Kim, and Kwang-yŏung Shin at various stages of writing this book.

The birth of this book would not have been possible without the generous assistance I received from Vassar College, including a one-year sabbatical leave and several faculty research grants. My appointment as a visiting scholar at the Korea Institute at Harvard University during fall 2002 and fall 2003 also facilitated my writing. My thanks go to Carter Eckert, Sunjoo Kim, and David McCann for cordially hosting me. I would also like to thank J. Reynolds Smith, my editor at Duke University Press, for appreciating my work for what it is and recognizing its relevance beyond Korean studies or East Asian studies. Although this book is a study separate from my dissertation, special thanks go to my mentors Gordon Fellman and Shulamit Reinharz at Brandeis University, who have given me enduring nurturance.

Joy Hyun Kim at the Korea Heritage Library at the University of Southern California and Angy Kim and Peter Owens, my student assistants at Vassar College, gave me reliable assistance for my research. I would also like to thank the late T'ae-wu Yi and Paek-kwan Sŏng for helping me to carry out research at the Institute for Defense Analysis.

For collecting the valuable pictures that appear in this book, I am indebted to In-Seob Kim and Chong-ch'ang Yi at Yonsei University libraries, who scanned old photographs I found. Ŭn-gyŏng Yi at Yonsei University library helped me to identify the journalists who took some of these pictures. I also owe thanks to Yŏngch'ŏl Kim and Sŏn-mi Kim at the Yonhap News Agency. T'ae-hyŏng Kim at Maeil Newspaper Company generously provided me with a complimentary copy of a valuable picture he took.

I owe immeasurable thanks to Farzin Vahdat for his love, care, and great sense of humor, which I needed often during the process of working on this project. He was my intellectual and emotional partner in the journey of developing and completing this book.

A NOTE ON KOREAN LANGUAGE CONVENTIONS

The romanization of Korean words and names in this book follows the McCune-Reischauer system except for a name whose personal orthography is publicly known. The transliteration of Korean names in the main text, as well as in parenthetical citations, notes, and references, follows the Korean way of writing surname and given name without a comma between them.

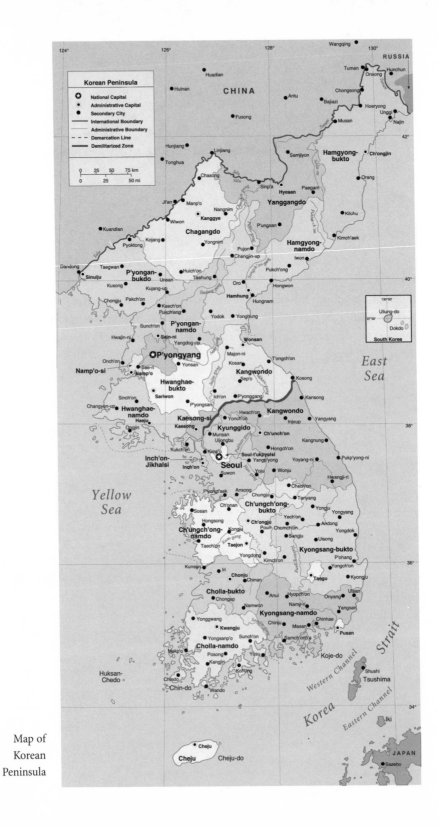

Map of
Korean
Peninsula

INTRODUCTION

*The Gender Politics of Nation Building and
Citizenship in South Korea*

The point is that countries which come late to the process of development possess social structures which must be understood in their own
terms rather than merely as "transitional stages" to the type of industrialized society exemplified by the English or, better still, the American case.

—Reinhard Bendix, *Nation Building and Citizenship*

This book is a postcolonial feminist study of the politics of
membership in the modern Korean nation. In this study, I adopt the notion
of modernity to engage in a critical reflection on the dramatic social transformation in South Korea for the past three decades or so. Drawing on insights
from cultural studies, I conceive of modernity as a "keyword," in Raymond
Williams's sense,[1] used by different social groups to describe a desirable (or
undesirable) direction of contemporary social change. While modernity can
be defined specifically as a set of normative values and social conditions drawn
from the theoretical and empirical discourse of modernity in the West, I prefer
to approach it as an array of global and local claims, commitments, and knowledge whose specific meanings are determined in the context of asymmetrical
power relations among (national) societies and (intranational) social groups.
This cultural approach to modernity allows us to open space for the study of
social change in "other" societies in their own terms. The cultural politics of
modernity do not reduce modernity to merely an empty sign, as semiotics may
suggest, that can be filled with any arbitrary permutations of meanings. Histories of colonialism and neocolonialism, as well as current power inequalities
among nation-states and among internal social groups in a given (national)
society, circumscribe the ways in which modernity is imagined and such mean-

ing is contested. Therefore, the interpretive and cultural approach to modernity highlights the global and local politics of the meanings of modernity and concerns itself with the following questions: Who imagines what constitutes modernity, and under what sociopolitical conditions is it imagined? How is the hegemonic meaning of (Western) modernity interpreted and reinvented by diverse local actors? To what extent is the meaning of modernity appropriated by the developmental state accepted, contested, or subverted by those who are mobilized by it in the name of national modernization?

During the military rule in postcolonial South Korea, the elites who controlled the state adopted the notion of modernity associated with a strong military and high productivity based on advanced technology that conservative nationalist leaders of the Chosŏn Dynasty had imagined at the end of the nineteenth century. In the context of the Cold War rivalry and military confrontation with North Korea, Park Chung Hee's regime pursued this interpretation of modernity as a nation-building project. I have conceived the notion of militarized modernity to illuminate the three related processes of sociopolitical and economic formation: the construction of the modern nation as an anticommunist polity, the making of its members as duty-bound "nationals," and the integration of the institution of male conscription into the organization of the industrializing economy. These processes were characterized by the amalgamation of violent coercion and Foucauldian discipline during the period of militarized modernity (1963–1987).

To build a wealthy and (militarily) strong nation as the embodiment of modernity required the state to mobilize its populace on a mass scale. We need to consider two points regarding mass mobilization. First, the path of mass mobilization was structured not only by the instrumental notion of modernity but also by a hegemonic understanding of the proper places of women and men in the modern nation. Underlying this understanding was the gender ideology that constructed man as a protector and family provider and woman as a reproducer of children and daily life. Accordingly, men were called on to perform mandatory military service and encouraged to become the primary labor force in the industrializing economy. In contrast, marginalized as a secondary workforce in the economy despite their economic contribution, women were exhorted to carry out birth control and the "rational management of the household." Second, the peculiar nature of the nation-state that generated the powerful perception of common destiny between rulers and the ruled turned such gendered processes of mass mobilization into moments of willing participation to varying degrees among different social groups.

In the context of the political transition from military rule to procedural democracy in the late 1980s and early 1990s, grassroots social movements began to replace the established practices of mass mobilization tinted with willing participation. Combined with the end of the Cold War elsewhere and globalization, procedural democratization led to the uneven decline of militarized modernity and became an enabling condition for the emergence of a new type of political membership, characterized by the struggle to monitor the powerful and demand rights vis-à-vis the state. Highlighting the willingness to fight to give substance to formal rights, I call this new type of political membership (substantive) citizenship. I argue that the emergence of citizenship is the unintended and dialectical consequence of gendered mass mobilization because women and men who were called to contribute to the process of nation building were commonly exposed to repressive discipline and violent punishment, and the specific paths of gendered mobilization shaped the ways in which women and men forged their new political subjectivity as citizens. My research indicates significant differences between men and women in terms of their citizenship trajectories. Women came to acquire citizenship through the autonomous women's movement to achieve equal employment, a movement that supported the concerns and interests of working-class and middle-class women. In comparison, men's emergence as citizens took two class-specific routes: college-educated middle-class men used new "citizens' organizations" that grew after 1987, and the upper segment of working-class men used "democratic labor unions." I argue that the gender distinction in class alliance is linked to women's marginalization, regardless of class, in the industrializing economy in almost all sectors of employment. Yet I do not intend to exaggerate this cross-class alliance in the women's movement; rather, such an alliance becomes meaningful in comparison with the visibility of class division in the trajectory of men's citizenship.

RETHINKING THE FRAMEWORK FOR STUDYING
SOCIAL CHANGE IN EAST ASIAN SOCIETIES

A majority of studies of contemporary social change in East Asia have focused on rapid industrialization within the framework of "economic development."[2] Recently, responding to the growth of civil society and the political transition to procedural democracy, some scholars of East Asia have begun to pay attention to the processes of "political development."[3] Emphasizing a replicable model of economic and political development, many studies of social change in East Asia within the framework of "development" studies have attempted to identify facilitators of, and constraints on, capitalist economy and procedural democracy. In doing so, these studies tend to assume that modernity is a "Western" phenomenon in the sense of being its property or heirloom, and therefore that social change in Korea (and other East Asian societies), as a latecomer in the pantheon of modern nation-states, is to be measured in terms of the fixed trappings of modernity observed in Western societies. Some of the development studies continue to suggest that non-Western societies achieve development by transplanting modern (read implicitly as "Western") institutions and values to their soil. Responding to the recent wave of industrialization in East Asia, however, others have generated a *culturalist* account for the "East Asian model of development," stressing "Confucian" values and the role of the authoritarian developmental state.[4] Retreating from the earlier version of the Orientalist dichotomy between the Western self, which is modern, advanced, and civilized, and the non-Western other, which is premodern (or antimodern), backward, and uncivilized,[5] this culturalist discourse tends to overlook historical change in (nationalized) cultures in East Asia and specific power relations defining what constitutes apparently uniform national cultures.[6]

In questioning the Eurocentric view of modernity and articulating a postcolonial view of it, I do not intend to essentialize cultural differences among societies as if they were devoid of histories, or to embrace relativism as if there were no intersubjective human experience, understanding, and knowledge, as certain strands of postmodernism imply.[7] Nor do I deny the influence, on forging modernities in non-Western societies, of hegemonic components of historically Western modernity such as instrumental rationality, bureaucratic institutions of capitalist economy and representative government, and the ideals of individual freedom and equality. Rather, by questioning the uniform and fixed meaning of modernity tied to the West as its privileged originator, I intend to highlight the politics of meanings that exist at the core of the dichotomous categorization of concepts and ideas—for example, Western/foreign versus non-Western/indigenous. I also intend to recognize the hybrid nature of modernity in specific national contexts, including Western national societies; modernity is neither purely Western nor purely indigenous to a specific local society.[8] Since the period of colonialism and imperialism, the notion of modernity has traveled across linguistic and cultural boundaries, and its meanings have been appropriated and reinvented by various social groups in a host society.[9] When we recognize the interpretive agency of local actors who are mobilized to transform their social worlds in the name of modernity, modernity becomes as local as it is "Western." This recognition enables us to investigate active responses to the notion of modernity in different local contexts and helps us illuminate the agency of women and men who contest hegemonic meanings of modernity in their historical and social contexts.

John Duncan's study of "the plasticity of Confucianism" in Korea throughout the late nineteenth century and the twentieth (2002) suggests that the politics of meaning are not limited to "foreign" concepts. (I enclose the term in quotation marks because it is not self-evident when what is imported becomes indigenous or remains foreign, and who draws such temporal and spatial boundaries.) Duncan shows that the meaning of Confucianism is not fixed but is reinterpreted by nationalist intellectuals, reformers, political leaders, and social activists in relation to their effort to reform Korea. What is noteworthy in these types of inquiries is that, unlike a normative definition of a concept, their focus on the reinterpretation and reinvention of concepts' meanings allows us to see the politics of meanings among various groups of interpreters in employing the dichotomous categorization of concepts and ideas.

The recognition of the hybridity of modernity and the interpretive agency of women and men allows us to decolonize knowledge produced about postcolonial societies.[10] The Eurocentric view of modernity that represents the West as its privileged originator also represents women and men in "other" societies as passive recipients or mere imitators of values, knowledge, and institutions associated with Western modernity.[11] Or worse, these women and men are represented as unable even to receive or imitate because of their "antimodern" culture, which is often essentialized as a body of fixed ideas and rituals.[12] The varying degrees of the Orientalist gaze at women and men in East Asian societies in the discourse of the so-called East Asian model of development obscure the complex processes in which they experience modernity beneath the appearance of passive mobilization by the authoritarian state.

Building on the scholarship on the cultural politics of modernity (and tradition), this study intends to understand the South Korean path to modernity in terms of the making and remaking of political subjectivities of women and men in the process of mass mobilization and its aftermath. To capture the slippery agency of women and men who are mobilized by the modernizing state in South Korea, beyond their interpretive dimension, requires the examination of the way in which the state constructed these women and men as "nationals" (*kungmin*) in its pursuit of modernity, and the extent to which they have emerged as citizens in the aftermath of this mobilization. This approach to social change enables me to place women and men affected by it at the center of my analysis.[13]

FROM GENDER AND INDUSTRIALIZATION TO THE
GENDER POLITICS OF MODERN NATION BUILDING

In critical responses to gender-blind studies of rapid industrialization in East Asia, during the past decade some students of East Asian political economy have examined gendered processes of industrialization.[14] Most of these studies focus on the impact of the economic transformation on various groups of women, and on gender relations in household and workplace. In particular, these studies investigate the patriarchal nature of industrial development of the "miracle" economies of East Asia, a perspective that marginalizes women in the industrializing economies.[15] Conceptualizing gender as an organizing principle in society, most of these studies go beyond the questions raised by women and development studies about women's experiences and the impact of industrialization on women. They also move away from the Marxist feminist reduction of women's subordination to the logic of capital accumulation.[16] They provide us with accounts of women's subordination in terms of their specific structural positions located in the interplay between the processes of production and reproduction, paying attention to the sexual division of labor rooted in the household as the core of the "social relations of gender" shaping industrialization (Elson and Pearson 1981).[17]

Yet the approach to industrialization primarily as the transformation of political economy tends to obscure the political and cultural dimension of this transformation, including the meaning of industrialization as a crucial requirement of modern nationhood and the extent to which the Cold War shaped the processes of nation building in decolonized or non-Western societies. The historical significance of the Cold War for the pursuit of modernity in these societies cannot be overemphasized, because the notion of economic development as the dominant path to modernity in the postwar era was born from a perception that poverty was the hotbed of communism.[18] Specifically, through economic development as well as military alliances, the "free world" was to "protect" its former colonies and new allies against impending threats from insidious communists. In other words, the idea of economic development was intimately linked to the strategic and political interests of the capitalist West in the Cold War rivalry. In this global equation, East Asia occupied a crucial geopolitical position because Japan, South Korea, Taiwan, and Vietnam (before its communization) functioned as frontline bulwarks against the communist Soviet Union and the People's Republic of China. After the collapse of the Eastern Bloc, the Cold War rivalry has been replaced by (economic) globalization. Yet the implications of the Cold War for nation building in East Asian societies still deserve serious attention. While social histories of the gender politics of modern nation building in relation to the Cold War in various East Asian countries are yet to be written, this book hopes to contribute to such inquiry by focusing on South Korea, which is arguably one of the countries most affected by the Cold War; in fact, as the eruptions of nuclear-weapons crises in 1994 and the early years of the twenty-first century indicate, the Cold War lingers on in the Korean peninsula in the post–Cold War era.[19]

Approaching industrialization as an integral part of modern nation building, I use the notion of militarized modernity to capture the peculiar combination of Foucauldian discipline and militarized violence that permeated the Korean society in the process of building a modern nation in the context of the Cold War. In particular, I focus on discipline and violence observed in the interplay between the militarized nation, constructed as the anticommunist self that is at war with communist North Korea, and its members, whose political identities were forged and contested in the process of mobilization and its aftermath. I argue that gender shaped the process of mass mobilization of Koreans, whom the modernizing state constructed as a unified people, and in turn the gendered paths of mobilization shaped the ways in which women and men obtained new political subjectivity as citizens in the process of the collective struggle to redefine the nature of their membership in the nation. This means that the asymmetry of gender relations in the economy and politics of contemporary Korea needs to be explained in terms of the specific ways in which women and men are incorporated into the nation.

Words of caution are necessary here to avoid possible misunderstandings about the notion of militarized modernity. I do not intend to reduce the complex phenomenon of South Korean modernity to militarization. I conceive militarization not as a single factor but as a changing process that has permeated various aspects of South Korean society.[20] Nor do I intend to overlook the importance of ongoing change to the nature of South Korean modernity, whose hegemonic meaning is challenged by competing commitments and knowledge concerning the desired direction of contemporary social change within the state and growing civil society. Rather, I use the notion of militarized modernity to illuminate the peculiar combination of historical circumstances under which modernity has been pursued in South Korea: national division, the civil war and the prolonged military confrontation between the two Koreas, postcolonial ambivalence to modernity, and the extreme sense of urgency about catching up with advanced countries.

RETHINKING CITIZENSHIP AND GENDER

A series of national and transnational political changes since the 1970s has generated growing interest in the study of citizenship.[21] These changes included (procedural) democratization in third-world countries and former Eastern Bloc countries, increasing transnational migration, and the rise of the new Rights in the West that was linked to the weakening of the welfare states. While debates about these changes tend to highlight the formalistic dimension of citizenship rights entitling one to access resources in a national community, some scholars have been interested in the notion of active citizenship, emphasizing citizens' political mobilization and participation. In line with this democratic view of citizenship, I find recent feminist scholarship on citizenship fruitful in moving beyond the formalistic and unilineal evolutionary model that has been dominant in the literature on citizenship.

Feminist scholars have pointed out that despite its universalistic locution, the application of the notion of citizenship and access to citizens' rights has varied from one social group to another, depending on the group's position embedded in the social structures of inequalities (Yuval-Davis 1997, 68; Lister 1997, chap. 3; Walby 1994, 384). Hence some feminists are cautious about the notion of citizenship, and others reject it as a male or masculinist concept and replace it with maternal thinking. Critically responding to this line of debate, Mary Dietz (1996) envisions a democratic view of citizenship thus:

> For a concept of citizenship, feminists should turn to relations and practices that are expressly contextual, institutional, and political, informed by and situated within particular cultures and histories, and oriented toward action. What this requires, among other things, is a project that conceptualizes politics . . . differently than the Liberal, the Marxist, or the Maternalist views. That conception I will loosely call "democratic" insofar as it takes politics to entail the collective and participatory engagement of historically situated and culturally constituted persons-as-citizens in the determination of the affairs of their polity. The polity is a public space, a locale or realm or arena: it may manifest itself at the level of the neighborhood (rural, urban, metropolitan, suburban), the town or city, the state, the region, the nation, or the globe, or even in "cyberspace." (34–35)

Similarly, going beyond merely arguing that citizenship is a masculinist concept, Ruth Lister reconstructs the notion of citizenship; she redefines it not only as a formal status, characterized by a set of rights and obligations vis-à-vis the state, but also as the practice of such rights and obligations, including the struggle to gain new rights and give substance to formal rights that already exist. At its heart, citizenship is an expression of the human agency to transform oneself and the social world governed by the nation-state (1997, 36–39, 41). In light of these insights, I define citizenship as a democratic membership in the body politic characterized by active struggle and negotiation to give substance to formal rights and redefine their boundaries.

MILITARY SERVICE AS A NODAL POINT IN MILITARIZED MODERNITY AND THE GENDER POLITICS OF MEMBERSHIP IN THE NATION

Rarely explored in studies of social change in South Korea, military service has been a pivotal component in the state's mobilization of gendered nationals and the emergence of citizenship in the aftermath of militarized modernity. Some scholars investigating Korean political economy from various perspectives have mentioned the striking resemblance between the modern military and large blue-collar and white-collar companies in their daily working and social relations (Koo 2001; Lie 1998; Janelli 1993; Choong Soon Kim 1992; Kearney 1991; Bae Kyuhan 1987). Yet these scholars' observations of business firms do not lead to an analysis of militarized modernity characterized by the construction of the militarized nation, the making of its members, and the integration of military service into the organization of the industrializing economy. There are certain historical and sociopolitical factors contributing to the peculiar function of military service in South Korea. First, South Korean society has been entangled in a prolonged military confrontation with North Korea for half a century, ever since the Korean War (1950–53). This situation contributed to the development of a postcolonial state that has exploited anticommunism as national orthodoxy and imagined modernity in terms of building a strong military to protect the nation. Here I do not intend to exaggerate Korea's peculiarity in militarized national security, since the modern nation-state tends to rely ultimately on military means to safeguard its claim to territorial sovereignty. Yet its quasi-religious fervor in ruthlessly persecuting dissidents and labeling them "communists," combined with the dominance of the issue of military security, particularly during the decades of repressive military rule, set South Korea apart from many other nation-states. A cornerstone of the

strong military in South Korea has been the "universal male conscription system" (*kungmingaebyŏngje*) that has mobilized the masses of young men.

Second, completely overlooked by scholarship on the political economy of
Korean industrialization, the use of conscripts as workers and researchers in
the industrializing economy was institutionalized under the military service
special cases law, enforced from 1973 onward. Although this practice still exists,
its economic and social significance as a means to build a nation has been un-
raveled, throughout the 1990s, by economic globalization and procedural democratization in South Korea. That is, the institution of military service was
an integral part of economic development pursued as a way to build a wealthy
and strong nation.

Third, it is important to pay attention to specific forms of military recruitment, because the form of recruitment shapes the relationship between the
nation-state and its gendered citizens. As social theorists have argued, the
process of state formation is embedded in war making and the attempt to
monopolize the means of organized violence (Tilly 1992; Giddens 1987). The
maintenance of the military through a specific method of recruitment is therefore central to the nation-state's sustained claim to territorial sovereignty, and
this territoriality in turn constitutes the very sociopolitical context in which
gendered citizenship is constructed, maintained, and potentially contested.
This emphasis on the military does not mean that the relation of the military
to the state remains constant as the state evolves in a specific social and historical context. The "civilizing process" (Elias 1939/1997) of "internal pacification"
(Giddens 1987) and the rise of "hegemony" (Gramsci 1971) certainly reduce
the relative importance of the military in domestic politics and social relations
among civilians. Yet the imperative to secure military power as the ultimate
recourse in both domestic and international politics makes military service a
significant factor to be reckoned with in any study of the gender politics of
membership in the nation.[22]

DATA COLLECTION

In this study I have made use of primary and secondary sources on the conscription system, the state's women's policy (*yŏsŏngjŏngch'aek*) and "administration of women" (*punyŏhaengjŏng*), and grassroots social movements to
democratize Korean society. While my primary sources were mostly textual
materials, they also included informal conversations and interviews I conducted with members of the Korean Women's Associations United, govern-

ment employees at the Office of Military Manpower, the Korea Women's Development Institute, and the Korea Institute for Defense Analysis, and personnel managers of three major *chaebol* companies (economic conglomerates). The bulk of my research was conducted during a field trip to Seoul between October 1998 and January 1999, during which Korean society was recovering from the shock of the 1997 economic crisis. A smaller part of my research was conducted during the summer of 1996 and winters of 2000 and 2001. Gathering information on the state's policies on military service and related issues was at times not easy, even in the present context of procedural democratization. A particular problem was that comprehensive statistics on military manpower are either unavailable or inaccessible, since they are considered "sensitive" to "national security." I was able to collect some government documents regarding military service policies from various libraries, and others I obtained from the Office of Military Manpower (OMM) and the Korea Institute for Defense Analysis (KIDA).

My access to the OMM was relatively smooth because the office has publicly tried to portray an "open" and "service-oriented" administration of military recruitment to improve the public perception of military service and the military in general in the period of civilian administration. This administrative effort to promote a new and more democratic image of the office definitely helped my access to it as an individual scholar.[23] My visits to the KIDA, on the other hand, were arranged through a personal connection, since this organization is not open to the public. Both the OMM and the KIDA were heavily masculinized apparatuses of the state. The only women at the KIDA were administrative assistants. A few more women worked in the General Affairs Division at the OMM, where information was collected, and more women in another building with service windows, where prospective conscripts and their families received information and assistance concerning the process of military recruitment.

OVERVIEW

Focusing on the period of militarized modernity (1963–1987), part 1 traces the mass mobilization of men and women as "dutiful nationals" (kungmin) in the process of building the modern nation and the extent to which this process was intertwined with the militarization of the nation and the labor market. Chapter 1 begins with a historical discussion of how nationalist leaders in Korea at the beginning of the twentieth century imagined modernity in their desire to construct a strong and wealthy nation. The historical discussion also explores the continuity between Japanese colonial rule and the postcolonial military rule in terms of specific tactics of disciplining the populace for mass mobilization. The chapter then goes on to examine the rise of militarized modernity in contemporary Korea, focusing on the militarization of the national identity and the labor market, and the molding of the populace into dutiful nationals (kungmin) through discipline and violent punishment. Chapter 2 analyzes the ways in which men were mobilized for mandatory military service and the building of the industrial economy. I argue that men's military mobilization and economic mobilization were intimately intertwined and that this combination contributed to the consolidation of the modern gender hierarchy, organized around the division of labor between man as provider and woman as housewife. Chapter 3 analyzes the ways in which women were mobilized as producers and reproducers. I argue that women's economic mobilization as factory workers in fact marginalized women in the industrializing economy and that women's membership in the industrializing nation was defined in terms of their roles as breeders and household managers.

The analysis of separate paths of gendered mobilization reveals the different ways in which women and men were integrated into the nation being built. Unlike the later discussion in part 2, the analysis in part 1 does not highlight class distinction but juxtaposes women as a group with men as a group, because the modernizing state de-emphasized class distinction within each gender group in its nationalist rhetoric of Koreans as a unified people. The analysis of the interplay between the state and grassroots women and men also reveals the extent to which the repressive rule of the modernizing state coexisted with the hegemony of the nationalist project of building a (militarily) strong and wealthy nation. That is, militarized modernity shows the coexistence of Foucauldian disciplinary power and the extensive use of violent punishment for those who did not conform.

Focusing on the period of postmilitary rule (1988–2002), part 2 explores the ways in which, and the extent to which, men and women forge their new political subjectivity as citizens. In this discussion, citizenship is defined not merely as a legal status conferred by the state but as democratic membership in the body politic, characterized by the human struggle to give substance to that formal status. From this perspective, a citizen is an actor willing to struggle and negotiate to obtain and protect rights and fulfill obligations and is thereby able to redefine the substance of entitlements and obligations. Highlighting the emergence of social movements in revitalized civil society in post-1987

Korea, chapter 4 discusses the uneven decline of militarized modernity and the rise of the counterhegemonic discourse of democratization generated by grassroots social movement organizations that envisioned a new membership in the democratic body politic. Chapter 5 examines the constraint that military mobilization poses for men's emergence as citizens and the significance of the labor movement for the trajectory of men's citizenship. I argue that there are two distinct paths to citizenship for men in Korea: one is the "citizens' movement" in which educated middle-class men forge their identity as citizens, and the other is the labor movement led by the upper section of working-class men in the heavy-industry sector. Yet the citizens' movement did not challenge men's military mobilization in the process of procedural democratization in Korea, whereas the labor movement challenges the fundamental construction of workers as duty-bound "nationals." The labor movement has also provided a model of a citizenship path for men and women who are employed in other industrial sectors. Chapter 6 examines the trajectory of women's citizenship in the process of contesting their economic marginalization caused by the gendered mobilization during the period of militarized modernity. I identify two distinct paths to women's citizenship: one is the factory workers' labor movement actively supported by interclass autonomous women's associations, and the other is the interclass and middle-class women's movements to obtain lifetime equal employment for women of all classes. What distinguishes the trajectory of women's citizenship from the trajectory of men's citizenship includes the central role of autonomous women's associations and the relatively interclass nature of the collective struggle for citizenship.

The analysis of the trajectory of gendered citizenship in part 2 is by nature preliminary because the transformation of women and men into citizens began only in the past decade. The decline of militarized modernity is significant and far reaching in the long run but in no way presents a radical rupture from the past. After the summit meeting between North Korea and South Korea in June 2000, the inter-Korea relationship has undergone some dramatic shifts, including the discussion of removing land mines from the Demilitarized Zone (DMZ), rebuilding railroads and highways across the DMZ, and increasing South Korean investment in North Korean economic development. Nevertheless, a crucial condition of militarized modernity such as the national division justifying the ideologies of anticommunism and (militarized) national security remains an underlying reality in the apparently demilitarized landscape of the vibrant consumer society in South Korea. For example, the National Security Law, the linchpin of the anticommunist national identity, which has frequently been abused in the persecution of political dissidents and labor activists, persisted even under Kim Dae Jung's regime. Although he, as a leading dissident, was repeatedly accused and prosecuted for violating this law by the military regimes under Park and Chun, Mr. Kim could not dismantle them, even after he became president, in the face of conservative social and political forces. Under the presidency of Roh Moo Hyun (2003–7) there has been deep division between those who support the law's elimination and those who oppose it. Recognizing these ambiguities, I hope to contribute to our understanding of the changing nature of membership in the body politic in South Korea and beyond.

MILITARIZED MODERNITY AND

GENDERED MASS MOBILIZATION,

1963–1987

1 THE HISTORICAL ROOTS AND THE RISE OF MILITARIZED MODERNITY

To build the economy and strengthen national defense, national solidarity and total unity are the most important things for us in confrontation with the communist North. The most harmful things for us are
corruption, impropriety, and the lack of discipline.
— Park Chung Hee, in a cabinet meeting on November 12, 1976

Historians of ideas usually attribute the dream of a perfect society to the
philosophers and jurists of the eighteenth century; but there was also a
military dream of society; its fundamental reference was not to the state
of nature, but to the meticulously subordinated cogs of a machine, not
to the primary social contract, but to permanent coercions, not to fundamental rights, but to indefinitely progressive forms of training, not
to the general will but to automatic docility.
— Michel Foucault, *Discipline and Punish*

Few dreams could be more enchanting to leaders of twentieth-
century Korea than that of building a wealthy and strong nation. Turning such
an ambitious dream into reality in the face of uneven domestic and international power relationships entailed the discovery of individual members of the
nation as useful bodies, and the remolding of those members into useful and
docile instruments of the nation-state. Indeed, it was a nightmarish process of
dehumanization that underlay the realization of the nationalist dream during
the period of military authoritarian rule, inciting popular protests by workers,
intellectuals, and students. This chapter traces how nationalist intellectuals
imagined the Korean nation and its members at the end of the nineteenth century and how Japanese colonial rule informed the Korean path to modernity

pursued by the postcolonial military regimes. Then it discusses the emergence of militarized modernity and its trajectory during the period of military authoritarian rule,[1] focusing on its defining characteristics: the construction of the Korean nation as the anticommunist body politic, the remolding of individuals into useful and docile members of the nation through "discipline" and physical force, and the integration of military service into the organization of the industrializing economy. The anticommunist national identity was crucial to disciplinary control over members of the nation in that it provided ruling regimes with ideological justification for the surveillance, normalization, and repressive violence exercised over the people. As discussed in chapter 2, the militarization of the economy resulted from the imperative to remold men to accept military service.

The development of militarized modernity as a sociopolitical and economic formation in the period of military rule resulted from the coordinated use of various techniques for discipline and punishment that have existed in Korea and elsewhere in an effort to build a modern nation under the peculiar combination of historical conditions of national division, war and military confrontation, postcolonial ambivalence to modernity, and the urgency to catch up with advanced nations. Emerging earlier than other characteristics of militarized modernity, the anticommunist national identity was consolidated in the 1960s through the Korean involvement in the Vietnam War, as well as the continuing military confrontation with North Korea. Park Chung Hee's regime also adopted new and old techniques of remaking the populace into useful and docile members of the nation in the 1960s, including the institution of the resident registration system, the ubiquitous display of anticommunist mottoes, the revival of administered mass organizations and the conversion system, and the use of schools and the television network. The military service extra-points system, an element of the militarized labor market, also began in the early 1960s. It was in the mid-1970s that other central elements of the militarized labor market, such as the enforcement of military service completion as a precondition for employment and the conventional recognition of military service as work experience, were established. The pursuit of militarized modernity reached its peak in the 1970s, the decade of extensive mass mobilization for building heavy industries and "self-reliant national defense," and began to show some signs of decline in the 1980s.

This historical discussion is intended to offer a larger context for understanding how the gender politics of membership in the nation have been intertwined with the pursuit of modernity. This discussion also suggests that, reflecting the dark side of modernity grasped by Max Weber and Michel Foucault, militarized modernity approximates the military dream of modern society, whose members are reduced to efficient tools of a machine producing national wealth and safeguarding national security. While disciplinary modernity in the West, Foucault argues, stemmed from the imperative to manage increasing multiplicities of humans and economic production (1979, 218), militarized modernity in South Korea sprang from the combination of the following conditions in contemporary Korea: that the postcolonial state had to cope with the exigencies of building a modern nation, via the establishment of a national identity and the discipline of its population, in a modern world characterized by increasing "rationalization," all in the context of national division, the Korean War, and the Cold War.

Having emphasized the peculiarity of Korea, I recognize that militarized modernity in South Korea shares crucial features with fascist modernities in Germany and Japan during the first half of the twentieth century, including the rule of authoritarian regimes involved in preparing and waging war, mass mobilization of the populace through administered mass organizations, and the latecomer's urgency to equal the progress of advanced Western nations. Yet postcoloniality and the national division in the context of the Cold War compel me to distinguish South Korea from Germany and Japan before World War II. Korea's colonization by Japan, the only non-Western colonizer, intensified South Korea's need to catch up with modern nations and its postcolonial ambivalence toward modernity that stemmed from the indelible historical connection between modernity and the advanced Western countries as dominant colonizers (Seungsook Moon 2002c, 483). Showing a historical parallel to South Korea, the divided Germany during the Cold War was followed by the rule of democratic regimes and the critical reflection on its fascist past.

IMAGINING MODERNITY AT THE TWILIGHT OF CONFUCIAN SOCIETY

The hegemonic meaning of modernity in postcolonial South Korea has hinged on this latecomer's perceived imperative to build a modern nation with an industrial economy and a strong military. The equation of modernity with economic and military strength is not peculiar to postcolonial Korea; this view of modernity has its roots in the violent encounter between colonizing powers and colonized societies in the past.

Facing the internal and external challenges of frequent peasant rebellions and of foreign powers who extracted economic and military concessions, the ruling elite of the Chosŏn Dynasty (1392–1910) was forced in the late nineteenth century to adopt some reformist ideas to maintain its privilege to rule. Those reformist ideas were articulated by a group of Confucian scholars known as the *kaehwap'a* (enlightenment faction), who advocated the adoption of Western technology to strengthen the nation. The enlightenment faction was divided into a radical faction, supporting the reduction of monarchical authority,[2] and a moderate faction, espousing the preservation of the Confucian monarchy. Kim Yun-sik (1835–1922), a Confucian bureaucrat and member of the moderate faction, articulated this second position in the notion of *tongdosŏgi* (Eastern way, Western technology).[3] Resembling the elite nationalist strategy of nineteenth-century Bengal (Chatterjee 1993), this notion separated the material sphere, in which the West was advanced, from the mental sphere, in which the East was supposed to be superior to the West. Accordingly, Kim used Western technology to establish an arsenal and manufacture new weapons but rejected other aspects of Western culture, including democratic ideas and institutions. At its core, the notion of tongdosŏgi was devised to deal with the double challenge of preserving the Confucian order while at the same time adopting advanced technology from the West to "modernize" the military and the financial system. Hence it ignored the urgency of implementing the broader social and political reforms advocated by the radical enlightenment faction.[4] Adopting this ideology after the Sino-Japanese War (1895), in which Japan had been victorious, the Chosŏn monarchy attempted to reinforce its power and renamed itself Taehanjeguk (the Empire of Korea). During the short period of Taehanjeguk (1897–1905), the ruling elite rushed into the importation of Western technologies to build power plants, streetcars, telephone lines, a telegraph system, and railroads (Kang Man-gil 1985).

The instrumental view of modernity implied in the precolonial notion of tongdosŏgi was embraced by the ruling elites of postcolonial South Korea. The hegemonic meaning of modernity highlighted the imperative to build a wealthy nation and a strong army. In particular, the significance of military power to the modern nation was so compelling in the age of colonialism that some nationalist intellectuals (historians, folklorists, and writers) displayed a militaristic orientation in writing a nationalist history. For instance, Shin Ch'ae-ho (1880–1936) and his admirers glorified the military tradition of honor and patriotism in Korean history against the backdrop of (effeminate) colonized Korea (Eckert 2000, 134). This historical legacy of imagining modernity primarily as military and economic superiority has had a lasting impact on the way in which the postcolonial state in South Korea imagined modernity, particularly during Park Chung Hee's rule (1961–79).

Coterminous with the notion of tongdosŏgi was the instrumental view of individual members of the modern nation among nationalist intellectuals. Introducing Western liberalism in his *Sŏyugyŏnmun* (Observations on a Journey to the West [1895]), Yu Kil-jun (1856–1914) imagined members of the Korean nation essentially as dutiful nationals subject to continuous mobilization and control, whose education and improvement were to be undertaken for the purpose of enriching and strengthening the nation-state. This view influenced many other nationalists at the turn of the century, including An Ch'ang-ho. During the first decade of the twentieth century, such dutiful members of the nation acquired a new name, *kungmin*, meaning, literally, "people of the state." Commonly used to refer to the members of the body politic in post-colonial Korea, this term was imported from Japan as a result of the increasing number of Koreans who were studying there in the 1900s. Noteworthy in the discourse of kungmin produced by nationalist newspapers is its connection to the military. *Hwangsŏng Newspaper* (1898–1910) stated that military service was the most important duty for kungmin otherwise entitled to rights given by Heaven. In its distinction between kungmin and *minjok* (ethnos), *Taehan Daily Newspaper* (1904–10) defined kungmin as the artificial formation of collective membership equipped with a barracks mentality constitutive of the strong state, contending that an ethnos could not survive in the modern world without transforming itself into kungmin. The nationalist discourse of kungmin constructed not only the self of the modern nation but also its external and internal others (Pak No-ja 2003, chap. 1). As discussed hereafter, this binary opposition of the self and the other operates as a central mechanism of disciplining kungmin to embrace anticommunism during the period of militarized modernity.

LEGACIES OF COLONIAL MODERNITY: SURVEILLANCE AND NORMALIZATION

The nationalist imagination of individual members of the nation as useful instruments for building a strong and wealthy state became a tumultuous reality during the period of Japanese rule, based on a "highly articulated, disciplined, penetrating colonial bureaucracy" (Cumings 1984, 487). In order to effectively control Koreans, the colonial government established the centralized national police and intelligence network (480). Yet colonial control was more than repressive domination leading to the painstaking disciplining of the colonized population to make them useful and docile instruments to enrich and strengthen imperial Japan. The police were not merely a repressive state apparatus but also a disciplinary institution controlling minuscule details of people's quotidian lives. The police oversaw the implementation of various programs to eradicate "indigenous lifestyles" and make people more useful and efficient, including campaigns for short hair for men, wearing colored clothes (as opposed to traditional white Korean dress), and saving money. The police monitored public hygiene, gathered a range of information about local people, and directed them in farming and in building and repairing roads (Chulwoo Lee 1999, 37). The sprawling expansion of the colonial government into the regulation of infinitesimal details of daily life enhanced Korea's "governability" as the government attempted to remold Koreans into colonial subjects of Japan (40). As I will discuss later, the postcolonial state under military rule appropriated similar disciplinary techniques in the name of building the modern nation.

While the intensification of the colonial state's disciplinary control over Koreans reflected a common feature of the modern state, there was a certain peculiarity in the Japanese version. The Japanese colonial state attempted to exercise control over the minds of its members, involving the "conversion" of ideological offenders and close surveillance of them, even after their conversion and release, during the decades of wartime mobilization in the 1930s and 1940s (Lee Chulwoo 1999, 47). This seemingly bizarre legal practice stemmed from the supralegal emperor system (*tennōsei*), which was reinvented through the Meiji reforms. In the name of promoting the "spiritual integration" of Koreans into the Japanese empire, the colonial state enforced thought control to maintain the integrity of the body politic (*kokutai*) (42). This sort of legal control of the individual mind began with the establishment of the 1907 Security Law that prohibited public meetings and associations, and spiraled down to the 1925 Peace Preservation Law that penalized real and attempted involvement in so-called anti-kokutai organizations (43, 45, 46). Indeed, the discourse of the kokutai reinvented the meaning of modernity in imperial Japan, opposing the liberal notions of social contract, democracy, and rule of law and stressing the integration of individual members into the totality of the state. According to this view, the expression of individual, class, and ethnic interests was not a healthy outcome of complex modern society but a threat to imperial integrity. While even Nazi Germany did not devise any such legal practice aiming at the conversion of thought criminals, postcolonial Korea inherited the "conversion system" (*chŏnhyangjedo*), which was applied mainly to communists, the others of the body politic.

Another colonial practice significant to militarized modernity that was pursued by the postcolonial Korean state was the use of "administered mass organizations" (AMOS), modeled after the modern army, with its hierarchical and national network, to implement state policy.[5] As Louise Young (1998) documents, the imperial Japanese state created numerous AMOS on the basis of residence, gender, age, and occupation to facilitate its access to local populations in Japan proper and in its colonies. Such semiofficial associations allowed the colonial state to develop more direct involvement with local populations and thereby facilitated the increase of its disciplinary power over the populace. For example, the Rural Revitalization Campaign (1932–40) in colonial Korea showed the changing relationship between the state and society, from a merely repressive one toward a more disciplinary one. Through this campaign designed to cope with the rural economic crisis, the colonial government greatly heightened its ability to reach villages. By the outbreak of the Pacific war in 1941, a national network of hierarchical and organic associations was in place that could be deployed for the wartime mobilization of the rural population (Gi-Wook Shin and Han 1999). In line with the Japanese view of modernity that denounced the politicization of the populace for collective or individual interests in favor of the unity of the Japanese empire, AMOS functioned to depoliticize the grassroots population or to preempt its political activation. After decolonization, the AMOS remained intact throughout the periods from the U.S. Army military government (1945–48) to the military regimes of postcolonial Korea.

Undeniably repressive and brutal, the Japanese colonial rule of Korea left not only an extensive infrastructure for industrialization but also military leaders deeply affected by Japanese militarism, particularly the Meiji belief in the role of a strong state in engineering society and solving problems, including the development of the economy (Cumings 1984, 479). A military career, even though it was usually confined to the lower ranks, was one of the few paths of upward mobility open to ambitious Koreans under Japanese colonial rule. The leading officers of the 1961 military coup d'état that resulted in the rise of the developmental state had started their military careers in the later period of Japanese colonial rule (Olsen 1986, 91).

THE RISE OF MILITARIZED MODERNITY

While the imagining of modernity as a social condition characterized by an industrial economy and a strong military in the framework of the nation-state has been shared by many ruling elites in postcolonial societies, the pursuit of modernity as such by the developmental state in South Korea since the early 1960s took a peculiar turn into the emergence of what I call militarized modernity. The core elements of militarized modernity involved the construction of the Korean nation as the anticommunist self at war with the communist other, the constitution of members of the anticommunist body politic through discipline and physical force, and the intertwining of the industrializing economy with military service. The militarization of national identity as such revolved around the ideologies of anticommunism and national security. In other words, South Korea was founded as an anticommunist nation against the "archenemy," North Korea. This ideological construction of the nation enabled the modernizing state to deploy disciplinary techniques of surveillance and normalization, as well as institutionalized violence, in its remolding of individuals and social groups. It also resulted in the ascendance of militarized national security over any other sociopolitical issues and justified the construction of the strong modern military and the integration of men's military service into the organization of the economy.[6]

The Militarized Construction and Maintenance of the Anticommunist Nation

The South Korean state was founded in a maelstrom of decolonization, national partition, and the rise of the Cold War. Born in tandem with the establishment of the state in 1948, the anticommunist national identity had remained hegemonic in the context of prolonged military confrontation between the two Koreas. Crucial to the making of this national identity was the political dynamic during the period of the U.S. Army military government in Korea (1945–48). At the outset of the Cold War rivalry between the United States and the Soviet Union, the USAMG attempted to establish a "friendly" regime in Korea, serving its own political and strategic interests, with a heavy reliance on coercive means. Upon its arrival in the southern half of the peninsula, the USAMG proclaimed that it was the only legitimate authority in the region. With the establishment of the military government, the euphoria of national independence soon evaporated and was followed by the partition of the Korean peninsula into north and south. Throughout its occupation, the USAMG militantly suppressed the indigenous grassroots political movements organized around the Korean People's Republic and the people's committees (Cumings 1981, 441–43).[7]

At the same time, the USAMG collaborated with the conservative landed class and bureaucrats in South Korea who had served the Japanese colonial government. This privileged minority was equally threatened by the mass-based movement aiming at the redistribution of land and other resources.

Therefore the conservative Korean elite and the USAMG shared a fervent anti-communism, to the point of equating any autonomous local movement in the South with communist insurgency sponsored by the Soviet Union, and eradicating it (Cumings 1981, 349, 380). This anticommunist fervor contributed not only to the division of the Korean nation but also to the absence of effective organized opposition to rigid anticommunism for decades to come. Although over time it had gradually given way to pragmatism in the area of foreign policy, anticommunism as the state ideology that defined North Korea as the "chief enemy that poses actual military threat" remained largely intact until the North-South summit meeting in June 2000 (Ministry of National Defense 1998, 51).

Upholding anticommunism as the state ideology, Syngman Rhee's regime (1948–60) continued, on the internal front, to suppress the left-wing press while exercising tight control over the remaining right-wing press under the National Security Law proclaimed in 1948 (Kang Chun-man 1998, 116). Externally, the regime displayed belligerent hostility to North Korea in the context of the escalating politics of the Cold War. As Kim Il Sung was explicit about his desire to "liberate" the South by force, so was Rhee about his desire to "restore" the northern territory by force (Hong Yong-p'yo 1997, 237; Cumings 1990, 388). The mutually militaristic rhetoric was accompanied by several skirmishes, initiated by both sides, including a serious battle near Kaesŏng in 1949 that involved thousands of troops (Hart-Landsberg 1998, 116).

It was, however, the Korean War, leaving more than four million casualties (Cumings 1990, 770), that shaped the modern national identity into its hegemonic form, which essentially revolved around, and was nourished by, fierce anticommunism directed toward North Korea. The war not only intensified the existing hostility between the two nations to the point of irreparability but also justified the paramountcy of militarized national security and therefore the need for a strong military for decades to come. During the Korean War, President Rhee advocated an irredentist march to the north of the thirty-eighth parallel. Although negotiation for an armistice agreement had been under way since July 1951, he ardently opposed any truce in favor of fighting to a victory by the allied forces over the communists and driving the communists out of the Korean peninsula.[8] Hence President Rhee was instrumental in devising popular phrases such as "victory over communism" (*sŭnggong*), which was later adopted as the title of an ethics textbook widely used in primary and secondary schools during the 1970s.

The exodus of Koreans from the North to the South during the period between decolonization and the end of the Korean War generated a large number of people who were or became ardent supporters of anticommunism in South Korea. During the first five years after decolonization, an estimated 740,000 North Koreans, who had been landowners, members of the Japanese constabulary, and employees of the Japanese colonial government, migrated to the South. In the context of the sociopolitical revolution in the North, these groups, who had collaborated with the Japanese colonial regime to varying degrees, "had all taken the opportunity to flee to the South" (Foley 2003, 30). The emerging North Korean regime also allowed those who opposed its policies, including religious groups, to leave for the South. During the Korean War, another estimated 650,000 North Korean refugees moved to South Korea (42, 56).

Reasserting anticommunism as an official doctrine,[9] Park Chung Hee's regime (1961–79) fortified the anticommunist national identity through its involvement in the Vietnam War from 1965 to 1973. Indeed, the North and the South fought a vicarious war in Indochina by actively supporting communist North Vietnam and capitalist South Vietnam, respectively. In the spirit of advocating a third-world nationalist struggle against imperialism, North Korea sent food, clothes, medicine, military supplies, and soldiers. South Korea, meanwhile, dispatched its troops in exchange for a pledge by the United States to modernize the South Korean military, purchase war supplies produced in South Korea, and offer new loans (Gills 1996, 109, 110, 152; Editorial Board 1994, 104). For the eight years of its military entanglement, South Korea sent more than 300,000 soldiers annually, representing the second largest ally to the U.S. forces after the South Vietnamese military itself (Sungjoo Han 1978, 893). One of the significant social consequences of this long-term involvement was the reinforcement of the unthinking acceptance of anticommunism among the populace, exposed as it was to mass mobilization and ideological propaganda. Students were exhorted to send comfort letters and comfort goods to Korean soldiers serving in Vietnam. The mass media produced a plethora of images and stories supporting the everyday mythology of brave and ferocious Korean soldiers fighting in the war. Yet in the face of the global spread of the antiwar movement in the late 1960s, no critical public discourse on Korea's role in Vietnam, let alone popular protest against the war, was formed. *Sasanggye* (Thought World), a major progressive intellectual magazine during the period, did not publish a single article critically reflecting on the war and Korean involvement in it (Kim Hyŏn-a 2001, 69).

Drastic changes in international relations in the early 1970s, characterized by the U.S. rapprochement with the People's Republic of China and détente with the Soviet Union, did not significantly modify South Korean anticommunism. Kim Il Sung and Park Chung Hee made a symbolic gesture to ease tension by declaring a joint statement for peaceful unification independent of foreign intervention in 1972. Park's regime also established diplomatic relations with some communist countries during the 1970s. At the same time, though, this regime maintained its anti-North stance and accelerated military buildup to catch up with the North, which had achieved military superiority over the South as a result of its own successful postwar reconstruction (Hart-Landsberg 1998, 146–47).

The anticommunist identity of the modern Korean nation was perpetuated in the reescalation of Cold War militarism caused by the election of Ronald Reagan and other conservative leaders in Western countries in the late 1970s and early 1980s. Yet some signs of the undermining of the anticommunist identity began to appear. Critical to this change were the Kwangju massacre (May 1980) and the U.S. role in establishing Chun Doo Hwan's military rule (1980–87).[10] Instrumental to the birth of the second military regime (1980–87) was the U.S. condoning of the 1979 coup d'état and the Korean army's brutal suppression of the citizens' uprising in the city of Kwangju. U.S. complicity in the Kwangju massacre, which left an estimated five hundred civilians dead (Gi-Wook Shin and Hwang 2003, xvii),[11] and the subsequent U.S. support for Chun's regime seriously damaged its claim to defending democracy in South Korea against the communist North. Consequently, the popular perception of anticommunism as part and parcel of democracy was eroded, particularly among political dissidents, and this erosion, in turn, contributed to the emergence of public skepticism toward the anticommunist national identity.

The Making of Members of the Anticommunist
Body Politic through Discipline and Violence

The amalgamation of discipline and physical violence in remolding the population into useful and docile members of the body politic distinguished militarized modernity in South Korea from Foucauldian modernity, characterized by the progressive decline of force in the context of growing disciplinary power. According to Foucault, as discipline became the dominant organizing principle of modern society,[12] the military, which lent various techniques, "from the control and exercise of individual bodies to the use of forces specific to the most complex multiplicities," to other modern disciplinary institutions such as the school, the factory, the hospital, and the prison, reduced its own prominence in domestic politics (1979, 167). Discipline is a sophisticated form of power that achieves maximum effect at a minimum economic and political cost. Exercised in the form of knowledge designed to improve individuals, disciplinary power aims at meticulous control over individuals to maximize their productivity and utility (as opposed to the renunciation of the world that was produced by premodern religious disciplines) and minimize their resistance. Therefore disciplinary power does not need to be violent; it is impersonal and rationalized power, to use Weberian terminology.

In contrast, the use of physical force was pervasive in South Korea during the period of militarized modernity, despite the expansion of the state's disciplinary power over individuals and social groups. It would be misleading, however, to confine the frequent use of physical force in South Korea to militarized modernity as if it testifies to the savagery of lesser modernity. Western modernities also blatantly used physical force to control colonized people. What distinguishes militarized modernity from Western modernities in this regard is the way in which the boundaries between civilization (the realm governed by law) and savagery (the realm ruled by physical violence) are drawn. To the extent to which they lacked procedural democracy and the process of "internal pacification," the military regimes relied on the use of organized violence against those who did not conform to the rule of the anticommunist nation.[13] At the same time, the developmental state used "surveillance" and "normalization," two great instruments of disciplinary power (Foucault 1979, 184), to discipline its members.

Reflecting the disciplinary technique of using reports and registers to exercise surveillance over the population (Foucault 1979, 213–14), in May 1962, Park's junta enacted the resident registration law and introduced the current system of resident registration (chumindŭngnokchedo). Under this system, each individual is given a unique and immutable number at birth, and this identification is used to monitor the population's movements for a wide range of purposes, including military service, taxation, criminal investigation, and recently the administration of social welfare services. The registration system enabled the modernizing state to keep comprehensive records on each individual member of the body politic, ranging from his or her address, marital status, and date of birth to his or her schooling, technical license possession, vocational training history, and reasons for changing his or her permanent address. Compared with state-administered identification systems in other modern societies, the Korean version is decidedly excessive, with its punctilious collection of 140 different items of individual information (Kim Ki-jung 2000).

Central to the development of the resident registration system was the imperative of military mobilization, rooted in the ideology of national security against communist North Korea. The first amendment to the law, issued in 1968, required all adult men and women to carry a fingerprinted card (*chumindŭngnokchŭng*) to document their resident registration. One of the main reasons for instituting the card was "to be fully prepared with anticommunist attitudes for easily distinguishing North Korean spies and impure elements and ferreting them out" (Kim Ki-jung 2000, 70). This disciplinary move was a response to North Korea's increasingly aggressive stance toward both South Korea and the United States in the escalation of the Vietnam War, indicated by a series of widely publicized incidents in 1968: its commandos' infiltration of the Blue House to attempt to assassinate President Park, the seizure of the USS *Pueblo*, and the infiltration by over 130 armed guerrillas of the eastern maritime towns. In the face of opposition by the Democratic Party to the institution of the resident registration card, the ruling Democratic Republican Party pushed through passage of the amendment in the National Assembly, along with the Homeland Security Force Establishment Law, in the absence of the opposition party. By the end of 1968, the modernizing state had issued the resident registration card to 15.74 million people.

Throughout the 1970s, the South Korean state reinforced the registration system in the name of strengthening national security and preparing for total war. In 1975, it lowered the age at which citizens were required to apply for the registration card, in order to enhance "the effective management of the civil defense forces, the homeland security forces and the national human resources" (Kim Ki-jung 2000, 70). In the mid-1980s, Chun Doo Hwan's regime modified the system for the effective control of the populace (see figure 1).

Another disciplinary technique for monitoring individual commitment to anticommunism was the use of anticommunist mottoes to alert the populace to communist infiltration and subversion and encourage them to identify North Korean spies and impure elements and report them to the police. Such anticommunist posters were ubiquitous along highways and streets, and in public transportation, public buildings, schools, apartment complexes, and business corporations. Anticommunist mottoes were printed on cigarette cases, lottery tickets, and movie tickets. Based on an analysis of numerous anticommunist mottoes, the scholar Kwŏn Hyŏk-pŏm argues that this ubiquitous, impersonal supervision generated an "anticommunist circuit" in popular perception that automatically makes the following associations. First, people tend to link a "suspicious" person to an "impure" element, and then to a "leftist," or to link

1. Men and women updating their resident registration cards, circa 1983. Photograph by Dong-A Daily Co.

a leftist to a supporter of North Korea and a spy. Second, people tend to equate confusion, division, and the lack of discipline with machination by the impure element, North Korean aggression, and national insecurity (2000, 55, 58). Although Kwŏn's study focuses on anticommunist mottoes collected in the 1990s, his analysis is relevant to earlier decades as well, because this disciplinary technique was more pervasive and conspicuous then. For instance, it was a common practice to mobilize a large number of men and women for anticommunist rallies (see figure 2).

The use of punctilious surveillance by the police was not, however, always connected to the constitution of the anticommunist members of the nation. One such exception was the regulation of the length of men's hair and women's skirts after a Lesser Crime Punishment Law (kyŏngbŏmjoech'ŏbŏlbŏp) became effective in 1973. Unacceptably long hair was defined as hair that covered the ears and touched a man's shirt collar; an unacceptably short skirt was defined as a skirt that was seventeen centimeters above the knee. Carrying a tape measure and scissors, policemen caught these "lesser criminals" on the streets and cut men's hair in public as punishment. While the regulation of miniskirts was not quite as strict, the police carried out annual campaigns throughout the 1970s during which they intensified the punishment of long-haired men (Kang Chun-man 2002, 2:110–15).

The modernizing state fortified its ability to supervise the population by organizing individuals into the hierarchical associations that I am calling administered mass organizations (AMOs). As discussed earlier, these organizations were a legacy of Japanese colonial rule, particularly during the 1930s and 1940s, the decades of wartime mass mobilization. The postcolonial state attempted to reach every corner of Korean society by creating and expanding the national network of numerous AMOs arranged by residence, gender, age, and industry. A telling example of this disciplinary technique was the use of the pansanghoe (residential association) in all urban and rural towns to monitor and indoctrinate local residents. During the second half of the 1970s, the Ministry of the Interior administered monthly assemblies of the residential associations, during which attendees were instructed in anticommunism, government policies, and the code of conduct for kungmin, including detailed guidelines about how to behave during an emergency and how to identify North Korean spies and report suspicious people. Local residents were also instructed to report "groundless rumors" and avoid "impure" conduct (Kang Chun-man 2002, 3:41). This disciplinary practice continued during Chun's rule (see figure 3). As examined in chapter 3, the modernizing state used vari-

2. Seoulites assembled for a large-scale anticommunist rally, 1984. Photograph by Yonhap News Agency.

3. A *pansanghoe* (local residents' assembly) scene, circa 1983. Photograph by
Yonhap News Agency.

ous women's AMOs to mobilize them for the successful implementation of government policy and campaigns.

The modernizing state's reliance on AMOs was conspicuous in its remolding of workers into useful and docile carriers of the labor power necessary for
building the industrial economy. The state attempted to secure its control of
labor in the following ways. First, it permitted only one labor union per firm
and required each union to be registered. Second, it organized labor unions
hierarchically for effective monitoring and control, requiring each local union
to belong to a nationwide industrial federation and ultimately to the confederation of industrial unions. Third, although collective bargaining was allowed
through the labor-management councils, the state retained the ultimate authority to impose its own resolution. Fourth, it promoted the *sampo* system,
originating in a Japanese colonial practice, under which a company financed
its labor union as a way to co-opt it (Ogle 1990, 14–15, 47; Sin Illyǒng 1988, 18).

As the resident registration system was intimately coupled with the ideology
of national security, so was control over labor. Under the Yushin Constitution
(1972–79), which suppressed a range of democratic rights, labor laws not only
became more repressive but also allowed for increasingly minute control of
workers in the name of national security. Shortly after the declaration of "the

state of emergency" in 1971, which was perfunctorily legitimized after the fact
by the issuance of the Special Laws concerning National Security, the state enacted "guidelines to manage the right of collective bargaining and adjustment
tasks under the state of emergency" in order to make collective bargaining
and collective action virtually illegal (Sin Illyŏng 1988, 19, 298). Labor control
carried out by the Ministry of Labor was transferred to the Ministry of Public Order and the Korean Central Intelligence Agency (KCIA). Since 1971 the
KCIA had virtually appointed the leadership of the Federation of Korean Trade
Unions and its industrial branches (Ogle 1990, 59–60). The state's labor control
also involved the imposition of a maximum rate of wage increase. Throughout
the 1970s the Economic Planning Board (EPB) adjusted wages and working
conditions under the Special Laws concerning National Security declared in
1971 (Yu Yŏng-ju 1982, 65). These practices continued during Chun's rule after
even more repressive labor laws replaced the Special Laws concerning National
Security in 1981. The National Security Planning Council, a successor of the
KCIA, and the Committee to Counteract Labor Insurgency were in charge of
close surveillance and suppression of labor movements (Ogle 1990, 103).

In the Free Export Zones, the police held daily briefings with company
management representatives (Ogle 1990, 60).[14] As it turned out, female Korean
workers were not as docile as foreign companies wished them to be in the
face of extremely exploitative working conditions. In 1968, the OAK Electronics Corporation, a small U.S. firm that employed about three hundred female
Korean workers in the Inch'ŏn area, became embroiled in a labor dispute over
low wages and authoritarian management. Blaming "high wages" and "irre-
sponsible" unions, the company closed its operations. In response, the Korean
state moved to safeguard the "docility" and "cheapness" of female labor by
enacting the Special Law on Trade Unions and Mediation of Labor Disputes
in Enterprises Invested by Foreigners in 1971. Until 1986, when this law was
abolished, the Industrial Estates and Free Export Zones boasted of their immunity to labor unions (23–25). Compared with the impersonal and bureaucratic system of resident registration, the state's control over workers was far
more violent and less discreet and therefore generated militant resistance from
workers.

The constitution of members of the anticommunist body politic entailed
the disciplinary technique of "normalization" to train individuals to become
anticommunists dedicated to protecting national security and building the
industrial economy. The modernizing state deployed its orthodoxy of anticommunism to make normalizing judgments on individuals. Producing "a

whole range of degrees of normality indicating membership of a homogeneous social body" (Foucault 1979, 184), those judgments distinguished legitimate members of the Korean nation from those who were not. Hence anticommunism as a state ideology was essential to the creation of the individual members of the nation, linking them to the body politic. Such disciplinary training involved the detailed regulation of individual attitudes, conduct, movement, and thoughts.

Schooling functioned as a mechanism for reshaping individual thoughts, attitudes, and conduct and for normalizing individuals as members of the anticommunist nation. Park's military junta (1961–63) announced the "pulverization of the communist invasion" as a main goal of higher education (Kim Chin-kyun and Hong 1991, 231). By using the national network of schools centrally controlled by the government, Park's regime tried to intensify the ideological inculcation of anticommunism directed against North Korea, and of the importance of militarized national security, into students at various levels of education. Major curriculum reforms carried out in 1963 and 1973 emphasized the formation of an unshakable anticommunist consciousness as a principal goal of education. This type of ideological control evolved from a narrow focus on anticommunism in the 1960s to the incorporation of "traditional" values such as loyalty and filial piety into curricula in the 1970s (233, 237). As a result, students were instructed in the following subjects: anticommunist morality (*pangongdodŏk*), victory over communism (*sŭnggong*), right living (*parŭnsaenghwal*), national ethics (*kungminyulli*), and national history (*kuksa*). These subjects essentially highlighted the danger and threat of communist North Korea and the need for unity under the military leadership.[15] Students were also regularly instructed to participate in contests for anticommunist posters, writings, and public speeches. Echoing the Japanese colonial practice during World War II,[16] students were advised to send "comfort letters" (*wimunp'yŏnji*) and "comfort goods" (*wimunp'um*) to the soldiers who protected the nation.

Chun's regime also tried to maintain the ideological control of students by implementing a "school curriculum reform" in 1981. This reform reasserted the anticommunist national identity as a crucial goal of education and designed more sophisticated ideological indoctrination in response to the growth of the anti-regime movement among college students. It relabeled anticommunist education, calling it "unification security education" (*t'ongilanbokyoyuk*) (Kim Chin-kyun and Hong 1991, 235, 237). Under this rubric, the blatant demonization of communism was replaced with an ideological critique in an attempt to control college students (Han'guk'kyoyungmunjeyŏn'guhoe 1989, 350–51). Yet as the explosive development of the militant student movement in the mid-1980s testified, this attempt was not very successful.

Crucial to the indoctrination and mobilization of individual members of the body politic for quotidian war preparations were the mass media, especially the national television network, which rapidly expanded throughout the late 1960s and early 1970s (Kang Chun-man 1998, 199–200). The 1970s were a time of societal militarization par excellence in which the entire population was mobilized for war preparation under the ideology of total national security (*ch'ongnyŏkanbo*) and total unity (*ch'onghwadangyŏl*). All sectors of society were drawn into war preparation in several ways. The populace was mobilized to participate in monthly civil defense training, introduced for the first time in 1971.[17] Employed men and women were required to pay a defense surtax (*pangwise*), instituted immediately after the communization of Indochina following the fall of Saigon and the ascendancy of the Khmer Rouge in Cambodia in 1975. The collection of this surtax lasted until 1990 and served to finance military buildup under the Yulgok project (Editorial Board 1994, 105–6).[18] Representing approximately 2 percent of the gross national product during the 1970s and 1980s, it served as a major source of financing for the modernization of the armed forces (Moon Chung-In 1998, 278) (see figure 4). Between 1973 and 1988, the national television network also played a central role in promoting campaigns to collect defense funds (*pangwisŏnggŭm*) among students, workers, and housewives, which resembled the Japanese wartime colonial practice (Kim Chin-gyun 1996, 298).

In the Korean nation unified under the banner of anticommunism, those who failed to conform to the norms of correct attitudes and conduct were subject to violent punishment. The categories of deviants in the anticommunist body politic included external communists, as well as internal communist followers and sympathizers. In 1956, the postcolonial state legally reestablished the conversion system (*chŏnhyangjedo*) used by the colonial state to reshape the beliefs and thoughts of North Korean spies and prisoners of the Korean War (Cho Yŏng-min 2001, 109). Bizarre on the face of it, the conversion system was a logical though extreme outcome of the disciplinary regulation of individuals, aiming to reduce the gap between rules and nonconformity. Foucault argues:

> The art of punishing, in the regime of disciplinary power, . . . refers individual actions to a whole that is at once a field of comparison, a space of differentiation and the principle of a rule to be followed; it differentiates

4. Eulji military exercise in downtown Seoul, 1985. Photograph by Yonhap News Agency.

individuals from one another, in terms of the following overall rule: . . . The perpetual penality that traverses all points and supervises every instant in the disciplinary institutions compares, differentiates, hierarchizes, homogenizes, excludes. In short, it *normalizes*. (1979, 182–83)

Under military rule, "nonconverted prisoners" (*pijŏnhyangsu*) were incarcerated in several designated prisons and exposed to excessive surveillance and ideological indoctrination. Yet these prisoners were also subjected to brutal violence involving terror and torture (Cho Yŏng-min 2001, 111), which separates the working of militarized modernity from Foucauldian disciplinary modernity. Even after "conversion," the prisoners were under close supervision, including the monitoring of their movements and telephone conversations. And under the "societal security law" (*sahoeanjŏnbŏp*) enforced between 1975 and 1989, converted thought criminals were kept in quasi prison even after their supposed release (122, 123).[19]

Whereas North Korean communists were external others, political dissidents and workers organizing democratic unions, often accused of being communist sympathizers, were internal others, who also needed to be punished. Although the Constitution and the Standard Labor Law formally upheld workers' rights to assemble and to take collective action, the technique of anti-communist normalization categorized workers involved in labor organizing as criminals undermining national security who existed outside the boundary of normal membership in the body politic. The Korean Central Intelligence Agency and later the National Security Planning Council played the major role in exercising extensive and detailed surveillance over the suspicious. However, surveillance was frequently coupled with brutal violence including torture and beating. By the beginning of the Yushin system in 1972, the KCIA had become "a complete rogue institution" that enjoyed enormous power to reward allies and punish foes at will (Cumings 1997, 365). Its agents were almost omnipresent, keeping watch not only over opposition political parties but also over mass-media corporations and college classrooms (366). A history of political perse-cution in South Korea shows ample examples of political dissidents who were executed or suffered enormously from anticommunist witch hunts.[20]

Day-to-day surveillance of individuals and their normalization, justified by the ideologies of anticommunism and national security, remolded them into useful and docile members of the anticommunist body politic. As discussed in chapter 4, the persistence of many of the techniques of surveillance and nor-malization into the era of procedural democracy suggests the largely successful constitution of individuals as kungmin to be mobilized for building the mod-ern nation. Yet the frequent use of violence and the repressive control of indi-viduals and social groups galvanized militant protests and, later, an organized oppositional social movement, called the *minjung* movement, in the 1980s (see chapter 4). The military regimes' frequent abuse of the ideologies of anticom-munism and national security in the service of suppressing protests against dictatorship, going as far as the execution of several journalists and dissidents, also undermined the effectiveness of anticommunism as the orthodoxy that justified the surveillance and normalization of the populace.

Dramatic economic growth also altered priorities among the general public in daily life. As ordinary Koreans became concerned with achieving and main-taining high standards of living in the context of economic expansion, they became less willing to be mobilized for war preparation. Unlike Park's regime, Chun's regime in the 1980s promoted the building of a "welfare society" by announcing its plan to implement, for the first time in South Korean history, a national pension system and a minimum wage system, and to expand the national health care system (Ch'oi Jang-jip and Ko 1989, 393). This kind of rhe-toric was accompanied by cosmetic but culturally significant changes in daily life: the lifting of the midnight curfew, the abolition of school uniforms (criti-

cized for being trappings of Japanese colonialism), and the beginning of professional sports leagues. This line of social liberalization was far less conducive
to popular mobilization for war preparation than was the previous regimes'
emphasis on "total security" and "total unity." While these discontinuities did
not entail the immediate decline of the anticommunist national identity, they
prepared the soil for further challenges to it in the following decade.

The Militarized Economy: The Integration of Men's Military Service into the Organization of the Labor Market

An aspect of militarized modernity far less recognized than the militant suppression of labor and the discipline of big business was the extensive integration of men's military service into the overall working of the labor market in
South Korea. Not only was the completion of military service the precondition
for any type of employment, including any self-employment that required the
state's approval, but military service was also recognized as work experience
in the conventional and legal practices of employment. As will be discussed in
chapter 2, although this coupling of military service with employment resulted
from the state's intention to establish the system of universal male conscription by penalizing evaders, its enforcement contributed to the development of
the militarized economy. There were three ways in which paid employment in
the industrializing economy was closely tied to military service.

First, military service was integrated into the workings of the labor market
in the process of recruitment. During the period of military rule, which was
before the enforcement of the Equal Employment Law (1988), business corporations commonly specified the completion of (or official exemption from)
military service as a criterion for applicants in their recruitment advertising.
This specification was a formal reminder of the Special Measure Law that contained penalties for the violation of the Military Service Law enacted in 1973.
Yet this criterion also came to mean that such job openings were reserved for
men. That is, although women were technically exempted from military service and therefore eligible, they need not apply. According to a study of the
recruitment advertisements of 683 firms published in a newspaper between
March 6, 1982, and February 28, 1983, over a third of these firms used the completion of military service as a necessary precondition for application. Military
service was the third most frequently printed criterion, after education and age
(Chang Chi-yŏn 1990, 168). This practice of excluding women from jobs ad-
vertised with the specification of military service was more prevalent among
"large" corporations (ones that hired more than three hundred employees and

provided better working conditions and better pay). According to the Korean Women's Development Institute's study of the gender-segregated recruitment practices of 1,217 corporations, over half of large firms required the completion of, or exemption from, military service for mere application (KWDI 1983, 51).

Second, recognizing military service as work experience, not only public but also private firms developed conventional practices of granting higher pay and faster promotion to veterans, an absolute majority of whom were former conscripts. The KWDI study of gender-segregated recruitment practices shows that over a third of all firms studied observed these conventional practices (51). These employment practices remained intact without challenge until the late 1980s, when the Equal Employment Law was enacted and provided at least a legal ground to contest them.

Third, the military service extra-points system (eliminated in late 1999 as a result of a women's movement and the democratizing court system) guaranteed veterans some advantages in employment tests and interviews in public sectors and some designated private sectors. Other private employers were encouraged to apply this legal practice. It is useful here to discuss briefly the legal evolution of the extra-points system, because it reveals the legal arrangement of connecting military service to employment, which had uneven ramifications for women and men in the presence of "universal" male conscription. The system was introduced under the Military Relief Recipients Employment Act (*kunsawŏnhodaesangja imyongbŏp*) promulgated in 1961. Initially, the extra-points system was adopted as the core element of national compensation for veterans and their families in the area of employment, in the absence of other substantive forms of reward. The Supreme Council for National Reconstruction, formed by General Park Chung Hee's military junta (1961–63), articulated a twofold rationale for establishing such an act: first, to provide a livelihood for those who had completed the "sacred duty of national defense," particularly disabled soldiers (*sangi kunin*) and families of soldiers killed in battle (*chŏnsajaŭi chikkyegajok*), and second, to elevate the national military's morale, undermined by the impoverishment of veterans. As a way to assist their employment, the law included an article specifying veterans' entitlement to extra points when they took public employment tests for positions in the government, public corporations, and other relevant organizations. According to Article 5 of the Employment Support Act, former conscripts were guaranteed extra points worth 5 percent of full marks, while one family member of each disabled or deceased soldier received 10 percent extra.[21]

The practice of granting extra points was modified after the Military Relief

Recipients Employment Act was replaced, in 1984, by the Honorable Treatment of Persons of National Merit Act (*kukkayugongja yeudŭngekwanhan pŏpyul*) (Kim Chong-sŏng 1997). Basically, this new law expanded the application of the extra-points system in terms of which employers were required to adopt it and which types of recruitment tests it applied to. According to Article 30 of this act, the category of employers included not only the public employers specified in the previous law but also private schools and firms defined as "organizations practicing employment protection" (*ch'wiŏppohosilsigigwan*).[22] Article 70 of the Honorable Treatment Act guaranteed extra points not only on written tests but also in other equivalent tests, such as job interviews and auditions. The act redefined "patriotic martyrs, patriotic fighters, and police-men and soldiers killed in the line of duty" as "persons of national merit." Compared with the earlier term, "military relief recipient," this euphemistic terminology seems to suggest the state's affirmative recognition of soldiers and their bereaved families. While families of disabled or deceased "persons of national merit" were entitled to receive an extra 10 percent of full marks on any given test, veterans — both conscripts and professional soldiers — received extra points ranging from 3 to 5 percent, depending on the length of their service.[23] (This differentiation reflected the development of two different types of military service — shorter supplementary service and longer regular service — beginning in 1969 [see chapter 2].)

In this sketch of the evolution of the military service extra-points system, the following points deserve further attention. First, its gradual expansion over time suggests the increasing symbolic significance of military service in the labor market in the 1980s. More categories of employers were expected to adopt it, and more categories of recruitment tests were included in it. While we have no reliable data by which to determine the total number of beneficiaries of the extra-points system, what is more important is the symbolic currency of the system as the expedient marker of the state's recognition of the hard-ship of military service. The state tried to use the system as a minimum reward or compensation for military service to sustain the universal conscription system. Second, it is worth discussing this seemingly esoteric system of military service extra points in a comparative manner. While it may sound peculiar to South Korea, it can be understood as one form of the kinds of incentives that every nation-state has to offer to ensure the supply of competent and will-ing soldiers for the smooth working of the military. The restrictive nature of military service necessitates certain forms of initiatives and rewards to attract potential recruits and to mitigate discontent among conscripts, depending on the availability of resources, the perceived state of "national security," and the form of the military recruitment system. Most states offer a combination of government pensions, monetary compensation, medical insurance, and educational and other employment aids to attend to the basic needs of veterans and their families. Moreover, some states grant veterans advantages in public employment, and the military service extra-points system implemented in South Korea can be seen as a specific version of that. For example, under the Veterans Preference Act (1944), honorably discharged veterans in the United States receive additional points on federal and state employment tests.[24]

For these three reasons (military service as a prerequisite for applying, higher pay and faster promotion for veterans, and the military service extra-points system), the organizational culture of large corporations under military rule (but with effects that are still present) was imbued with militaristic values and practices. Corporate culture in major business firms was characterized by rigid hierarchy based on rank, the command mode of one-way communication, and a collective ethos used to justify individual sacrifice. These aspects of corporate culture underlay interactions among workers and managers in offices and on shop floors.[25] In addition, orientation and on-the-job training programs in large corporations for college-educated, white-collar employees often included endurance training (marching and collective gymnastics in athletic uniform), which mirrored military training, in their regimented daily schedule. Choong Soon Kim (1992) and Roger Janelli (1993) documented militarized corporate culture in a blue-collar factory and a white-collar firm, respectively, in their ethnographic studies of large corporations based on fieldwork conducted during the second half of the 1980s.

CONCLUSION

Militarized modernity as a sociopolitical and economic formation emerged in the 1960s when new and old techniques for discipline and punishment came together, reached its peak in the 1970s, and showed some signs of decline in the 1980s. The rise of militarized modernity as the Korean path to modernity stemmed from South Korea's particular circumstances of national division, the Korean war and prolonged military confrontation, and the postcolonial exigencies of building a modern nation via the establishment of a national identity and the discipline of its population. These historical conditions modified the general trend of modernity characterized by increasing rationalization and internal pacification in various spheres of human life, generating a society ruled by the fusion of discipline and pervasive force. The pursuit of militarized modernity in the process of nation building involved not only authoritarian imposition on the populace but also the mass mobilization of men and women, consolidating the political subjectivity of kungmin, "dutiful nationals" who were expected and willing to forgo their rights for the sake of the nation. In the following chapter, I discuss specific ways in which men were mobilized as soldiers and as a permanent workforce in the militarized economy of the 1970s and 1980s.

2 MOBILIZED TO BE MARTIAL AND PRODUCTIVE

Men's Subjection to the Nation and the Masculine Subjectivity of Family Provider

In his film *Fools' March* (1975), the late Ha Kil-jong, one of the most controversial directors in the history of Korean cinema, portrays the lives of college students during the height of militarization in the mid-1970s. The youth are represented as alienated and lost in the midst of an escalating military dictatorship that defines even men's long hair as an insidious threat to "national security." Tracing the tragic eclipse of hope and freedom under the repressive rule, the film narrates the demise of two male protagonists: Yŏngch'ŏl commits suicide by riding a bicycle into the sea, and Byŏng-t'ae enlists for military service. In a scene toward the end of the film, Byŏng-t'ae anxiously shares a farewell kiss with Yŏng-ja, his girlfriend. In this romanticized scene of separation, he is aboard a train carrying loads of young conscripts like himself, and she is outside on the platform. This somewhat sentimentalized scene suggests two aspects of the deeply gendered institution of military service in South Korea. First, men are the protectors who leave home for the barracks, and women are the protected who stay behind and watch their men leave. Second, men are the insiders in the militarized national community, whereas women are the outsiders.

However, this scene simultaneously undermines the gender dichotomy around military service and membership in the nation. Byŏng-t'ae's enlistment, in the context of the film, does not actually symbolize the heroic act of a masculine protector, but rather represents the renunciatory act of a hopeless young man. He is far from the glorified image of a virile soldier willing to endure the hardship of military service and die for the nation. After all, the director uses military enlistment as a metaphor for the end of youth. Similarly, the militarized national community symbolized by the train conjures up the mechanism of control and confinement that suppresses individuality. Hence, one would rather stay outside if one could choose. The visceral sense of belonging that Benedict Anderson (1991) discusses in various versions of nationalism is missing from Byŏng-t'ae's compulsory membership in the barracks community. He is not quite an insider, or at best, he is a reluctant and helpless one. His ambivalent relation to conscription as evoked in the film offers a useful entry point for a feminist study of the mass mobilization of men in pursuit of militarized modernity, leading to the construction of men as dutiful nationals willing to perform military service.[1]

Words of qualification are needed here. Since the critical view of military service in the film is articulated around the lives of college students, a privileged sector of society, especially during the 1970s, one might point out that such a view is not representative of the relationships that a majority of less-privileged young men have toward military service in South Korea. However, I am using the vignette from *Fools' March* not to convey the "typical" relationship between South Korean men and military service but to illuminate complexities beneath the hegemonic construction of military service as "men's national duty" that had remained unquestioned until the late 1990s. The film's evocation of men's ambivalent relationship to conscription raises questions concerning the specific ways in which the modernizing state disciplined and rewarded different groups of men to mobilize them as soldiers. The analysis of the institutional mechanism to discipline and reward men in the 1970s and 1980s can illuminate the ways in which men are incorporated into the nation differently from women in the pursuit of militarized modernity.

This chapter examines the modernizing state's use of repressive surveillance over the body of prospective conscripts and its use of ideological indoctrination through schooling and the mass media to establish military service as men's national duty. Interwoven with men's mass mobilization for mandatory military service was their mobilization for the industrializing economy, especially after 1973. In lieu of military service, tens of thousands of men were employed annually in heavy industries crucial to industrialization and the building of self-reliant defense. The intertwining of military service and paid employment in the process of men's integration into the nation had implications for the modern gender hierarchy organized around the gender division of labor between dependent housewife and provider husband.

THE UNIVERSAL CONSCRIPTION SYSTEM AND BARRIERS TO THE ESTABLISHMENT OF MILITARY SERVICE AS MEN'S NATIONAL DUTY

The enactment of the Military Service Law in 1949 marked the introduction of the universal conscription system (*kungmingaebyŏngje*), but its implementation was delayed until 1957 owing to the Korean War and postwar instabilities (Kang Kyŏng-hwan 1996, 68). Although conscription in practice has resulted in an uneven burden for lower-class men, the principle of universal conscription was significant because the entire category of men as a group was theoretically required to perform military service.[2] According to the Military Service Law, universal conscription constructed military service as "men's national duty." In premodern Korea, it had only been certain categories of men, such as commoners and a hereditary group of warriors, as opposed to all men as a presumably homogeneous group, who performed military service.[3] This militarization of masculinity in South Korea was intimately linked to the building of the postcolonial nation-state in the context of the Cold War. During the Korean War (1950–53), the South Korean army expanded exponentially, from 100,000 to 650,000 (Se Jin Kim 1971, 37–40). Under the Agreed Minute of Understanding, formulated during the 1954 summit conference between the Republic of Korea and the United States, the United States called for the Korean military to be dominated by the army (Sŏ Chin-t'ae 1998, 1:13–15).[4] Representing over 90 percent of the military's personnel, the gigantic army was to be manned primarily by male conscription.

During the military rule, the conscription system required all able-bodied young men aged eighteen or above to serve in the military for around three years. After numerous revisions over the decades, the length of mandatory service was reduced to twenty-six to thirty months, depending on the types of forces (Ch'oi Kwang-p'yo 1997, 99).[5] After completing active service, men continue to serve in the Homeland Reserve Force for an additional eight years, during which they receive regular annual military training (Kim Chae-il 1996; Yi Yŏ-song 1996).[6]

The mass mobilization of men for conscription is a difficult task for a new state because men do not naturally embrace military service as their national duty. In spite of the enduring symbolic link between masculinity and military service in various societies, many men are reluctant to perform mandatory military service for various reasons, ranging from pacifism and fear of death to the loss of years of youth and their economic obligation to their families. According to comparative and historical studies of conscription in the Middle East and Central Asia, popular resistance toward the new form of military recruitment was a norm rather than an exception (Zürcher 1999). In South Korea, the state achieved the mass mobilization of men for military service through aggressive and coordinated efforts to alter popular resistance toward military service. In particular, they involved the daunting task of transforming the deeply negative associations that military service held among the grassroots population, shaped by neo-Confucian tradition, Japanese colonial rule, and the deadly civil war, as well as the absence of any substantial sociopolitical and economic rewards for mass military mobilization.

Neo-Confucianism, adopted as the state ideology by the Chosŏn Dynasty (1392–1910), was fundamentally a philosophy of ruling by cultivated scholars. In the Chosŏn court, men of the pen enjoyed political dominance over men of the sword (Palais 1996). It was a gentleman scholar (*sŏnbi*), not a martial warrior, who represented "hegemonic masculinity" under the Confucian order (Connell 1995, chap. 3).

This lack of respect and prestige for soldiers was superseded by a more active avoidance of soldiering under Japanese colonial rule. The Japanese Imperial Army, particularly during the 1930s and the first half of the 1940s, developed extremely severe discipline, pursuing a policy that promoted the beating of soldiers by officers. The frequent infliction of pain was designed as a technology to subjugate foot soldiers to officers' orders. This process is poignantly captured in an account given by a Japanese soldier: "Having been subjected to cruel and irrational punishments, we were trained to act without thinking in response to orders" (Edgerton 1997, 308). It is not difficult to infer that Koreans in the Japanese Imperial Army suffered even more, as this harsh discipline was compounded by racism against the colonized. Furthermore, conscription by the colonial authorities in the midst of Japan's imperialist war in Manchuria, and later in the Asia-Pacific region, meant becoming cannon fodder for the oppressor. This memory is still vivid among older-generation Koreans.[7]

The Korean War reinforced this common perception of military service as merely a cause of severe injury and death, particularly because the army's ill-prepared involvement in the civil war forced ordinary men into battle without proper training and equipment, leaving countless soldiers and civilians dead. To replenish the drastically shrinking armies during the war, even civilian refugees in flight were coerced onto the battlefield (Ki 1995; Ryu 1989). At the same time, sons of high government officials were commonly exempted from the draft (Pak Myŏng-sun 1997, 25). This kind of irregularity fortified the sense of military service as an unequal burden borne by the powerless. The perception of military service as a cause of severe injury and death also conflicted with the strong legacy of Confucian patrilineage, working against the willing acceptance of military service as men's national duty. In the patrilineal order, a "legitimate" son was indispensable to the continuation of the family lineage. Therefore, in the interest of patrilineal households, sons could not be spared for soldiering, which was highly conducive to severe injury or death.[8] During the Korean War and the immediate postwar decade, numerous families, regardless of their economic standing, were eager to send their sons to college in order to avoid the draft, as student status allowed young men to postpone military service.[9]

In fact, South Koreans in the postwar decade lacked any historical experience of the kind of mass military mobilization that led to sociopolitical empowerment, as documented in histories of revolutionary or independence wars during which common men were transformed into citizens through soldiering.[10] This positive legacy of military service fostered the birth of the civic republican idea of military service as a citizen's duty, rather than merely a coercive burden imposed on the ruled.[11] Although some Koreans were actively involved in the armed nationalist struggle during the colonial period, inside and outside the Korean peninsula, the decolonization of Korea was not achieved through an independence war that mobilized the masses of men and women, but was rather a byproduct of Japan's surrender that ended World War II. Nor had Korean veterans and their families enjoyed any generous economic entitlements in the postwar decade in exchange for mass military mobilization during the Korean War. This historical experience stands in contrast to the treatment of the veterans of World War II and their families in the United States.[12] The absence of the historical experience of mass military mobilization as an avenue to socioeconomic entitlement contributed to the negative popular perception of military service as merely a dangerous and coercive burden, to be avoided if possible.

From the implementation of male conscription in 1957 to the beginning of the 1990s, the single most significant factor contributing to young men's distaste for military service had been the conditions of barracks life in the South Korean military, characterized by a daily routine of subjection to extremely harsh bodily discipline (Yi Sŏng-ch'an 1998; Kwŏn Sŏn-jin 1997; Kim Tŏk-han 1996; Kim Sun-kwŏn 1991). Before the military reform of the 1990s, the Korean military that conscripts encountered displayed the same common practices of severe and repeated punishment and abuse that the Japanese Imperial Army had practiced. This continuity needs to be understood in relation to the historical circumstances under which the South Korean military was created and developed. Although the U.S. Army military government (1945–48) directed the process of instituting the modern military, the elite of the South Korean military consisted mainly of officers who were trained by, and had served in, the Japanese Imperial Army, including Park Chung Hee himself. Controlling the military and domestic politics until the late 1970s, this group of military officers had molded a rigidly authoritarian culture in the military. As a result, while its formal organizational structure closely resembled that of the U.S. military, social relations among soldiers in their daily routine mimicked those in the Japanese Imperial Army (Sŏ Hyo-il 1995, 2:72; Yi Tong-hŭi 1982, 264, 265, 317).

The organizational identity of the military in general as an armed fighting machine generates a collective ethos that justifies the sacrifice of individuals for the sake of a larger goal, that is, the military security of a nation. To make civilian individuals willing to accept their sacrifice, military establishments have generally assumed that civilians have to be transformed into foot soldiers willing to carry out orders without critical thinking and reflection. This transformation is to be achieved through intense and repetitious physical discipline and indoctrination, as well as the daily routine of collective living in barracks. The discipline that transforms men into soldiers exploits male gender identity, the lowest common denominator of recruits from diverse socioeconomic backgrounds, to compensate for the physical hardship involved in military service and to inculcate the elementary sense of solidarity necessary to deal with stressful situations on the battlefield. While military culture in a given (national) society is internally differentiated among various groups of soldiers divided by tasks and stratified by rank, the masses of recruits, especially conscripted privates, are exposed to the cult of tough and aggressive masculinity, which also emphasizes obedience to military authorities. As Klaus Theweleit (1987) argues, the cult of tough and aggressive masculinity reduces the female body and "feminine" traits to essential markers of otherness to be conquered and destroyed by soldiers. It is a standard that basic military training transforms civilian recruits—both conscripts and volunteers—into soldiers by regimented corporal discipline seasoned with songs and rhymes that often contain the explicit and implicit degradation of women and sexualized violence against them. Routine military drills and marches, for example, are often peppered with such songs and exclamations (Hilsdon 1995; Sturdevant and Stoltzfus 1992). The Korean military is no exception in reflecting the misogynistic construction of the masculine soldier (Cho Sŏng-suk 1997). Memoirs of military service written by officers and conscripts report that ideas and practices of masculinity are frequently used as a means to control and discipline rank-and-file soldiers, and as a trope for interpreting military service experiences.[13] It is noteworthy that "Real Men" (*chinjja sanai*) is the title of one of the most popular songs used during basic training and marches in the Korean military. The term *sanai* connotes a man at the pinnacle of his physical strength, supporting the visceral exuberance of courage. This category of man is meant to embody the unadulterated essence of masculinity. This song is so familiar, even to civilian ears, that many can easily recognize its tune and sing along. Its lyrics portray soldiering as the most glorious and honorable act men can ever perform.

These general features of military culture were accentuated in the South Korean military as shaped, to a great extent, by the fascistic culture of the Japanese Imperial Army. Before the recent gradual change in military subculture began, strenuous discipline often took the form of repeated physical assault and psychological abuse to break down an individual conscript's will and subject him to the orders of his superiors. For instance, habitual practices of abuse ranged from verbal humiliation and severe beating to depriving subordinate soldiers of meals and sleep. Absolute obedience and the performance of personal services such as washing and ironing clothes or running errands governed the relationship between subordinates and superiors.[14] These routine aspects of the military subculture indicate that popular acceptance of military service as men's national duty was not grounded in any genetic inclination of males to violence but stemmed rather from a "cultural inclination to obedience that would permit [a man's] integration into the highly hierarchical military system" (Sebesta 1994, 39). This process of bodily subjection, though it is designed to promote obedience, is likely to generate resistance toward military service, instead, if it is not accompanied by substantial rewards, a sense of entitlement, or a sense of fairness in bearing this burden.

The following section examines the ways in which Park's regime managed to alter the negative social meaning of military service and establish it as men's national duty through conscription policy and other related policies, and how Chun's regime maintained this mass mobilization of men as soldiers in the face of emergent resistance in the 1980s. The historical discussion of these policies allows us to see both ideological and coercive mechanisms by which men were mobilized for military service in the pursuit of militarized modernity.

DISCIPLINING MEN AND THE GENERAL POPULATION TO ACCEPT
MILITARY SERVICE AS MEN'S DUTY TO THE NATION

Manufacturing Hegemony through
Schooling and the Mass Media

Popular acceptance of military service as men's national duty requires the inculcation of militarized patriotism in young students and the routinization of military training. In the late 1960s and early 1970s, Park's regime distributed state-approved textbooks on new mandatory subjects such as "anticommunism" and "defeating communism" (Kim Chin-kyun and Hong 1991). In the midst of escalating military tension between the two Koreas in the late 1960s, Park's regime enacted a law in 1969 establishing a new subject, "educational drill" (*kyoryŏn*), and requiring all healthy male students in secondary schools and colleges to receive military training (OMM 1986, 206). Reflecting the normative view of gender dichotomy, female high school students were instructed in emergency nursing skills. The Ministry of Education considered military drill a contribution to "the cultivation of students' character" and a "wholesome atmosphere in school." In 1972 the American-style ROTC was introduced and, in association with the educational drill, became the basic structure for the military training of students (207). Alarmed by the communization of Indochina in 1975, Park's regime also revived the National Protection Students Corps (*hakdohogukdan*), a paramilitary organization of male high school and college students, originally created by President Rhee and then abolished in 1960 when his regime was overthrown. This organization was used not only for military training but also for monitoring student dissident activities on college campuses (Kim Chin-kyun and Hong 1991, 243). This variety of military requirements and organizations, directed at all male students, was designed to prepare men to accept military service as their duty.

The mass media supported the inculcation of militarized patriotism by emphasizing real and fabricated invasions or attacks from North Korea (Kang Chun-man 1998, chaps. 7–10). The North Korean threat culminated in the failed 1975 attempt by a North Korean agent to assassinate President Park, in which Park's highly regarded and popular wife was killed. In conjunction with the impending threat of war in the Korean peninsula, the changing contour of international relations in the 1970s generated a heightened sense of the importance of national defense among South Koreans. Popular sentiments were affected by a series of international events, including the Nixon Doctrine, which resulted in the withdrawal of twenty thousand U.S. soldiers stationed in South Korea, America's abandonment of Taiwan and its rapprochement with China, the withdrawal of the American military from Vietnam, and the consequent communization of South Vietnam. This turn of domestic and international events worked in favor of the efforts to establish military service as men's duty.

Surveillance of the Body of Prospective Conscripts
To mobilize men to defend the nation threatened by the communist enemy in the North, the South Korean state had to deal with the problem of popular resistance to military conscription, expressed in the negative social perception of military service. The military regime under Park Chung Hee (1961–

79) managed to achieve the goal of establishing military service as men's duty through strengthening its surveillance of the body of prospective conscripts. Throughout the 1960s, the regime attempted to improve its ability to identify conscription evaders. In 1966, it formed councils devoted to investigating evaders and their collaborators (such as medical professionals, employers, and government employees) in Seoul and major provincial areas.[15] The regime embarked on a large-scale national investigation of military service corruption between December 1969 and March 1970 (Ki 1995; Ryu 1989). It also launched campaigns in 1969 and 1970 during which evaders were encouraged to surrender in exchange for immunity. These campaigns brought in a total of 20,675 and 50,613 evaders, respectively (OMM 1986, 802), representing approximately 22.4 percent of the 318,000 men subject to the conscription test in 1970 (Pak Sang-wŏn 1995, 17).

The crackdown on conscription evasion in the 1960s was only partially successful given a social milieu characterized by the absence of militarized patriotism or the technological infrastructure necessary to control hundreds of thousands of prospective conscripts. The regime tackled these problems throughout the 1970s, the peak decade of militarized modernity, strengthening the infrastructure necessary for effective surveillance of the body of prospective conscripts. Upgraded as an independent organization outside the Ministry of National Defense (MND) in 1970, the Office of Military Manpower (OMM) played a central role in administering all affairs concerning conscription. In particular, by improving techniques for the physical examination of prospective conscripts and monitoring their overall supply and identification, the office contributed to the drastic reduction of draft evasion over time (Pak Sang-wŏn 1995).

Park's regime also implemented a series of initiatives to eradicate the evasion of military service throughout the 1970s. In 1973 it enacted the special law to penalize violators of the Military Service Law. It embarked on intensive campaigns to crack down on violators, organizing central and local councils dedicated to investigating military service corruption. Evaders were now subject to more severe punishment than before.[16] As a result, the number of evaders dropped after that year and remained very low (though probably not quite as low as portrayed by the official statistics on conscription evasion).[17] A highly effective deterrent to evasion was the practice of prohibiting employers from hiring men who did not complete military service. The violation of this regulation also subjected employers to heavy fines and withdrawal of the state approvals necessary to run a business (Ki 1995; Ryu 1989).[18] In conjunction with the militarized patriotism promoted through schooling and the mass media, these severe punitive measures contributed to the formation of the popular opinion that military service was necessarily and inevitably men's national duty. The change in the social meaning of military service is captured in a popular saying that "a man has to serve in the military to play a man's role" (*namjanŭn saramgusilharyŏmyŏn kundae katdawayahanda*) (see figure 5).

Yet the military mobilization of men as a group made possible by increasing surveillance of the body of prospective conscripts and the ideological indoctrination of the general public did not always succeed in securing young men's willingness to comply. Chun's regime faced this problem among male college students, whose number almost doubled as a result of the regime's educational reforms. Throughout the 1980s, during the vibrant and militant height of the student movement, some male student activists refused to take the military drill course established during the previous decade under Park's rule. They demanded the removal of compulsory drill, perceived to be an instrument of the military dictatorship, and also refused to take the annual trip to the military barracks for more intensive military training. In response, on the one hand, the regime used the conscription system to punish student activists: serving a certain amount of time in prison had excluded one from military service, but that amount of time was now decreased, so that more young male dissidents not only had to complete prison terms as punishment for their dissidence but then also had to serve in the military once their prison terms were completed (KNA 1991, 11). This kind of abuse of military service added to the lingering negative perception of military service among young men and their families. On the other hand, the OMM under Chun's rule adopted a "service-oriented" administration of conscription to promote popular willingness to perform military service. Under this new approach, the manpower office tried to improve its treatment of recruits and their families during the process of enlistment. For example, it tried to accommodate individual conscripts' preferences for enlistment dates. The office computerized the procedure for physical and psychological tests to dissipate mistrust of their results (Ki 1995).

This softer approach, however, was not completely effective in eliminating resistance to military service. In particular, resistance to military service on lofty philosophical grounds developed among college students starting in the mid-1980s. A tiny minority, a group of conscientious objectors who "refused to carry guns" on religious grounds, emerged as a new phenomenon (KIDA 1995a, 155–51).[19] Since this category was not recognized by the South Korean state, these resisters were sentenced to imprisonment for violating the military service law.[20]

Nevertheless, according to a 1985 survey report on military service and the

5. Family visits to conscripts at the Nonsan training center, circa 1988. Photograph by Seoul Newspaper Co.

socialization of young men, a majority of male college students, who have been generally more critical of military service than other social groups, accepted martial duty and reported that they learned patriotism, endurance, and masculinity through military service. They also indicated that they learned negative attitudes such as passivity and the use of tricks to avoid extra work, since the military tended to discourage individual initiative (Hong Doo-Seung 1996, 43). The hegemonic view of military service as men's national duty, despite some lingering resistance, is attributable to the imperative of military security in the context of hostile confrontation with North Korea during the 1980s. It also suggests that the hegemonic view of military service as men's duty to the nation may be more fragile than it at first appears. Now let us turn to a discussion of the state's use of male conscripts in the industrializing economy in an effort to bring together the twin goals of militarized modernity: a strong military and an industrial economy.

COUPLING MEN'S MILITARY MOBILIZATION
WITH THEIR ECONOMIC MOBILIZATION

Since 1973, when Park's regime introduced the Military Service Special Cases Law, tens of thousands of conscripts annually have worked in factories and research centers designated by the state in lieu of mandatory military service. Although this practice persisted throughout the 1990s and today, I focus on the 1970s and 1980s, when it remained instrumental to the building of national defense and heavy industrialization pursued by the modernizing state. In particular, I discuss the ways in which male conscripts were deployed as "industrial soldiers" during this period and analyze the extent to which this practice contributed to the masculinization of the skilled workforce and thereby served to reinforce men's subjectivity as family providers.

The Use of Conscripts in the Industrializing Economy

Drawing little attention from either Korean feminists or scholars of the Korean political economy, the universal conscription system has nevertheless played an important role in segregating the labor market by gender. Instrumental to institutionalizing the practice of deploying conscripts as workers in heavy and chemical industries was the Military Service Special Cases Law, enacted in 1973. This law was consciously designed to build a strong military and an industrial economy, the two main goals of militarized modernity, by collapsing the distinction between soldiers on the one hand and workers, engineers, and researchers on the other. In fact, factory workers were commonly called industrial soldiers (sanŏpyŏkkun) in South Korea. The OMM explained the legislation of the Special Cases Law as follows:

> [The state] faced the urgent problem of obtaining skilled labor in its pursuit of national development through building foundational industries, defense industries, and heavy and chemical industries. This law was established as a countermeasure to deal with this problem by making an *effective use* of a *surplus* of conscripts. (OMM 1986, 177; translation and italics mine)

The notion of a surplus of conscripts assumes that the periodic fluctuation in the total number of prospective conscripts is not to be affected by the separate ideal of an optimum size of military manpower. That is, even when the military cannot absorb the entire pool of prospective conscripts in a given year, all of them are to be processed through the conscription system to sustain the principle of universal male conscription; all healthy young men in South Korea must serve in the military. Hence the management of a surplus of conscripts is crucial to the stability of the universal conscription system.

According to the Military Service Special Cases Law, the following categories of prospective conscripts were permitted to substitute paid employment for military service: (1) engineers and "craftsmen" (kinŭngsa) working in military supplies factories, weapons assembly and maintenance factories, or military research centers; (2) licensed engineers and craftsmen working in strategic industries such as heavy and petrochemical manufacturing, mining, construction, and energy industries; and (3) students of the Korea Advanced Institute of Science and Technology (KAIST) (OMM 1986, 177). To apply for the special cases, individual young men had to obtain training and licenses and to be employed by companies designated by the state before they were drafted. After receiving basic military training, all these categories of conscripts, except for students of KAIST, were obliged to work for employers designated by the state for five years instead of mandatory military service; KAIST students were required to work for three years after graduation (MND 1988, 343–44). Although there were several revisions of the law throughout the 1970s and the 1980s, its basic structure as described earlier remained largely constant (MND 1990, 286–87). The following remarks by a senior researcher working for the Military Recruitment Council represents an official view behind this practice. In a short article on the influence of military service on industrial development, he writes:

> Our nation's military has contributed to modernization in two ways. First, it was instrumental in developing the human resources that played a cen-

tral role in achieving economic development. Second, it has produced technology and the *mentality necessary for industrialization* and urbanization by functioning as an educational setting that has provided opportunities to learn technical training and management technique. (Pyŏng-du Ch'oi 1991, 47; translation and italics mine)

This view echoes a main theme in the literature of the modernization school: that the military played the role of a modernizer in "developing" societies.[21]

From its inception, the defense industry in South Korea consisted of a loose collection of production firms fostered by the state in the midst of heavy and chemical industrialization during the 1970s. The majority were large-size factories set up by the business conglomerates known as *chaebol.* In 1982 there were eighty-five defense companies; their number decreased slightly, to eighty-two, in 1990 (Nolan 1986, 65; MND 1991, 260). Although their exact numbers during the 1970s are not available, it can be inferred that they might have been close to these figures, for at least two reasons. First, the 1970s were definitely the formative decade for defense industrialization. Under the Yulgok project (1974–81), Park's regime invested $5 billion to build defense industries (Hamm 1999, 83). Second, the state, as their only customer, tightly controlled the operation of these firms, protecting them with preferential loans, special interest rates, tax exemptions, and handsome annual profits (Moon Chung-In 1989, 159; Nolan 1986, 113, 114). In other words, defense firms could enjoy stability, since they were largely immune to vagaries of the market and to competition. These military contractors recruited a large number of male conscripts, who had either already been trained under public vocational training programs or were trained after recruitment under in-plant training programs. While there are no reliable statistics on the number of workers in these enterprises,[22] we can get a glimpse of the extent to which conscripts were hired by the military contractors from an ethnographic study of Poongsan Company, one of the top thirty enterprises in South Korea and a major defense and metal business (Choong Soon Kim 1992). According to this study, conducted between 1987 and 1990, Angang plant, the largest of Poongsan's four plants, had 4,050 employees, who were predominantly blue-collar male workers, along with a handful of managers. Almost three-quarters of all employees were under thirty years of age. Kim explained this high concentration of young male workers as follows:

> The Korean government exempts from active military duty all those who work in the defense industry, and many young men of draftable age (18 years old and older) seek employment in the Angang plant to be exempted

from military duty. Currently, nearly 15 percent of the workers at the Angang plant fall in this 17- to 20-year-old age group. (1992, 74)

The percentage of economic conscripts in this plant would of course be far
higher if we also counted older workers initially recruited through the same
channels.

The cumulative number of industrial conscripts employed in heavy industries reflects the extent to which skilled labor was masculinized in conjunction with compulsory military service. Here I am not suggesting that skilled
labor would not have been masculinized without the economic use of male
conscripts. In the absence of a male conscription system, gender as a symbolic order naturalizing hierarchical relations among binary opposites would
influence us to associate metal and chemical industries with masculinity and
the so-called light industries with femininity.[23] In the case of South Korea, the
masculinization of skilled labor in the heavy industries was rigidly institutionalized through the mechanism of vocational training programs, the technical
license system, and the economic use of male conscripts with such training
or licenses. Consequently, women workers were marginalized from the initial
stage of recruitment and job training in a labor market sharply segregated by
gender.

The Economic Substitute for Conscription and the Masculinization of Skilled Labor in Heavy and Chemical Industries

The masculinization of skilled labor in conjunction with the economic use of
conscripts was embedded in the process of building a self-reliant national defense through developing strategic heavy and chemical industries.[24] This industrialization, which was initiated by Park's regime in the early 1970s and
modified by Chun's regime,[25] necessitated a continuous supply of workers
adequately trained in manufacturing iron, steel, machinery, petrochemicals,
ships, and automobiles. To meet this challenge, the state established the technical license system and vocational training programs under the Vocational
Training Law, which was enacted in 1967 and subsequently revised in 1974,
1976, 1981, and 1987 (ML 1989, 188). Throughout the 1970s, the state, in collaboration with the private sector, acted as a major agent of vocational training,
but by the 1990s the private sector had become the major agent. The combined
use of vocational training programs and the technical license system in conjunction with the economic use of male conscripts contributed to the gendered
formation of skilled labor in heavy and chemical industries.

6. President Park Chung Hee's visit to a vocational training center, 1975.
Photograph by Yonhap News Agency.

According to the 1967 Vocational Training Law, vocational programs were, from their inception, intended to produce the skilled labor necessary for the defense industry, as well as foundational heavy and chemical industries (Cho Pyŏng-t'ae 1975, 89). As initial steps, Park's regime founded vocational training centers in the Seoul-Inch'ŏn industrial district (1968) to produce instructors, and in the Pusan area (1971) to train male workers in metal processing, mechanical assembly, lathing, and welding (ML 1989, 188; Bureau of Labor 1971, 32, 36). The state expanded such training facilities in major industrial cities throughout the 1970s and modified them in the 1980s (ML 1989, 197, 198, 206). Major fields of vocational training included metal processing and manufacturing, electricity, electronics and communications, and construction (199).

The state and employers have played the central role in training industrial workers in heavy and chemical manufacturing. As table 1 indicates, the numbers of industrial workers trained by the state and the private sector multiplied during the first half of the 1970s with the launching of defense industrialization and the implementation of the Military Service Special Cases Law (see figure 6). The numbers of these workers continued to grow throughout

Table 1. Vocational Training by Agent

Years	Public*	In-plant**	Authorized***	Total
1967–71	36,317 (36.7)	48,225 (48.8)	14,321 (14.5)	98,863 (100.0)
1972–76	81,294 (26.0)	177,350 (56.7)	54,092 (17.3)	312,736 (100.0)
1977–81	120,117 (24.2)	337,388 (68.1)	38,234 (7.7)	495,739 (100.0)
1982–86	121,044 (43.8)	114,773 (41.6)	40,370 (14.6)	276,187 (100.0)
1987–91	113,802 (31.0)	163,230 (44.4)	90,584 (24.6)	367,616 (100.0)

Source: Ministry of Labor, *Nodongpaeksŏ* [White Paper on Labor] (1997), 219.
Note: Percentage of total is indicated in parentheses.
*Public agents include the Korea Manpower Agency, the central government, and local administrations.
**In-plant agents include private firms and their commissioned organizations.
***Authorized agents include commercial training institutes and social welfare bodies. See Ministry of Labor, *Nodongt'onggyeyŏn'gam* [Labor Statistics Yearbook] (1992), 346.

the 1970s, a decade of defense industrialization. However, during this period, private firms trained far more workers than the state. Yet this should not be construed as a sign of the dominance of private business. Rather, the state delegated the task of training industrial workers to the expanding economic conglomerates (chaebol) that it was fostering. Toward the late 1970s, however, the further expansion in the role of private firms resulted not so much from this delegation by the state as from the rapid growth of private business. That is, the growth of private business during the 1970s undermined the "developmental" state's dominance over domestic capitalists, and their relationship became increasingly competitive in the 1980s (Kim Eun Mee 1997).

According to the Military Service Special Cases Law, (male) workers in heavy and chemical industries and defense firms had to obtain licenses in their technical fields (before or during their employment) when they applied for the exemption from mandatory military service. Public and in-plant vocational training programs prepared male workers for the state-administered qualification tests.[26] The numbers show that, indeed, the fields in which licenses were required for exemption from military service were in fact the fields in which licenses were acquired, in great numbers. The largest field of vocational training programs, representing over two-fifths of the total number of skilled workers, was machine manufacturing, and the next five largest fields consisted of electricity, communications, chemical engineering, construction, and electronics,

Table 2. Vocational Training by Sex and by Agent

Year	Public		Private (in-plant)		Private (authorized)	
	Women	Men	Women	Men	Women	Men
1978–82	6,289	127,035	99,051	209,729	11,462	22,066
	(4.7)	(95.3)	(32.1)	(67.9)	(34.2)	(65.8)
1983	983	23,278	3,256	17,704	3,825	2,646
	(4.0)	(96.0)	(15.5)	(84.5)	(59.1)	(40.9)
1984	1,052	21,751	3,187	17,577	4,146	4,133
	(4.6)	(95.4)	(15.3)	(84.7)	(50.1)	(49.9)
1985	924	21,659	4,388	19,488	3,745	5,181
	(4.1)	(95.9)	(18.4)	(81.6)	(42.0)	(58.0)
1986	1,005	21,857	4,680	14,362	3,808	5,146
	(4.4)	(95.6)	(24.6)	(75.4)	(42.5)	(57.5)
1987	927	21,313	4,903	9,405	3,083	6,175
	(4.2)	(95.8)	(33.8)	(66.2)	(33.3)	(66.7)
Total	11,180	236,893	119,465	288,265	30,069	45,347
	(4.5)	(95.5)	(29.3)	(70.7)	(39.9)	(60.1)

Source: Adapted from Sin Yong-su, *Yŏsŏng nodongsijangŭi chungjanggi chŏnmangkwa kwaje* [A Mid- and Long-Term Prospect on the Women's Labor Market and Its Problems] (Seoul, 1991), 31.
Note: Percentage of total is indicated in parentheses.

in descending order. These areas largely overlap with the fields specified in the Military Service Special Cases Law. Between 1979 and 1987, the average number of craftsmen newly licensed each year was approximately 13,000 to 14,000. The field of metal processing consistently generated the largest number of licensed craftsmen, close to 10,000 each year on average (ML 1989, 199)

The majority of workers trained by the state in the 1970s and 1980s became economic conscripts, that is, entered the fields that government was making available as alternatives to military service. The absolute number of male workers trained in public vocational training programs remained largely constant during the 1980s (following the growth of the 1970s) (see tables 1 and 2). While Chun's regime (1980–87) virtually abandoned defense industrialization, purchasing advanced weapons from the United States and other Western countries instead, the mechanism of economic conscription, coupled with vocational training programs and technical licenses, was sustained during the period. Until the beginning of the 1990s, paid employment in heavy industries in lieu of military service was highly appealing to young conscripts. The state used various incentives to attract young men to the expanding industrial sectors. Male recruits to public vocational training programs were provided with free training and free dormitory living, as well as guaranteed employment (ML 1989, 203). There is an additional reason for the popularity of economic conscription; most companies designated for the military service special cases were large firms, with three hundred employees or more, which could provide relatively good working conditions (Hŏ Sang-gu 1990, 62). To lower-class young men with a secondary education, secure employment in heavy and chemical industries, handsomely subsidized by the state, must have been an appealing alternative to military service.

It is more difficult to assess how many of those trained by private companies during the period between the mid-1970s and the late 1980s were economic conscripts. There are no reliable statistics on this. According to a senior researcher in the KIDA, 10 to 20 percent of the annual cohort of prospective conscripts served under the military service special cases each year, depending on the size of the surplus of recruits that year. It can be estimated that both public and in-plant vocational training programs during this period trained between 20,000 and 40,000 conscripts annually.[27]

While public or in-plant vocational training programs supplied skilled workers as "industrial soldiers," universities, for their part, were expected to provide natural scientists and engineers to be recruited by public and private research centers.[28] That is, as a large number of prospective conscripts were integrated into vocational training programs after completing secondary education to fuel the heavy and chemical industries, a far smaller number of conscripts were to serve as engineers and researchers in the place of mandatory military service. The South Korean state did not merely rely on the existing system of higher education to procure engineers and scientists. In 1973, Park's regime inaugurated the Korea Advanced Institute of Science and Technology (KAIST) as a special graduate school to educate high-quality natural scientists and engineers indispensable for continuous industrial development. To increase its academic autonomy and creativity, KAIST was placed under the control of the Ministry of Science and Technology, not the Ministry of Education. Opening with 105 master's program students, KAIST soon founded a Ph.D. program, in 1975. The total number of graduate students multiplied over time, from 618 in 1978 to 2,168 in 1987.[29] During the period of military rule, KAIST recruited a predominantly male student body that was given full schol-

Table 3. Female College Students by Field of Study

Year	Total (% of all students)	Engineering (% of all engineering students)	Arts (% of all arts students)	Teachers' training (% of all teachers' training students)
1971	36,074 (23.2)	266 (0.7)	5,332 (74.7)	7,890 (49.7)
1975	55,349 (26.5)	569 (1.3)	7,912 (77.2)	16,514 (52.9)
1980	90,634 (22.5)	1,303 (1.2)	14,222 (76.3)	25,356 (47.5)
1985	209,674 (26.8)	5,389 (2.7)	29,243 (67.8)	53,844 (56.8)
1990	296,447 (28.5)	14,605 (6.1)	33,620 (63.4)	39,098 (57.6)

Sources: Adapted from Korean Women's Development Institute (KWDI), *Yŏsŏngbaeksŏ* [White Paper on Women] (1991), 458; and KWDI, *Yŏsŏngbaeksŏ* [White Paper on Women] (1985), 507–9.

arships and living expenses. In return, the students were required to work in research institutes designated by the state for three years after graduation, in lieu of military service.[30]

The masculinization of this elite-course science and technology education represented an accentuated version of higher education in general. As table 3 illustrates, women were extremely underrepresented in this field of study throughout the 1970s and 1980s, the decades of rapid industrial development. Although it grew significantly over the 1980s (increasing fivefold), the proportion of women in engineering still remained very low in 1990.[31] This minuscule representation stands in sharp contrast to the concentration of women in the arts, and, to a lesser degree, in teaching. This gender-segregated higher education led to the scarcity of women among licensed engineers under the technical license system.[32]

The large segment of the economy that was militarized by the hegemonic practice of using conscripts as industrial workers and researchers, in conjunction with vocational training programs and the technical license system, worked in favor of establishing men as primary family providers by institutionalizing the masculinization of semiskilled and skilled workers in heavy industry. In general, the vocational training programs and the technical license system excluded the majority of women workers in manufacturing industries from heavy industries. In particular, the economic use of prospective conscripts in conjunction with the vocational training programs and the technical license system ensured the flow of male workers into these industries. The combination of paid employment and virtual exemption from military service (aside from several weeks of basic training) worked as a strong incentive to draw prospective conscripts. Although obligatory employment in the place of military service froze occupational mobility for the required period of service, it was highly sought after by many young men during the 1970s and 1980s (KIDA 1995b, 155–48).[33] To be clear, this military and economic mobilization did not protect blue-collar workers from exploitation. South Korean workers generally worked longer hours and earned wages far lower than those of their counterparts in comparable countries before the explosion of labor strikes in the late 1980s. Nevertheless, these men's relatively stable employment in large firms contributed to the formation of the modern masculine subjectivity of the family provider among upper-part working-class men.

MEN'S SUBJECTIVITY AS FAMILY PROVIDER: MAKING THE MODERN GENDER HIERARCHY

As we have seen, the masculinization of skilled labor in the rapidly industrializing economy facilitated by the economic use of prospective conscripts was closely related to the marginalization of women in the economy, which will be discussed in the next chapter. This gendered making of the industrial economy was central to the remaking of the modern gender hierarchy based on the division of labor between housewife and husband-provider. Modern notions of femininity and masculinity, based on this hierarchical gender division of labor, became popularized through formal schooling and the mass media, two major mechanisms of socialization that construct gendered subjects. Even after the recent curricular reform in 1995, textbooks used in social studies represented sharply dichotomous images of women as consumers and housewives and men as historical heroes and productive workers (Pak Myŏng-sun 1997, 126–30). In South Korea, the production of textbooks was tightly controlled by the state under the military rule. Teachers had to use state-approved textbooks in primary and secondary education. This uniformity increased the influence of pervasive images of women as housewives among young students. The almost uniform representation in the textbooks of women as housewives, meanwhile, contrasted the diverse images of men. Adult men appeared in all occupations except those of household manager and nurse. At the same time, all the diverse images of men that were presented shared the fundamental role of family provider as well (Pak Myŏng-sun 1997).

The mass media also tended to represent women primarily as housewives. Programs targeted to female viewers reflected this tendency. For example, prime-time sitcoms or soap operas, for which women made up the majority of the audience, depicted married women as housewives (Song Yu-jae 1984; Pak Suk-ja 1997, 256). A content analysis of three major women's magazines published between 1968 and 1981 reveals that the typical heroine of fictional stories was an attractive but unhappy single woman in her twenties whose main work was housekeeping or who was at times employed in a low-status white-collar occupation. Married women appeared as the second-largest category in the fictional representation of women in these women's magazines. Both single and married women portrayed in these magazine fictions faced feminized problems of love and family (Song Yu-jae 1985).

In the process of rapid industrialization, emergent urban middle-class families adopted the normative gender division of labor. Studies of urban families conducted in the 1970s and early 1980s illustrate the following pattern. Although they were occasionally involved in children's education, family consumption, and family outings, the primary role of husbands was nevertheless financial support of their families. In contrast, wives performed housework and child rearing and often exercised authority in household decision making that was delegated by their absent and busy husbands. Even the paid employment of some wives rarely changed the rigid division of labor by gender, since these women worked only as long as their employment did not interfere with their domestic responsibilities. Furthermore, these working wives' employment (in the absence of an urgent need for money) tended to undermine their bargaining power with their husbands in any conjugal conflict. Professional women were inclined to feel grateful about their husbands' "permission" or "understanding" for their employment outside the home (Cho Uhn 1983).

After two decades of industrialization, by the 1980s, the normative gender division of labor between husband-provider and housewife became firmly established. Elaine Kim's study (1997), conducted in the late 1980s and based on in-depth interviews of fifty-four married South Korean men between the ages of twenty-four and sixty-nine, illustrates the central role of family provider in these men's perception of masculinity across class and age. While these men display varying degrees of misogyny and sympathy toward women, they converge in their perception of manhood, defined primarily in terms of financial abilities. A series of small-scale case studies based on interviews and surveys offers glimpses of the extent to which modern gender hierarchy was accepted by women as well. Even rural or urban poor women who had to work to assist family income tended to view themselves as housewives. According to a 1987 study of rural families whose economic conditions did not support the urban middle-class gender division of labor, only 10.1 percent of the women answered that they were entirely farmworkers. The majority of the women interviewed (57.8 percent) responded that they were solely or primarily housewives, and 30.7 percent that they were both housewives and agricultural workers (Kim Chu-suk 1990, 279). Similarly, a study of urban poor families in Ch'ungju, a provincial city, shows that a majority of the women considered their husbands the primary providers, despite the fact that other family members worked in order to maximize family income, and that the wife often contributed nearly half of it. Among these married women, 55.2 percent indicated that their husband was the primary breadwinner, whereas 12.4 percent indicated that they were (Kim Mi-suk 1990, 169).

The modernization of gender hierarchy in industrializing South Korea during the period from the 1960s to the 1980s hinges on the construction and maintenance of femininity and masculinity, tied to the ideology of housewife and husband-provider and the gender division of labor. Masculine identity in this structure is grounded in men's privileged access to the labor market, rigidly segregated by gender. Several mechanisms have been at work to ensure men's access to stable and full-time jobs, ranging from the state's policy and institutional arrangements to individual practices in business firms and factories, as well as the inculcation of modern gender ideology through family life, schooling, and the mass media.

In association with these cultural mechanisms for constructing men as family providers, the convergence of military and economic mobilization of men by the modernizing state functions to reinforce the masculine subjectivity, particularly enabling a large number of working-class men to gain access to secure employment. In the large scheme of the militarized economy, the economic use of prospective conscripts as semiskilled or skilled workers served as a reward for those who complied with men's martial duty, while the evasion of military service was punished with the denial of access to employment, even self-employment. This rewarding of martial duty was an integral element of the militarized economy that also recognized military service as work experience and translated it into extra pay, faster promotion, and the extra points for public employment tests (see chapter 1). In constructing men as dutiful nationals through economic and military mobilization, the modernizing state compensated men for their subjection to military service with economic advantage over women and thereby contributed to the establishment of men's subjectivity as family provider, especially among upper-part working-class men who would otherwise not be able to live out the middle-class norm of the nuclear family.

The coupling of military service with employment during the period of military rule remained unchallenged for two reasons. First, by exploiting the context of acute military confrontation with North Korea, repressive military regimes prohibited any public discussion of military service issues. Second, the rigidly gender-segregated labor market had rendered the connection invisible. In other words, segregated at the stage of recruitment, most working women were employed in feminized sectors of the labor market. They could not see the contributing role of military service to the masculinizing of skilled labor in strategic chemical and heavy industries.[34]

CONCLUSION

The modernizing state incorporated men as conscripts and primary workers into the nation being built through the multiple mechanisms of indoctrination, surveillance, training, and punishment. Subjecting men to the nation, the coupling of military and economic mobilization empowered men as family providers in the industrializing state. In the next chapter, I will examine women's incorporation into the modern nation, which constructed women as marginalized producers and primary reproducers.

3

MARGINALIZED IN PRODUCTION
AND MOBILIZED TO BE DOMESTIC

Women's Incorporation into the Nation

On the "labor day" I cannot but think about my reality as a worker and woman. There are numerous women, ranging from factory workers to college graduates, who cannot find work and therefore cannot contribute to society. I wonder how much "pride" these women feel as workers. Societal perception of women and their treatment in the workplace do not allow them to feel pride. Families, relatives, and the whole society are forcing women to stay within marriage. It is absurd that even family planning campaign centers, promoting the slogan "Let's have two children regardless of their sex," hire only men in "open hiring." . . . We are told that "labor is valuable, labor is life, humans exist through production, and production is done through labor, and human beings ought to work to live meaningful lives." But in this kind of social milieu, these really right words lose their persuasive power for women.

—woman working in a reading room of Chohŭng Bank, quoted in *Chungang Daily*, March 10, 1977

A new academic year has begun. Recently, each school has begun serious regulation of students' lunchboxes, to contain rice mixed with barley (the ratio is seven to three) to cope with rice deficiency and achieve nutritional balance. Yet it is likely for those students unfamiliar with this mixed meal to feel painful about eating such a lunch. This special column is created to provide readers with great recipes for delicious barley lunchboxes. Children can enjoy their lunchtime, which is the most pleasurable time of any school day.

—recipes given by the president of the Central Association of National Housewives' Classes, *Hanguk Daily*, March 4, 1976

The vignettes from the 1970s quoted in these epigraphs provide us with glimpses of women's marginalization as workers in the industrializing economy, along with the modernizing state's call for women to be wise mothers who can cook a delicious and nutritious lunch while saving rice to contribute to building the modern industrial economy. Women's mobilization in the pursuit of militarized modernity took a path quite different from men's mobilization during the period of military rule. In the absence of systematic policies and programs to train women as a permanent workforce for the industrializing economy, the only continuous policy and program directed to women during this period included "family planning" (a euphemism for population control) policy and the campaign to promote "rational management of the household." Reflecting the underlying assumption about women as reproducers confined to the domestic sphere, the family planning policy cast women as breeders, and the campaign for the rational management of the household cast them as housewives. Although these initiatives never received any material and ideological investment by the military regimes comparable to the investment in the military and industrial mobilization of men, they reveal the distinct ways in which women were incorporated into the modern nation to boost the strong military and the industrial economy.

This chapter outlines women's economic marginalization in manufacturing industries during the 1970s and 1980s as a backdrop to their mobilization as mothers and housewives. Then it examines the ways in which the state monitored women by surveillance and normalization practices; women were mobilized to control their fertility and manage their households "rationally" so they could contribute to the building of the modern industrial economy. It is my contention that women's membership in the modern nation being built hinged on their role as reproducers despite their significant contribution to the economy as producers. Economic marginalization of women became visible in their persistent exposure to domesticating instructions and their exclusion from vocational training programs during the period of heavy industrialization in the 1970s and 1980s. At the same time, it was during this period that population control in the name of family planning was the single national policy targeted at women that the modernizing state considered as integral to economic development.

THE MARGINALIZATION OF WOMEN IN THE INDUSTRIALIZING ECONOMY

Women in Manufacturing Industries

In the three decades of economic growth from the 1960s to the 1980s, women's participation in the labor market expanded in both absolute terms and relative terms. As table 4 shows, between 1960 and 1989 the number of "economically active" women who were able and willing to work increased from approximately 2.2 million to 7.3 million. The number of these women as a percentage of the total number of women who were socially defined as capable of working grew from 26.8 percent to 46.7 percent. During the same period, the number of these women as a percentage of the total economically active population grew from 28.6 percent to 43.5 percent.

However, as table 4 also shows, the percentage among women of economically active women and the percentage of women in the economically active population contracted between 1975 and 1985. The increase in women's economic participation between 1985 and 1989 reflected the explosive growth of service industries, absorbing a massive number of women. The decrease in the percentage among women of economically active women between 1975 and 1985 was largely attributable to the rise in women's educational level. As an increasing number of young women attended high school, junior college, and four-year college during this period, the ratio of women willing to work was reduced. However, this change does not explain why the percentage of women in the total economically active population was reduced with respect to that of their male counterparts, whose level of education was higher than women's and also on the rise. The contraction of the proportion of women workers in the expanding labor market reflects the specific pattern of industrialization in the 1970s and the 1980s, that is, aggressive building of heavy and chemical industries. In particular, this path of industrialization was integral to defense industrialization during the 1970s. This overall picture of industrial development strongly suggests a connection between the economic use of conscripts in the process of heavy industrialization and the marginalization of women in the economy.[1]

It is noteworthy that the formation of the mechanism for training male workers by the state and business (discussed in the previous chapter) coincided with the massive entry of women into the expanding areas of textile and textile-related manufacturing (*Kiŏpkyŏngyŏng* 1967, 68). During the first half of the 1970s, the state launched a project to employ 420,000 female workers, which resulted in record growth in young women's participation in the labor mar-

Table 4. Women's Economic Participation

Year	Total number of women over 14 years old (in thousands)	Number of EAW** (in thousands)	EAW as percentage of the total number of women over 14 years old	Percentage of women in economically active population
1960*	8,054	2,156	26.8	28.6
1970	9,629	3,625	37.6	34.9
1975	11,319	5,175	45.7	38.8
1980	12,945	4,973	38.4	36.6
1985	14,867	5,218	35.1	35.9
1989	15,576	7,274	46.7	43.5

Sources: Korean Women's Development Institute (KWDI), Yŏsŏngbaeksŏ [White Paper on Women] (1991), 463; KWDI, Yŏsŏngbaeksŏ [White Paper on Women] (1985), 510; Kang I-su and Pak Ki-nam, "Yŏsŏngkwa nodong" [Women and Labor], in Yŏsŏnghak kang'ŭi: Han'guk yŏsŏng hyŏnsilŭi ihae [Women's Studies Lectures: Understanding Korean Women's Reality], ed. Han'gukyŏsŏngyŏn'guhoe (Seoul: Tongnyŏk, 1991), 137.
*Numbers for 1960 include thirteen-year-olds.
**Economically active women. EAW refers to the number of women who are able and willing to work; thus it includes the number of unemployed women as well.

ket as factory workers (Kim Chang-ho 1986, 135; Kim Ok-yŏl and Kim T'ae-hŭi 1973, 2). Yet there were few public training programs for these women workers. They were mobilized merely as temporary and "cheap" workers for labor-intensive manufacturing. As heavy and chemical industrialization proceeded throughout the 1970s and 1980s, therefore, the ratio of women workers in manufacturing industries declined again.[2] The growth of women production workers between 1975 and 1983 was negative in the expanding economy (Kim Chang-ho 1986, 135).

The masculinized pattern of vocational training in conjunction with the use of male conscripts as industrial workers becomes clear when training programs are broken down by sex. Although comprehensive statistics over time are not available, the following information supports the trend. As table 2 indicates (see chapter 2), public vocational training programs focused on male workers throughout the 1980s.[3] The proportion of women in public vocational programs remained constant at between 4 and 5 percent of the total trainees. Private companies also focused on male workers during this time, albeit to a lesser degree than the state. It is noteworthy that the percentage of women workers trained by private businesses actually dropped during the mid-1980s, when these businesses enjoyed record growth in heavy and chemical manufacturing as a result of increasing export to the international market. All these characteristics, taken together, indicate that heavy and chemical industrialization, requiring skilled workers and generating relatively better-paying jobs, was accompanied by the masculinization of skilled labor.

Women workers' marginalization in public vocational training programs was not just a matter of numbers. The content of state-run training programs directed at women differed greatly from that of programs aimed at men. First, the public vocational programs for women were designed primarily for a specific category of "women who require the state's protection," which referred to prisoners and poor single mothers (Sin Yong-su 1991, 32). These programs were designed to teach women feminized skills such as embroidery, cooking, and sewing. Second, female workers were excluded from technical training in masculinized fields such as metal processing, electricity, construction, wood processing, and transportation and construction equipment, the fields in which the state trained the largest number of workers. Third, female trainees were segregated by their feminized skills and confined to low-paying, labor-intensive jobs such as sewing, embroidering, dyeing, weaving, spinning, operating telephones, dressing hair, and producing handicrafts (Cho Pyŏng-t'ae 1975, 90). This tendency to segregate and exclude women workers hardly changed throughout the 1970s and 1980s. As late as March 1988, the majority of women trainees in public programs (729 women) were ghettoized in the following areas: electronics assembly (24.8 percent), hairdressing (23 percent), dressmaking (13 percent), weaving (7.8 percent), machine embroidery (6 percent), and hand embroidery (5.2 percent) (Sin Yong-su 1991, 33).

Similarly, women workers trained by private companies and other authorized agents tended to be concentrated in feminized skills such as the operation of spinning or weaving machines, sewing, and electronics assembly (Sin Yong-su 1991, 35). The relatively higher percentage of women workers trained by in-plant training programs between 1978 and 1982 (see chap. 2, table 2) reflects the residual significance of light industry to private business before the explosive growth of heavy industry in the mid-1980s.

The gendered working of these vocational training programs resulted in a scarcity of women with state-approved licenses in heavy and chemical industries. Introduced in 1975, the technical license system was an integral part of supplying skilled workers necessary to heavy and chemical industrialization. Indeed, public vocational training programs prepared workers for state

Table 5. Women Licensees in the Categories of Craftsman

Category	Women as percentage of total number of skilled workers			Number of skilled women workers in each category (%)		
	1976	1980	1984	1976	1980	1984
First-class craftsman	0.3	0.2	0.3	51 (0.26)	73 (0.15)	155 (0.18)
Second-class craftsman	15.1	11.2	11.2	19,144 (98.6)	47,089 (97.6)	85,512 (96.7)
Assistant craftsman	0.7	1.0	1.7	229 (1.14)	1,068 (2.25)	2,790 (3.12)
Total	10.9	8.7	9.1	19,424 (100.00)	48,230 (100.00)	88,457 (100.00)

Source: Adapted from Korean Public Corporation for Vocational Training, "Annual Statistics of the State's Technical Certification" (1985).

examinations to obtain engineers' and craftsmen's licenses. In 1987, women comprised only 4 percent of the total applicants for these qualifying examinations and 3.9 percent of the total number of 660,726 licensed workers (Sin Yong-su 1991, 37–38). This implies that women exhibited almost exactly the same rate of success as men in passing the tests, and that the low representation of women is therefore attributable primarily to various mechanisms to discourage or disqualify women, rather than to their ability.

The cumulative size of the skilled labor force with technical licenses increased from 180,000 in 1976 to 980,000 in 1984. Yet as table 5 illustrates, women represented only 10.9 percent of the total number of licensed craftsmen in 1976, with the ratio decreasing even further, to 9.1 percent, in 1984. This confirms the decrease in the percentage of women workers trained by private firms during the expansion of heavy industry in the mid-1980s. It also confirms the masculinization of skilled workers through public vocational training programs. When the aggregate category of craftsman is further divided into "master craftsman," "first-class craftsman," "second-class craftsman," and "assistant craftsman," the trend appears to be even more striking. No women appear in the subcategory of master craftsman. Among the remaining three categories, the absolute majority of women (over 96 percent) are concentrated in the subcategory of second-class craftsman (ikŭp kinŭngsa), which did not require rigorous qualification criteria.[4] There was also a very small propor-

Table 6. Skilled Workers by Field and Sex in 1985

Field	Women	Men
Machine manufacturing	1,247 (1.4)	413,951 (42.4)
Electricity	91 (0.1)	105,263 (10.8)
Communications	80,526 (91.0)	94,290 (9.6)
Chemical engineering	1,624 (1.8)	93,236 (9.5)
Architecture	244 (0.3)	65,302 (6.7)
Electronics	772 (0.9)	61,657 (6.3)
Applied industries	1,614 (1.8)	47,777 (4.9)
Civil engineering	27 (0.03)	28,212 (2.9)
Mining	15	27,509 (2.8)
Metal	18	25,427 (2.6)
Textile	2,128 (2.4)	10,537 (1.1)
Information processing	62	1,582
Shipbuilding	1	1,444
Ocean	88	768
Aviation	0	262
Total	88,457	977,217

Source: Korean Public Corporation for Vocational Training, "Annual Statistics on National Skill Licenses" (1985).
Note: Percentage of total is indicated in parentheses.

tion of women in the category of assistant craftsman, since this rarely provided opportunities for better employment.

When the content of women's technical licenses is broken down, the pattern of gender-specific segregation and exclusion emerges clearly. As table 6 shows, there is a conspicuous disparity between the number of women and of men in the major fields of heavy and chemical industries actively promoted by the state. The only exception to this general trend is the category of communications, in which 91 percent of the skilled women workers are concentrated and the number of women uniquely approximates that of men. This is because 82.2 percent of these women work as telephone operators, a heavily feminized occupation. This has been a more or less consistent pattern since the mid-1970s, when the majority of women workers who received technical training were also telephone operators (Cho Pyŏng-t'ae 1975). Only a fraction of them operate communications machines. This demonstrates that during the 1970s and most of the 1980s, when the expansion of heavy and chemical industries demanded skilled labor, women workers remained in marginalized light industry and some labor-intensive sectors of heavy and chemical industry such as soap, rubber, and paint.

Domesticating Women Workers

While marginalizing women workers by means of discriminatory training and repressive labor control (see chapter 1), the state provided them with domesticating instructions through the Factory New Village Movement, working women's classes (kŭloyŏsŏngkyosil), workplace classes (chikchangkyosil), and ladies' university (sungnyŏdaehak) starting in the mid-1970s. Common to all these programs was a type of class teaching single women workers household management, womanly etiquette concerning speaking, dressing, and overall conduct, and domesticating hobbies such as flower arranging, handicrafts, and calligraphy. This suggests that the state intended to inculcate the reproductive and domestic subjectivity of mother and housewife in single women workers. This tendency was well expressed in the following statement by the Ministry of Labor: "Women workers need common sense, civility, thrift, wisdom as well as their duty as workers because they are mothers of future generations" (ML 1983, preface).

The Factory New Village Movement, which started in the mid-1970s, was an extension of the New Village Movement. Intended to depoliticize young single women working under extremely exploitative conditions, this movement involved the manipulation of reproductive and domestic femininity to make women docile and productive for the sake of building the industrial economy. A main component of the movement included four-night-and-five-day training camps at state-sponsored centers for working youths or at women's centers, during which women workers received instruction in domestic skills as well as propaganda for patriotism and "peaceful" worker-employer relations. Sixty to eighty women workers were trained at a time, and training was carried out semimonthly, over the course of one year (MHSA 1981b, chap. 6). The camp training also encouraged women workers' participation by means of small-group discussion concerning "worker-employer cooperation" and productivity. Although camp training recruited both male and female workers, women were treated differently from men because of women's essentialized identity as prospective wife and mother, articulated as follows:

"Women workers are housewives-to-be who carry out the New Village Movement in the household. Therefore, factories should play the role of a training center for the New Village Movement in the household" (249).

The working women's classes, workplace classes, and the ladies' university were variations of the instructional programs aimed at single female workers in Free Export Zones or Industrial Estates. The Ministry of Labor required firms that hired a certain number of young women workers to organize these classes and published instructional texts for them. The curriculum comprised sex education for population control, feminine etiquette, and basic skills for home management and child rearing, as well as propagandistic messages concerning anticommunism, the urgency of economic growth, and "industrial peace."

It is noteworthy that the domesticating programs began at the same time as the state instituted the licensing system to secure the supply of skilled labor. It appears that the state devised gender-specific training programs: domesticating programs for women workers on the one hand, and technical training for male workers on the other. Regardless of the actual effects of feminizing instructions on women workers, the persistence of such domesticating programs in their variations is suggestive of the extent to which the modernizing state was involved in the construction of gendered nationals (*kungmin*) in the pursuit of militarized modernity. An underlying assumption here was that whatever women might do and wherever they might be, they were ultimately reproductive and domestic beings represented in the role of wife and mother.

As a result, despite the quantitative expansion of women workers in manufacturing industries and their crucial role in the earlier phase of export-oriented economic growth, their subjectivity as full-time, permanent workers was overshadowed by the normative feminine subjectivity of the nonproductive housewife. This is well illustrated by the characteristics of female workers employed in manufacturing industries during the 1970s and 1980s. First, women workers are concentrated in labor-intensive industries such as textiles, clothing, sewing, tobacco, food, and electronics assembly (Chang Ha-jin 1991, 55; Kang Isu and Pak 1991, 142; *Kiŏpkyŏngyŏng* 1967, 67).[5] Women in these industries were generally defined as "unskilled" labor. Even within these industries, male workers occupied the relatively high-status positions involving supervision, sales, or technical skills. Similarly, in certain labor-intensive subsectors of masculinized heavy and chemical industries, such as rubber, plastic, paint, and soap, women represented between one-third and one-half of the total workforce. This contrasts women's underrepresentation in the capital- and technology-intensive areas of metal and petrochemical processing. In these areas, women represented less than 10 percent of the total workforce (Shim 1988, 120–24). As discussed in the previous chapter, these are the areas where men in general and prospective conscripts in particular were recruited and trained.

Second, women workers in manufacturing industries were paid extremely low wages and were specifically underpaid in comparison with their male counterparts. In 1972 the average wages of female workers employed in manufacturing companies with ten or more employees (where women represented 81.4 percent of the labor force) were among the lowest for all Korean workers, who as a group were already paid far below international standards. These women earned a monthly income — 10,445 won — which was below the average wages of female workers in all sectors — 11,784 won.[6] In 1985, women working in the manufacturing industries earned an average of 156,000 won per month, only 46.8 percent of the average earnings of their male counterparts, despite the fact that female workers worked six to seven hours more per month than their male counterparts (KWDI 1997, 200; 1985b, 4).[7] Although the labor strikes in the late 1980s substantially raised average monthly wages for all workers, women's wages continued to lag behind men's. In 1990, women in manufacturing industries earned an average of 353,000 won per month, 51.1 percent of men's wages in the same industries (KWDI 1997, 200).

Third, age and marital status were crucial factors affecting women's employment in manufacturing industries.[8] Young and unmarried women workers represented a majority of the labor force in manufacturing. In 1970, 77.5 percent of 541,200 female workers studied by the Center for Human Resource Development were single (Kim Yong-su and Lee Yong-ok 1976, 90). In 1978, 71.9 percent of 3,105,320 female workers hired by 62,217 firms with five or more employees were between eighteen and twenty-four years old (Yu Yŏng-ju 1982, 160). In 1983, 72 percent of women working in manufacturing industries were between eighteen and twenty-four years old. In the cases of feminized industries such as textiles, garments, and electronics, this ratio was slightly higher, between 74 percent and 77 percent (Kim Kyu-ch'ang 1985, 365). These figures imply that women's employment was often temporary or intermittent, which both reflected and in turn contributed to their marginalization in the economy.

During the second half of the 1980s, however, the number of older and married female workers grew noticeably. This reflects the changing industrial structure of the Korean economy, characterized by the flow of young female workers into the service sectors that were growing explosively during this period. Young women's distaste for highly exploitative and stigmatized factory work opened a space for older women whom employers had previously avoided. This trend becomes quite visible when we compare 1985 and 1990. In 1985, female workers between the ages of fifteen and twenty-nine comprised 55.8 percent of the total number of female workers in manufacturing industries, whereas those between the ages of thirty and forty-nine comprised 35.3 percent. In contrast, in 1990, the younger group made up only 42 percent of the total, while the older group grew in size to 45 percent (KWDI 1997, 150).

The characteristics of women workers in manufacturing industries, the fastest-growing sector of the industrializing economy during the period under examination, reflected and in turn reinforced the normative gender division of labor between husband-provider and dependent housewife. The economic marginalization of women became conspicuous as the focus of industrial development shifted from the manufacturing of light consumer goods to that of heavy and chemical industrial products, and the drive to build self-reliant national defense was unleashed. In sum, women workers remained untrained or trained with feminized skills and therefore "cheap," temporary, and secondary sources of labor. This should be understood against the background that labor-intensive manufacturing industries continued to be crucial to the Korean economy in the 1980s. The flip side of the drastic growth of the so-called capital-intensive export goods in the 1980s is the persistent feminization of labor-intensive manufacturing industries. This tendency is directly related to the state's attempt to recruit married women to compensate for the shortage of young female labor in the gender-segregated labor market.

ORGANIZING WOMEN AS MOTHERS AND WIVES

In an attempt to reach out to the entire population of adult women to accomplish the project of militarized modernity, the developmental state established new women's organizations and used the existing national network of women's organizations. Before the emergence of autonomous women's associations in the mid-1980s, the state organized mothers and wives as its quasi-official instrument. Formally civilian and voluntary organizations, all of these organizations registered with the state and received financial support from it. This kind of administered mass organization (AMO) of women included the Korean National Wives' Association, the Korean Federation of Housewives' Clubs, the Central Association of National Housewives' Classes, and the New Village Women's Association. During the later decades of colonial rule, Japan transplanted the AMOs as a mechanism to control the masses of colonized

Koreans, organizing them on the basis of place of residence, gender, age, workplace, and industry (see chapter 1). After decolonization, the U.S. Army military government (1945–48) continued to exploit the various AMOs for the same purpose. Subsequent postcolonial regimes in Korea adopted this established practice to keep civil society in check. In fact, women's AMOs can be seen as feminine counterparts of the masculinized organization of the ruling political party. As political parties in Korea served as instruments of personal power without their own institutional continuity, so have the women's organizations. In association with the mass media, which were kept under the state's tight control until the late 1980s, these women's organizations facilitated the state's access to women as mothers and wives.

The modernizing state built women's centers (*yŏsŏnghoekwan* and *punyŏbokchikwan*) in major urban areas. The idea of building women's centers emerged during the military junta period (1961–63). The Supreme Council for National Reconstruction funded the construction of the National Women's Welfare Center that was built as the first women's center in 1963 (MHSA 1987a, 175). During the following three decades, the state established women's centers in the capital cities of all nine provinces and four other major cities, namely, Pusan, Taegu, Kwangju, and Inch'ŏn. Many of them were built in the second half of the 1960s when the state expanded its women's networks (MHSA 1992, 1982b). As of January 1992 there were sixteen state-sponsored women's centers in major cities. Each center was a two- to six-story building with public facilities such as an auditorium, a refectory, bedrooms, classrooms, a library or an information room, a child-care unit, a beauty parlor, and a counseling center. These centers offered classes not only for mothers and wives but also for brides-to-be and grandmothers. The centers also held seminars, conferences, and workshops for the so-called women leaders.

In 1967 the Ministry of Health and Social Affairs instituted women's classes (*punyŏkyosil*) to organize the largely married women between twenty and sixty years of age in both urban and rural areas. By 1977, when they were merged into the New Village Women's Association, they claimed to have 2,150,000 members in 44,049 branches (MHSA 1981b, 47, 55). Other national women's organizations through which the state implemented the family planning policy and the campaign for the rational management of the household were the National Association of Korean Wives (Han'gukpuinhoe), the Korean Federation of Housewives' Clubs (Taehanjubuclŏbyŏnhaphoe), and the Central Association of National Housewives' Classes (Chŏngukchubukyosiljung'anghoe). Initially formed as the Great Korean Wives' Club around the time of the establishment of the Republic of Korea (1948), and later dissolved during the military junta period, the National Association of Korean Wives was revived under the latter name in 1964. Instituted in 1971 as an organizational base of the urban housewives' New Village Movement, the Central Association of National Housewives' Classes offered continuing education for adult women through housewives' classes starting in 1971 and housewives' university (*chubudaehak*) starting in 1977. These classes propagated the ideas and practices of birth control and the rational management of households (Yi Sŭng-hŭi 1991, 311–12; MHSA 1981b, 78).

Another state-controlled women's organization for implementing the family planning policy and the campaign for the rational management of the household was the New Village Women's Association (Saemaŭlbunyŏhoe). Created in 1973 as a branch organization of the New Village Movement, a major rural development project that started in the early 1970s, this organization was to cope with the problems of poverty and demoralization in rural communities caused by urban-centered economic development for a decade.[9] The association expanded to urban areas starting in 1977 by absorbing other women's AMOs, including the Clubs for Improving the Conditions of Living, the Women's Classes, and the Mothers' Clubs for Family Planning (KWDI 1990, 149; MHSA 1987a).

Intended for more effective and tight control of women's AMOs, this merger made the New Village Women's Association the only women's AMO during the Fifth Republic (1980–87). All education and training of women for the New Village Movement was to be carried out only by the New Village Women's Association (MHSA 1981a, 19). After the integration, the association played a central role in implementing the family planning policy and the campaign for the rational management of the household by publishing its educational materials every year, booklets for so-called women leaders every two years, and its monthly magazine, *New Village Women's Association*, whose circulation reached 100,000 in March 1978 (MHSA 1987a, 110). In the 1980s every rural village and every *t'ong*, the lowest urban administrative unit, had its New Village Women's Association made up of women between twenty and sixty years of age (MHSA 1989a; 1981a). Although its size and activities shrank toward the end of the 1980s with the beginning of the Sixth Republic (1988–92), this organization continued to be one of the largest women's organizations.

WOMEN'S INTEGRATION INTO THE MODERN NATION

Women's Membership in the Nation via Fertility Control

The idea of family planning was introduced in Korea by the International Planned Parenthood Federation (IPPF) in 1960. With the financial and technical assistance of the IPPF, the Planned Parenthood Federation of Korea (PPFK) was formed in April 1961. At the outbreak of the military coup in the following month, this civilian organization was dissolved, but it was soon revived with the strong sponsorship of the military regime, which subscribed to the idea that unchecked population growth in underdeveloped countries would endanger economic development by "draining" scarce resources and "undermining" fruits of economic growth.

The Supreme Council for National Reconstruction (SCNR), the core of the military junta (1961–63), appointed Yang Jae Mo, the founder of the PPFK, as a planning member for population control. He submitted a proposal for family planning with statistics showing that $2 billion could be gained by 1971 from successful family planning (Jae Mo Yang 1966, 307). The members of the SCNR unanimously accepted family planning as a strategy of economic development (PPFK 1983, 78; 1975, 37, 53). In November 1961 family planning was formally adopted as a major element of the first Five-Year Economic Plan (1962–66) (PPFK 1975, 54). From that time on, it was the single most important policy directly involving women in the period of militarized modernity.

The modernizing state had to launch aggressive propaganda for family planning because the idea of contraception was foreign to most Koreans, who tended to believe that having many children meant good luck and that every child would bring his or her own food into the world. To alter this customary idea, the state made extensive use of hierarchical organizations in administering the family planning policy. It coordinated interministerial actions, especially during the early stage of family planning projects in the 1960s. For example, the Economic Planning Board (EPB), the Ministry of Health and Social Affairs (MHSA), and the Ministry of Public Information at the level of central government and Public Information Rooms of municipal or local governments issued educational materials on family planning in the form of pamphlets, broadcasting, and films (PPKF 1975, 70). In 1963 the state created an intraministerial team exclusively dealing with family planning, which was upgraded in 1970 and 1972 (69). This administrative organization remained intact until 1981, when the state reduced the size and number of intraministerial agencies to pursue a more centralized policy (153).

7. A population control
campaign at a downtown
crossing, circa 1983. Photograph by Dong-A Daily Co.

The state also worked closely with the PPFK to change the public perception
of birth control, establishing a department of public relations in 1970 to make
the idea and practice of contraception familiar to the populace. The PPFK increasingly relied on mass media (radio, television, newspapers, magazines, and
educational texts of its own) to disseminate positive images and information
about families with a small number of children. To encourage popular participation, the PPFK organized popular contests of various kinds, ranging from
posters, songs, and slogans to stories of personal experiences by mothers and
wives concerning contraception.[10] The state issued commemorative stamps, as
well as lottery tickets and cigarette cases with messages about family planning.
In addition, the PPFK sponsored seminars, conferences, workshops, and sym-
posiums for medical professionals, journalists, scriptwriters, religious leaders
(especially women missionaries), corporate leaders, and military officials as a
way to generate an authoritative public opinion favorable to family planning.
It also sponsored large-scale popular gatherings and on-the-street campaigns
in cities and towns, aimed at married couples, mainly mothers and wives in
their mid- to late thirties (see figure 7). These campaigns were usually followed

by free vasectomies and free IUD insertions. The state and the PPFK sponsored such cultural events with financial and technical assistance from international agencies such as the IPPF and the United Nations Family Planning Agency (UNFPA), the Population Council (PC), the United States Agency for International Development (USAID), and the Swedish International Development Agency (SIDA) based in the first world (PPFK 1983, 1975).

In 1962 the state launched the family planning projects by dispatching to 183 local health clinics (*pokŏnso*) female family planning staff, who would introduce the idea and practice of contraception to local visitors to the clinics (MHSA 1981b, 279; PPFK 1975, 64; Yang Jae Mo 1966, 307). In 1964 the state began recruiting female family planning agents to facilitate its access to individual mothers and wives (PPFK 1975, 34). The female agents were auxiliaries to the leading male family planning staff, who were commissioned to serve at the existing local health clinics. They were usually local residents of the towns or villages where they were assigned to work, because neighborhood familiarity facilitated their access to fertile mothers and wives. They distributed free IUD coupons among neighboring mothers and wives in rural or poor urban areas, sometimes with persistent persuasion to use the IUD as a "patriotic" form of contraception (Yi Mi-Kyŏng 1989).

The state also sponsored the foundation of research organizations for family planning. The Ministry of Health and Social Affairs instituted a team for evaluating family planning research in 1966 (PPFK 1983, 108). With financial assistance from SIDA, the state established the National Research Institute for Family Planning in 1970. This organization was merged with the Research Institute for Health Development and became the Research Center for the Population's Health in 1981 (PPFK 1983, 352). While the Ministry of Health and Social Affairs planned, regulated, and supervised contraceptive services through the national network of health clinics, the Research Institute for Family Planning specialized in policy-oriented research, evaluation, and training of family planning staff and leaders of women's organizations (PPFK 1983, 208; 1975, 3–42).

Once perceived as crucial to state-led economic development, family planning was implemented within the framework of instrumental rationality. Accepting the simplistic causality between a low population growth rate and a high standard of living, the state set a specific rate of population growth to be achieved during each period of family planning in accordance with the Five-Year Economic Development Plan. The state employed the following steps to increase the use of contraceptives among married couples (usually wives).

First, the state-desired fertility rate was statistically calculated on the basis of demographic data. Second, on the basis of a preset rate of fertility and the actual fertility rate up to then, it was statistically estimated how many fertile couples should be subject to the use of contraceptives. Third, depending on available contraceptive methods, the number of married couples to use each contraceptive method was calculated (PPFK 1975, 1983; Kyu-taik Sung 1978).

The state agencies had reached out to given numbers of fertile couples—usually wives—in rural and urban poor areas until the mid-1970s (Foreit et al. 1980, 83; Kyu-taik Sung 1978). It used mobile vans, provided by the IPPF and SIDA, to perform IUD insertions and vasectomies (there were usually less than one-tenth as many vasectomies as IUD insertions) (PPFK 1983, 107). By the end of the 1970s, the state mobilized even the Marine Corps to reach out to the isolated islanders.

Reflecting its reliance on instrumental rationality, the state preferred one-shot and permanent contraception to conventional methods such as jellies, foams, and sponges. Shortly after the family planning projects were launched, IUDs replaced conventional contraceptives. In the mid-1960s, the state distributed 300,000 Korean-made loops for the first time. Large numbers of para-medics and some general practitioners were trained to insert IUDs because of the scarcity of gynecologists and obstetricians. The state chose 1966 as a Great Year of Family Planning and targeted and achieved the goal of 400,000 IUD insertions and 20,000 vasectomies (PPFK 1983). In 1968 oral pills were introduced to alleviate the side effects caused by IUD insertions. In the same year, 1,300,000 cycles of oral pills, supplied by SIDA, were distributed in rural areas. Yet throughout the 1960s, the IUD was the dominant and "ideal" form of contraception applied to Korean women (Taek Il Kim and Syng Wook Kim 1966; Takeshita 1966, 707; Foreit et al. 1980, 80).

In the second half of the 1970s, female sterilization was introduced and aggressively applied to fertile women in the form of free one-shot surgical sterilization. Necessary postsurgical care was often ignored. The practice of female sterilization reached its peak in 1979 and then decreased. Perceiving this decrease as a crisis, the state accelerated its sterilization campaign in the 1980s, into what can only be described as a sterilization mania. Between 1982 and 1987, two million women were sterilized, making up 58 percent of the total cases of sterilization during the past twenty-five years. Statistics in 1988 indicated that 48 percent of all fertile married women were sterilized. Sterilized women also made up 63 percent of all female contraceptive users. In addition, 83 percent of these women had been sterilized for free by the state's agencies, operating primarily in the form of mobile services. The semiforced mass sterilization led to abrupt reductions in the fertility rate and the rate of population growth in the 1980s. According to official statistics, the average number of children an adult woman would bear during her lifetime dropped from 6.3 in the early 1960s to 1.6 in 1988 (Yi Si-baek 1990, 4–6; Kim Eun-sil 2001, 317).

A major strategy of population control in the 1980s was sterilization complemented by various incentives. In 1981, confronting negative economic growth for the first time since 1962, along with a decrease in the number of sterilization accepters, the state issued "Countermeasures to Population Growth." These measures were characterized by incentives to a family with one or two children: priority in getting housing loans and business loans, monetary support of low-income families, and free medical service for the first visit. During the 1980s, variations of these kinds of incentives were introduced almost every year.

The state's organizational work was not limited to its own bureaucracies. The state was actively involved in forming women's organizations to encourage women's participation in implementing family planning policy beyond the coercive imposition of the state project of national modernization. In 1968, with the introduction of oral contraceptive pills, the Ministry of Health and Social Affairs and the PPFK created a women's organization called the Mothers' Clubs for Family Planning as a way to monitor rural mothers' use of contraception (Yoon 1977, 160). The state recruited 139 county managers (kun kansa) as administrative organizers of the club in every rural administrative unit. The Mothers' Clubs spread to urban areas after 1972, although not everywhere.

Initially, 16,868 clubs, comprising 194,617 mothers, were formed throughout rural areas. The organization grew every year and expanded to 27,292 clubs with 749,647 members by 1977, when it was merged into the New Village Women's Association. Although this large membership may include nominal members who were not active, the existence of such a sprawling organizational network indicates the extent to which the state intended to exhort women to become dutiful nationals by participating in family planning. Each Mothers' Club was composed of around fifteen members, who advocated the idea and practice of contraception. Each club had one leader, who had usually had experience working in the state-led Women's Clubs for National Reconstruction during the military junta period (PPFK 1983, 133–35). The state also regularly monitored the working of Mothers' Clubs.

The Mothers' Clubs published a house organ, Kajŏngŭi pŏt (The Friend of Home), which was distributed free between 1969 and 1980 and widely circulated, reaching 70,000 readers per month in 1973 (PPFK 1983, 326, 348). It was intended to be a monthly magazine for the modernization of rural families, containing information not only about family planning but also about modernized management of the household and "cultured wifery," which will be discussed in the following section (PPFK 1975, 247).

Major activities performed by the Mothers' Clubs indicate the extent to which the state depended on mothers and wives for calculated population control. The members exchanged information and shared their experiences of contraception with one another. They also indirectly became agents of state policies, as they worked to educate and persuade acquaintances who did not practice contraception. This role was crucial to the state's family planning projects because the female family planning agents, recruited as auxiliaries to the male staff, showed high turnover rates owing to low payment and low job security (PPFK 1975, 34, 42). Club members worked as intermediaries between local mothers and the county managers by facilitating state-sponsored local campaigns, distributing oral pills and monitoring their use. In this regard, the role of the leaders of the Mothers' Clubs was so crucial that they were trained for seven to ten days each year (PPFK 1983, 134).

Merged into the New Village Women's Association in 1977, the Mothers' Clubs for Family Planning became the family planning section within the Women's Association. Coinciding with a shift in economic-development policies, this organizational restructuring for tighter control over women's AMOS was accompanied by a major shift in family planning policies characterized by more centralized and intrusive approaches to fertile mothers and wives. Accordingly, the state renamed family planning policies "population policies." Experiencing a series of significant changes in international relations (e.g., the opening of diplomatic relations between the United States and the People's Republic of China and the U.S. withdrawal from Taiwan, two world oil crises, and the communist victory in Vietnam), the government decided to build heavy industry for industrialization as a basis for self-reliant defense. As discussed in chapter 2, it launched ambitious plans to establish its steel industry and shipbuilding as a steppingstone in this process. It borrowed large amounts of capital from international financial agencies. In this context, national women's organizations were merged into the New Village Women's Association.

The organizational change was accompanied by a project under which each fertile mother—a married woman between the ages of twenty and forty-four, and later between fifteen and forty-four—was supposed to keep a record of her pregnancy and contraceptive practices. In rural areas, 866,456 members from

12,742 New Village Women's Associations were initially registered through health-record keeping in 1977. In the following year, 1,510,000 women who had been "left out" in the initial project were registered. On the basis of rural success, this kind of project expanded to urban areas, except for the cities of Seoul and Pusan, where more residents had a higher level of education than the rest of the country, were less susceptible to government propaganda, and had already begun to change their reproductive behavior as a result of rapid urbanization and commercialization. In addition, leaders of the New Village Women's Associations in both rural and urban areas were trained on a regular basis by the PPFK (PPFK 1983; MHSA 1981b, 203).

The administrative hierarchy descending from the Ministry of Health and Social Affairs to the New Village Women's Association remained largely intact after the organizational restructuring of 1977. In 1989 the administrative hierarchy was composed of the Ministry of Health and Social Affairs, the PPFK, municipal or provincial hospitals of the PPFK, provincial managers, and the New Village Women's Association, in descending order. In this fashion the state could maintain its access to mothers and wives and its close monitoring of their contraceptive practices.

The state's dependence on mothers and wives for calculated population control was not limited to the two women's organizations with national networks, which initially focused on rural areas. In urban areas, pro-regime women's organizations and the "mothers' classes" of elementary schools were used in a less blatant way. Organized in each elementary school to establish an image of "learning and working" mothers, the mothers' classes dealt with the issue of family planning (MHSA 1981b, 74). Urban mothers acted as quasi-state agents by working voluntarily in public relations for family planning or at least willingly performing "patriotic" forms of contraception. The Federation of Women's Organizations carried out educational campaigns directed at fertile mothers and wives in the 1970s (MHSA 1975b). The Korean Federation of Housewives' Clubs, an urban women's organization financially supported by the state, started campaigns for no pregnancy and male contraception in 1975, when the United Nations announced the Women's Decade to deal with women's issues (MHSA 1975b, 41). Starting in the mid-1970s, the state expanded its family planning projects to cover married and unmarried men as well as unmarried women. It used the national networks of the standing army, reserve army, and schools to disseminate information about birth control (Research Center for Population Health 1986).

Within the instrumentalist framework of family planning policy that I have discussed, the actors appear to be male administrators, male professionals, and male family planning staff. Women and their fertility were perceived as the object of control and manipulation by the largely masculinized agents of population control. Family planning policy publicly highlighted women's domestic role as wives and mothers, suggesting that women's integration into the modernizing nation and its industrializing economy hinged on their contribution as biological reproducers. The target group of married women in rural and poor urban areas was merely a set of statistical numbers for IUD insertion and sterilization. Women were visible either as fertile mothers and wives or as temporary and underpaid family planning staff at the bottom of the hierarchy of family planning projects. At the same time, the existence of the Mothers' Clubs for family planning in local villages and towns implies that the modernizing state attempted to induce active participation of women in its project of nation building. The Ministry of Health and Social Affairs, in educational texts for women, hailed women as the dutiful nationals willing to practice contraception. Echoing neo-Confucian gender ideology, the contemporary version of these female instruction texts states:

> Family planning should be put into practice on the basis of consensus between husband and wife, and parents' [in-laws'] permission. . . . When it comes to real practices of contraception, women's role and effort are most important. (MHSA 1981b, 201; translation mine)

> At this time when population becomes an obstruction to national development, women who are in charge of childbirth need to display their power by actively participating in family planning projects. (MHSA 1975a, 11; translation mine)

This demand of the modernizing state reveals that it cannot maintain its calculated policy of population control without fertile mothers and wives willing to use certain forms of contraception as "patriotic" forms of family planning.

Population control pursued within the framework of instrumental rationality appears to have been successful at least from the point of view of the state, in that it achieved the objective of reducing the fertility rate. In addition, the Korean case is sometimes represented as a showcase in other developing countries. The modernizing state manages to achieve its policy goal by means of calculated plans and effective use of organizational networks. Yet success seems to come not only from women's subjection to family planning policy but also from their willing participation in practicing "patriotic" forms of contraception. In the late 1980s, the rate of contraception practice among married couples was as high as 77.1 percent, and popular methods of contraception among them were female sterilization and male sterilization, which were aggressively promoted by the state. During the 1980s, one slogan widely disseminated among the public was "Family planning shortcuts, vasectomy and female sterilization" (Kim Eun-sil 2001, 315, 319). Women's (and men's) acceptance of contraception reflected the shifting social meanings of children — from additional farmhands to family members requiring additional resources for extensive education and care — in the process of urbanization and commercialization. Ironically, there was a convergence of women's interest in reducing pregnancies and childbirths and the state's interest in controlling women's fertility.

It is also noteworthy that the modernizing state focused on women's identity as biological reproducers in constructing women's national duty while it also pursued industrialization, which incorporated women as wageworkers. The state's use of women as such is more than a mere reflection of already existing gender relations because social relations of gender are continuously shaped and reshaped. Decades of population control suggest that women's integration into the modern nation was predicated on their role as breeders, and women's national duty was epitomized by the patriotic control of their fertility. Against the backdrop of industrialization, which would potentially challenge reproductive femininity by incorporating women into the labor market as paid workers, this emphasis on women's fertility highlights the extent to which women's economic marginalization was integral to nation building.

WOMEN'S MEMBERSHIP IN THE NATION VIA THE RATIONAL MANAGEMENT OF THE HOUSEHOLD

Building a modern nation involves more than the industrial transformation of the economy characterized by the construction of factories, power plants, highways, and urban centers. It requires an overall transformation of daily life toward rationalization. In South Korea the modernizing state promoted the rationalization of quotidian practices of running the household as a crucial aspect of this transformation and linked it to economic development. The national campaign for rational management of the household involved the tailoring of daily practices like cooking, shopping, and consuming various goods, and observing ceremonies and holidays according to the needs of the nation's industrializing economy. To streamline daily life for economic growth based on its export-promotion strategy, the state manipulated the normative gender division of labor stemming from the cultural ideal of "wise mother and good wife." This ideal was used to facilitate economic growth and to minimize its negative impacts on households. The Ministry of Health and Social Affairs articulated the state's reliance on mothers and wives as follows.

> To build a self-reliant economy, government, business, and households should collaborate. In particular, it is of foremost importance for the housewife to manage the household economy frugally and to save for the accumulation of domestic capital. We should remember that the splendid economic growth of developed nations is based on their housewives' frugality and savings. . . . From time immemorial the prosperity and decline of a family has depended on the housewife's hands. The desirable housewife who respects parents [in-law], raises children to be great people, keeps house thriftily, and supports her husband wisely will not change although time may change. . . . But contemporary society, which is an open society, requires the housewife to play a wide range of roles. . . . [She] cannot manage the household wisely without knowledge and information about the economy, pollution, consumer issues, and so on. (MHSA 1984, preface by the minister of health and social affairs; translation mine)

This kind of call for mothers and wives was common in industrializing Korea.[11] The underlying message was that the rational management of households could save valuable resources and absorb the negative impacts on society caused by dependent capitalist economic growth.

For this purpose, reflecting the pervasive use of instrumental rationality as the core technique of ruling, the state relied on the combination of mass media and women's AMOS to generate a social atmosphere saturated with the emphasis on the role of mothers and wives in nation building. While the mass media were used to disseminate the idea to the general public through news programs, daily shows, and special shows, the women's AMOS discussed earlier targeted women in specific local areas.

One element of the rational management of households was the "scientific improvement" of cooking and eating. With instructions on nutrition and food-resource saving, mothers and wives were strongly encouraged to consume wheat, brown rice, or grains other than white rice. In association with the mass media, the state-sponsored women's centers and women's organizations held rice-saving campaigns and bread-making workshops and introduced recipes that used wheat flour and mixed grains (MHSA 1987a, 105; 1982a). "Scientific" cooking and eating were designed to alleviate the problem of decreasing self-sufficiency in grains by replacing rice, the staple grain, with other grains like wheat, barley, and legumes. The rice shortage resulted from an economic strategy that placed priority on manufacturing while ignoring agriculture. In fact, most technocrats of the modernizing state perceived agriculture as a declining sector that did not have a comparative advantage in the international market and therefore had better shrink to the point at which a few rich farmers could specialize in mechanized farming (Bello and Rosenfeld 1990, 78). The expansion of industry at the expense of agriculture led to the problem of a drastic reduction in self-sufficiency in grains, including the staple of rice. Overall self-sufficiency in staple foods and grains plummeted from over 91.1 percent in 1965 to 50.7 percent in 1980 (Kwack 1986, 80). The rate dropped further to 42.9 percent in 1989 (KWDI 1990b, 11). Against this background, mothers and wives were called on to practice "rational" cooking and eating.

Another element of the rational management of the household was the "wise" consumption of goods and resources. For the three decades of rapid industrialization from the 1960s to the 1980s, mothers and wives were exhorted to alleviate the problem of scarce natural resources in the densely populated nation by "wise" consumption and savings. They were also strongly encouraged to plan household budgets and keep records of their spending. The state promoted the image of "modern" and "cultured" mothers and wives who had knowledge of the national economy and international politics and managed their households accordingly. Mothers and wives were expected to recycle used goods and to save valuable resources like running water, electricity, and paper. They were also supposed to make mixed lunchboxes for their children and help them collect used newspapers to take to schools on a regular basis.

With regard to saving resources to be invested for industrialization, mothers and wives as managers of the household economy were encouraged to observe modified familial ceremonies and traditional holidays. Historically, Confucianism in Korea produced strict and meticulous rules concerning life rituals, considered an essential measure of one's moral uprightness and integrity as well as social prestige. Therefore the major life ceremonies tended to involve ostentatious consumption. Starting in the early 1960s, family ceremonies concerning weddings, sixtieth birthdays (hwankap), funerals, and ancestor memorials, which were rooted in Confucian rites, were the objects of state concern. Immediately after the coup d'état in May 1961, the military junta launched a "New Living Movement" by setting up a month for practicing "new living," which referred to the modernization of habits of living in general and the adaptation of simplified and standardized forms of familial rituals in particu-

8. The Democratic Justice Party meeting to discuss the observance of family rites, 1984. Photograph by Yonhap News Agency.

lar. In 1969, presidential decrees on the guidelines for modified familial rituals were proclaimed. Yet the decrees were not regulatory but recommendatory, because the state was cautious about the possibility that an abrupt change in the nation's deep-rooted ritual practices would cause an "undesirable" reaction and resistance from the populace. It gradually implemented some punitive measures, and the standardized rules of the familial rituals underwent several changes in the 1970s and 1980s (see figure 8).[12] Throughout this process, reflecting the Confucian role of women in preparing family rituals, the primary responsibility for observing "rationalized" life rituals fell on women as mothers and wives.[13]

Another element of the rational management of the household was not to hire domestic help. This took place at a time when domestic service and factory work provided the most job openings for young rural women who were thrust out of their impoverished families in the process of urban-centered industrial development. As one study of working women in manufacturing industries indicates, between 30 percent and 50 percent of women factory workers had worked as domestics before their factory jobs (Kim Ok-yŏl and Kim T'ae-hŭi 1973, 10). This percentage was likely to be higher in reality, because young women were reluctant to reveal their experience of domestic work, due to the stigma attached to the occupation. By asking urban middle-class mothers and wives not to hire domestic servants, the state attempted to control the supply of "cheap" female labor for expanding light industry in the 1960s and early 1970s.

The emergence of consumer society in South Korea in the 1980s began to undermine the old notions of thrift and saving. As numerous newspaper articles on the problem of "overconsumption" among the new rich in the 1980s suggest (Nelson 2000, chap. 2), this type of campaign to promote savings and thrift might not have been very effective in persuading women of the affluent new middle class, and even less-well-off women of the lower classes, who were increasingly exposed to commercial messages to consume. Apart from its actual effectiveness over time, however, assuming women primarily as consumers, the campaign to promote the rational management of the household constructed savings and thrift as women's national duty.

The willingness and ability of mothers and wives to make their families' ends meet were crucial in the face of chronic inflation caused by several factors. First, Korean currency was purposefully devalued in order to make Korean products cheap in the competitive international market. Second, the double pricing policy for grains (under which grain prices were artificially set below production cost to provide cheap grains to urban workers so that their wages could be kept low, and farmers were subsidized to offset the low grain prices) was abandoned in the early 1980s because of pressure from the International Monetary Fund, and this change added to the state's budget deficit. The state tended to fill the gap by borrowing from the Korean Bank — that is, by issuing more money — rather than by relying on tax revenue (Korean Rural Community Research Center 1989, 233). Third, wage increases in the late 1970s, caused by the construction boom in the Middle East and the expansion of manufacturing industries, which demanded more workers than ever before, exacerbated the nation's chronic inflation (229). Hence the modernizing state called on women to perform their national duty to be rational managers of their households, to minimize the impacts of high inflation on individual households and thereby shift its responsibility for social welfare to women as reproducers.

CONCLUSION

The modernizing state marginalized women as workers despite their crucial economic contribution and mobilized them as biological and domestic reproducers. In contrast to the economic mobilization of men, the massive incorporation of women into labor-intensive manufacturing industries did not transform women into a permanent workforce in the industrializing economy of the 1970s and 1980s. While the modernizing state excluded women workers from vocational training programs and the technical license system, it called on women to be dutiful nationals performing patriotic forms of contraception and managing the household rationally. As the implementation of male conscription showed, the implementation of family planning policy required the modernizing state to make the populace accept the unfamiliar idea of contraception through the combination of aggressive public relations, economic incentives for the practice of contraception, and monitoring of local women. Through the mass media, the state disseminated messages and images linking the idea of having a small number of children with modernity, affluence, and a happy nuclear family. Ironically, this national call to women appealed to them because the state's interest in population control converged with women's interest in reducing pregnancies and childbirths in the context of urbanization and industrialization. In combination with the campaign for the rational management of the household, the family planning policy articulated the reproductive nature of women's membership in the nation.

In the second part of the book, I will examine the ways in which, and the extent to which, the construction of women and men as dutiful nationals was resisted and, in the process of democratization, how different social groups of women and men forged their new political subjectivity as citizens.

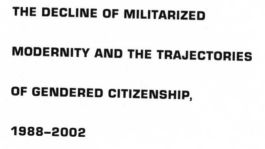

THE DECLINE OF MILITARIZED

MODERNITY AND THE TRAJECTORIES

OF GENDERED CITIZENSHIP,

1988–2002

4 THE DECLINE OF MILITARIZED MODERNITY
AND THE RISE OF THE DISCOURSE OF
DEMOCRATIZATION

> The founding members of the People's Solidarity for Participatory De-
> mocracy believed that to obtain the fruit of long efforts for democ-
> ratization, we must begin a movement to monitor the specific daily
> working of power beyond the anti-dictatorship struggle. . . . Genuine
> democracy is possible only when all citizens actively seek out their lost
> rights and bring together wisdom and professional expertise to build
> solidarity.
> — People's Solidarity for Participatory Democracy

In late summer of 1988, South Koreans were reveling in their
hosting of the Games of the Twenty-fourth Olympiad. Since their revival by
Pierre de Coubertin in 1896, the Olympic Games have often functioned as
an international coming-out ball debuting a newcomer to the club of modern nation-states. While Korea's arrival as Olympic host signified the apparent
realization of the nationalist dream of building a strong and wealthy nation,
its tumultuous journey through militarized modernity involved enormous
human cost and generated resistance from those who lived under its shadow.
This popular resistance dialectically grew in response to repressive discipline
and violent punishment by military regimes and merged into the discourse
of socioeconomic democratization articulated by grassroots social movement
organizations that developed in the late 1980s and 1990s, when militarized
modernity showed its uneven decline. As discussed in chapter 1, the pursuit of
militarized modernity as the hegemonic version of modernity in South Korea
stemmed from the selective appropriation of multiple meanings of modernity by the Korean elites throughout most of the twentieth century. Their
instrumental approaches to modernity in coping with foreign and domestic threats to their rule suppressed and marginalized its emancipatory mean-

ings contained in the notions of democracy, citizenship rights, and equality among individuals (and social groups). Periodically surfacing in popular protests against repressive regimes during the decades of authoritarian rule (1948–87), these counterhegemonic meanings of modernity were later absorbed into the discourse of democratization that envisioned a new form of membership in the nation by grassroots associations in the 1980s and 1990s, when dramatic sociopolitical change took place, establishing a full-blown consumer society based on the industrial economy and ending the almost three-decade-long military rule.

In this chapter, I outline the counterhegemonic meanings of modernity that were observed in popular protests against the authoritarian regimes and in works of intellectuals during the 1970s and 1980s. Building on the historical legacy of struggle against militarized modernity, four major grassroots social movements and organizations articulated the counterhegemonic discourse of democratization in the post-1987 era. This counterhegemonic discourse re-envisions grassroots women and men as citizens, active participants in the body politic who monitor the state and struggle with it to protect their rights and obtain new ones. This new view of membership in the body politic emerges as lofty and even utopian when compared with the actual state of citizenship in contemporary Korea — a formal status conferred by the nation-state.

IMAGINING MODERNITY IN POPULAR PROTESTS AND
WRITINGS AGAINST THE AUTHORITARIAN REGIMES

A brief history of spontaneous and organized popular protests against authoritarian rule illustrates the periodic resurgence of subjugated meanings of modernity during the period of civilian and military authoritarian regimes. The first of these events took place in April 1960, when college (and some high school) students, joined by other citizens, protested against gross presidential election irregularities committed by Syngman Rhee's regime, leading to the overthrow of the First Republic. This event, called the April revolution (*sa-il-guhyŏngmyŏng*), or the April 19 students' righteous uprising (*sa-il-guhaksaengŭigŏ*), became a symbolic landmark in the history of the democratization movement in South Korea.[1] The demands made by students for a new election and the end of Rhee's regime suggests that they viewed procedural democracy as a pivotal meaning of modernity (Cumings 1997, 344; Lee Ki-baik 1984, 384, 385).

The popular struggle for procedural democracy central to the growth of civil society in South Korea escalated during the Fourth Republic (1972–79), established through the Yushin Constitution, which suspended democratic ideas and practices such as civil rights and elections. This constitutional revision enabled Park Chung Hee's regime to replace direct presidential elections with an electoral college (*t'ongiljuch'e gungminwiwŏnhoe*) and to appoint all levels of administrative officials, from top posts all the way down to the heads of villages and urban residential units. The beginning of legal dictatorship triggered a series of protests by college students, religious leaders, writers, and antiestablishment politicians, and these protests intensified as the regime tightened its grip on suppressed civil society. The grassroots protests of the 1970s took various forms, ranging from street demonstrations and signature collections to repeal the antidemocratic constitution, to the announcement of democratic charters in public gatherings.[2] The state responded to these oppositional activities by deploying riot police and issuing a series of emergency decrees, finally declaring any criticism of the Yushin regime a violation of national security and arresting and imprisoning numerous political dissidents.

During the 1970s, a small group of writers and intellectuals, radicalized by the intensification of repressive rule, gave voice to the criticism of militarized modernity and thereby suggested a counterhegemonic leitmotif of nation building beyond (procedural) democracy. Reflecting the monopolistic appropriation of the term "modernity" by the ruling regime in its hegemonic discourse of "national modernization," this critical discourse did not directly refer to the notion of modernity. Instead it expressed the desire and the need for a humane and just society for the marginalized in the process of pursuing militarized modernity. In a series of poems and other writings, Kim Chi-ha, a highly regarded poet, criticized the moral bankruptcy of the ruling elites (identified as military generals, legislators, government ministers, capitalists, and other high-ranking officials who promoted militarized modernity) and voiced the pain and suffering of the powerless. He also called for national independence and unification, peace, and freedom, questioning the core elements of militarized modernity — anticommunist national identity and militaristic industrial growth at high human cost. Writers such as Hwang Sŏk-yŏng, Cho Se-hŭi, and Yun Hong-gil illuminated the contradictions of the militarized modernity pursued by Park's regime by narrating experiences of factory workers and the urban poor who fueled the nation's development (Chŏng Su-bok 1994, part 2, chap. 2).[3] Highlighting the plight of oppressed and marginalized social groups, these writers expressed a yearning for a humane and just society as an alternative to the nation of militarized modernity.

During the same decade, some factory workers, particularly superexploited young single women in labor-intensive light industries, inspired by the advocacy of progressive Christian churches, imagined a society where powerless workers like themselves were treated as human beings in their labor-organizing struggles (Ogle 1990; Cho Hwa Soon 1988; Chung Hyun-baek 1985). Largely disconnected from the collective and literary protests mentioned earlier, these women workers fought for human dignity literally with their whole bodies in the face of violence committed by male workers and thugs hired by their employers as well as the police force itself. The women's plea for humanity resonated in Chŏn T'ae-il's last shout that workers were not machines and needed basic human rights (Chŏn 1988).[4] The notion of human dignity central to these workers' pleas in their collective struggle directly challenged militarized modernity, whose achievement and maintenance relied on the transformation of human beings into instruments for building a strong military and industrial economy.

During the Fifth Republic (1981–87), popular protests continued to grow in response to the increasing control of emerging civil society by Chun Doo Hwan's regime. Attempting to tighten its grip over the mass media, the regime purged over seven hundred "disloyal" journalists and merged news agencies, newspapers, and periodicals for effective control; it also nationalized two of the three television networks and semi-nationalized the third one, taking ownership of approximately 70 percent of its stock. In addition, the regime revised laws concerning civil liberties in order to suppress civil society and prevented hundreds of politicians from joining political parties. These harsh measures galvanized fierce and growing protests by various social groups.[5] Confronting mounting popular resistance to its repressive rule, the regime was forced to make some concessions, including lifting the ban on politicians. In 1985, a national election mirrored widespread popular discontent with the regime, turning the New Democratic Party (NDP), a newly assembled opposition party, into the majority in the National Assembly for the first time in contemporary Korean history. After this political change, a constitutional amendment to restore procedural democracy became the central issue in the confrontation between the regime and civil society. In November 1986, a popular gathering in support of such an amendment was suppressed with the deployment of seventy thousand riot police (Hart-Landsberg 1993, 298). Massive popular protests spread throughout the nation when the regime announced its opposition to the amendment in April 1987.

Although the main actors of civil society were initially college students and factory workers, their struggle for democratization expanded to the middle class and to politicians. In the midst of mounting clashes between riot police and protesters, the body of a college student tortured to death by the police was discovered. This incident galvanized the participation of the conservative middle class in the opposition, thereby augmenting the antiregime protests. In June 1987, the alliance among various sectors of civil society succeeded in obtaining a concession from the regime for a direct presidential election. This election marked the beginning of the Sixth Republic under Roh Tae Woo (1988–92), who was handpicked by Chun Doo Hwan but elected because the opposition failed to provide a single candidate (Yi Hyo-jae 1997, 154–55).

It was during the mid- and late 1980s that, building on the critical legacy of the dissident movement against military rule and the labor movement of the previous decade, critical intellectuals adopted the term *minjungundong* (people's movement) to encompass a wide range of popular struggles that grew organically from the daily experiences of suffering among workers, farmers, the urban poor, students, women, and intellectuals. Although Korean minjung theorists differed in their interpretation of who exactly constituted minjung as the agent of social change, they tended to see it as a broad stratum of people who suffered from injustice, gained awareness of their situation, and struggled to bring about radical change in society (Cho Hŭi-yŏn 1995, 309). Therefore, populism was inherent in the very notion of minjung. While this notion of minjung populism can be traced to the 1880s, when the Tonghak (Eastern learning) movement was spreading in southern Korea (Wells 1995, 17), the populist movement of the 1980s sprang from the radicalization of students and intellectuals in response to the reappearance of military dictatorship, whose ascendance involved the massacre of civilians in the city of Kwangju, and the "economic liberalization" promoted by the Reagan administration that revealed Korea's economic dependence.

On the one hand, college students formed underground networks to overthrow the military regime, while thousands of activist students, after dropping out of college or being expelled for dissident activities, worked with factory workers and farmers to build solidarity with them (Abelmann 1996, chap. 6; Yu P'al-mu and Kim Tong-ch'un 1991, 404).[6] On the other hand, some scholars in the disciplines of theology, history, sociology, and economics began to articulate a counterhegemonic discourse to militarized modernity, stressing democratization (*minjuhwa*), resolution of national division (*minjokpundan*), and liberation of the oppressed (minjung) and their role as the agent of radical social change. In line with theologians like An Pyŏng-mu and Sŏ Nam-dong, the sociologist Han Wan-sang conceptualized the minjung as an inclusive category of social groups oppressed by economic, political, and cultural structures. This wide spectrum of the subordinated would encompass not only factory workers but also peasants, the poor, the disabled, and women. Yet as the minjung undong became ideologically rigid in the mid-1980s, the multilayered conception of the oppressed as the agents of social change was reduced to the Marxist notion of factory workers and the urban poor (Chŏng Su-bok 1994, part 2, chap. 2). A combination of domestic and international factors affected this shift over time. The Marxist framework appealed to dissident students and intellectuals living under the anticommunist authoritarian rule and the growing collusion between the state and big capitalists. The U.S. demand for economic liberalization also made the Marxist framework relevant to social analysis.

What distinguished the minjung movement from the social movements of previous decades was its self-conscious concern with radical social change and the utility of theory in guiding collective action. Followers of the minjung movement combined their theoretical inspiration, mainly drawn from Marxism, with the "indigenous" folk culture of the Korean people. At its core, as Kenneth Wells (1995) persuasively argues, the minjung movement can best be understood as a form of cultural nationalism that attempted to prescribe the Korean people's action in the time of crisis on the basis of populist readings of the past and present. Indeed, during the early 1960s, college students' identification with "the people" emerged in their search for the "indigenous" way of life to be preserved in rural Korea. After the suppression of the April revolution by Park's military coup, politicized college students and intellectuals redirected their energy to the reconstruction of folk culture such as farmers' music and mask dance as a medium to raise critical consciousness and mobilize the masses. As a result, by the beginning of the 1970s, students in most colleges in Korea formed circles to learn and perform mask dance. Throughout the 1980s, farmers' music, mask dance components, and shamanistic rituals became a common aspect of street protests (Abelmann 1996, chap. 3; Choi Chungmoo 1995).

The minjung movement, as a collection of radicalized opposition movements of the 1970s and 1980s, contributed significantly to the decline of militarized modernity and the rise of the discourse of democratization since the late 1980s in the following ways. First, not explicitly rejecting the notion of modernity, its counterhegemonic discourse took an unequivocally oppositional stance toward the militarized modernity pursued by the ruling regimes and thereby generated alternative spaces for imagining the nation. Instead of using the term "modernity," which had been appropriated by the ruling regimes, the minjung movement highlighted specific social groups who had been sacrificed to fuel militarized modernity. More importantly, it envisioned the oppressed not just as victims of militarized modernity but as actors who could obtain critical consciousness and fight for radical social change. It also envisioned solidarity between the oppressed and intellectuals by identifying with the interests and causes of the oppressed. Although this idea was closely connected to the elitist role of intellectuals as the vanguard of the radical social movement, it was a positive step in the discussion of how to build a just society. Second, the militant and organized protests resulted in the revitalization of civil society where the discourse of democratization emerged in tandem with various social movement groups, loosely called the "citizens' movement," in the post-1987 era. Although the Korean debate on civil society in the early 1990s tended to polarize the people's movement and the citizens' movement along class lines, there is continuity between them in terms of the composition of leadership and the concern with democratic social change (Yu P'al-mu and Kim Ho-gi 1995). The presence of these various forms of popular protest reflected the high political cost involved in the pursuit of militarized modernity, which led to its uneven decline in the post-1987 era.

THE UNEVEN DECLINE OF MILITARIZED MODERNITY

The Emergence of Public Skepticism

The combination of the growth of civil society in South Korea and the end of the Cold War elsewhere contributed to the emergence of grassroots skepticism to the anticommunist national identity guarded by the National Security Law and the Anticommunism Law. The most dramatic change in this regard was observed in activism among some members of grassroots social movements directed at socioeconomic democratization in growing civil society. A left-wing camp among these movements, inheriting the minjung movement, transgressed the boundary of the anticommunist national identity (to be militarily defended against North Korea) as a step toward peaceful reunification. Reverend Moon Ik-hwan, a senior advisor to the National Democratic Movement Federation, visited Kim Il Sung in March 1989. In the same year, Im Sukyŏng, from the Association of University Student Representatives, and Father Moon Kyu-hyŏn, from the Association of Catholic Priests for the Realization of Social Justice, went to North Korea to participate in the Thirteenth World

Festival of Youth and Students, convened in Pyongyang. All three of them were arrested and imprisoned upon their return to the South for violating the National Security Law and the Anticommunism Law (Hart-Landsberg 1998, 198).

Such bold grassroots challenges to the anticommunist national identity were not isolated incidents but were symptomatic of the bifurcation of U.S. policy and the South Korean policy toward North Korea in the post–Cold War era. On the one hand, the United States softened its deterrence-science militarism against North Korea. On the other hand, it reaffirmed its commitment to South Korean military security (Hart-Landsberg 1998, 161–64). The Korean government also became divided between the hard-liners (the Ministry of Defense) and soft-liners (the National Unification Board and the Ministry of Foreign Affairs) on dealing with North Korea (Kim Cha-ju 1994).

Popular attitudes toward the primacy of the military security of the anticommunist nation changed significantly during the 1990s. According to eight national surveys on security perception among South Koreans, conducted by public and private research centers between 1989 and 1995, the general public had become more concerned with sociopolitical stability and economic competitiveness than with military security.[7] This finding corroborates the public perception of the threat from North Korea as reported by another national survey. According to this study, the majority of those surveyed (53.7 percent) responded in the negative when asked about the possibility of a North Korean invasion, whereas 36.8 percent replied positively. The younger, more educated, and wealthier the respondents were, the more likely they were to reject the possibility of a military attack from the North (Yi Suk-jong 1995, 55). In the context of growing civil society, an emerging peace movement began to address taboo subjects such as arms reduction,[8] the unequal military alliance between South Korea and the United States,[9] the gradual withdrawal of U.S. troops and their criminal activities against South Korean civilians, and grassroots-level exchange between South and North (*Hangyŏre 21* [Seoul], July 13, 2000).

This recognition of the growing popular skepticism toward the militarized anticommunist national identity does not mean to ignore the contradictory and uneven course of the decline of militarized modernity during the past decade or so. The specter of the Cold War has lingered on the Korean peninsula. This has been poignantly observed in counteroffensives from conservative forces in various sectors of society such as the government, the military, the mass media, and business and education. The 1993–94 nuclear crisis provided a compelling rationale for the conservative forces within the administration to press President Kim Young Sam to return to a hard-line position (Hart-

Landsberg 1998, 202). The conservatives also exploited the arrests of two North Korean agents, who had been prominent university professors for decades, and the exposure of their spy rings, to roll back the development of progressive social movements. The government resumed its crackdown on radical students and unionized workers for violating the National Security Law and the Anticommunist Law. For instance, deploying riot police for a week, it arrested hundreds of students among those who convened at Yonsei University to host the Grand Unification Festival in August 1996. Similarly, equating large-scale workers' strikes with a communist attempt to "overthrow the government," Kim's administration, in early 1997, declared worker-organized labor unions illegal and arrested striking workers (203).

Counteroffensives to the progressive changes within the state and society continued until Kim Dae Jung's administration was inaugurated in February 1998. Implementing the "Sunshine Policy" to facilitate reconciliation with North Korea, his government, which was an odd coalition of conflicting political forces, was cautious not to alienate large segments of conservative constituencies. The dramatic summit meeting between President Kim Dae Jung and Chairman Kim Chŏng-il in June 2000 boded well for the demise of the militarized anticommunist identity of South Korea in the long run. Yet the promise of the summit meeting has been largely stalled in the face of shifting U.S. policy toward North Korea after the inauguration of the second Bush administration (2000–2004) and the recent exposure of the funneling of huge sums of money into Kim Chŏng-il's bank account in Singapore by South Korean corporations, which strengthened the conservative opposition party and conservative sectors in society (*Korea Times*, February 13, 2003). Despite the significant change in public perception of military security, a sizable portion of the population, especially older generations who experienced the Korean War, remains anticommunist and anti-North. According to a national survey conducted by Sejong Research Center in 1995, 75.6 percent of those surveyed supported the continuing existence of the National Security Law, either as it is or with some modification, despite repeated abuse of it by all previous regimes in the persecution of dissidents. While this percentage decreases as a respondent's age goes down and his or her education goes up, the majority of respondents in various subcategories still preferred the law's continued existence to its abolition (Yi Suk-jong 1995, 75–76). As will be discussed in chapter 5, the conservative public perception of national security is linked to the overall absence of any social movement to challenge mandatory military service in the decade of democratization, during which men have acquired the new subjectivity of citizens in the aftermath of their mass mobilization as soldiers and industrial workers.

The Uneven Decline of Surveillance and Normalization
To the extent to which the anticommunist national identity has been questioned, the Korean state's use of violence and discipline to remold individuals into useful and docile members of the nation has declined. What disappeared in the sociopolitical landscape of post-1987 Korea were the extremely violent punishment of political dissidents carried out by intelligence agencies and the intrusive surveillance over individual appearance and conduct by the police. A change even more significant to the rise of the discourse of democratization was the replacement of the AMOs by numerous civic associations, or the transformation of the AMOs into such associations. The restoration of procedural democracy facilitated the dramatic expansion of civil society, characterized by the formation of numerous voluntary associations autonomous from the state, particularly after the inauguration of Kim Young Sam's civilian government (1993–97). The number of "citizens' movement organizations" grew to 4,023 in late 1999 from 2,181 in 1994 (Pak Chae-ch'ang 2002, 45). The remarkable expansion of civil society was also observed in the explosion of the labor movement and the proliferation of labor unions, particularly between 1987 and 1989.[10] This growth of the labor movement, however, was accompanied by the state's continued deployment of repressive measures to cope with fervid labor strikes precipitated by the absence of any tradition of labor-management dialogue and the persistent association of the labor movement with communism.[11] At the same time, the legitimacy of the ruling regimes has subdued the militant antiregime protests that were characteristic of the suppressed civil society of the pre-1988 period. This shift can be observed in the decline of radical underground organizations advocating the revolutionary overthrow of the ruling regimes and capitalist society, and the multiplication of legal organizations pursuing the improvement of the quality of everyday life by means of institutional reform and continuous education of the public on various social issues, ranging from the human rights of women, workers, rural farmers, migrant foreign workers, and sexual minorities, to peace and unification, the environment, and antinuclearism.

It is important to stress that the growth of civil society illuminates a noteworthy new development in the process of the uneven decline of militarized modernity but does not connote a radical rupture from the past (see figure 9). Despite their quantitative and qualitative growth, an absolute majority of the

9. Military-style punishment on a college campus, 1995. Photograph courtesy of
Kim T'ae-hyŏng.

new social movement organizations have a small membership. The combined
membership of all the new social movement organizations in South Korea, exclusive of union membership, was estimated at around 1.5 million in 1999, but
fewer than half of these are active dues-paying members (Cho Tae-yŏp 2000,
294). Active members of social movement organizations are predominantly
educated members of the middle class (mostly men) and those who were previously involved in dissident activism during the period of authoritarian rule
(256). Kim Sŏng-guk points out the structural constraints of civil society in
South Korea as follows:

> Unlike the West, civil society in Korea has faced the tradition of strong
> statism; incomplete nation building stemming from the national division;
> fragmentation by the dominance of the particularistic social network based
> on hometown, blood, and school; the persistent alliance between the state,
> capital, and the mass media; a weak foundation for the establishment of
> the welfare state; and low grassroots participation in citizens' movements.
> Due to these structural constraints, civil society has yet to achieve internal
> maturity beyond the external growth. Hence the ruling groups tend to dele-
> gitimize demands from civil society as regional egotism and attempt to co-
> opt resistance and criticism from civil society by granting state-sponsored

projects [to citizens' associations]. Although violence has lessened in civil society, the state and capital continue to maintain the indomitable golden alliance that undermines it. (2002, 98; translation mine)

The overall profile of membership and the structural limitations of civil society suggest that despite its dramatic growth and qualitative transformation, civil society in Korea remains an unfamiliar dimension of the public sphere to the majority of Koreans.

As I discuss hereafter, these civic associations, small as they are, have played a pivotal role in transforming kungmin, useful and docile members of the nation, into citizens, active participants in building a democratic body politic. However, the decline of the AMOs and the revitalization of civil society during the 1990s and the present decade have coexisted with specific techniques of surveillance and normalization from the era of militarized modernity, suggesting the conservative nature of democratization in South Korea. Under the resident registration system, civilian regimes have continued to compile extensive information on individuals, who are identified by immutable numbers assigned at birth. In May 1999, Kim Dae Jung's government (1998–2002) began collecting a photograph and fingerprints from each individual in order to replace the paper-form resident card with a new plastic card. Some citizens' associations criticized fingerprinting as a form of human rights violation. Attempting to collect signatures to refuse this old practice, these organizations received a lukewarm response from the public. Instead, within two months, 25 million adult Koreans spent their own time to submit their pictures and have their fingerprints taken. This means that 70 percent of the adult population was willing to comply with the demand from the government. According to a survey done by these civic associations, the public, including educated professionals, tended to believe that fingerprinting was necessary for the effective investigation of crime and societal security. The survey also revealed that people tended to be anxious about noncompliance with the state's instructions and potential disadvantages they might face resulting from not having a new resident card (Kim Ki-jung 2000, 65).

Anticommunist mottoes, which alert members of the nation to guard against communists and impure elements or encourage these groups to report themselves to the authorities, have continued to decorate streets, highways, public transportation, and public buildings. In the 1990s hundreds of thousands of anticommunist billboards were displayed every twenty to thirty kilometers along streets and highways throughout South Korea. Along seashores and roads near the Demilitarized Zone, such billboards appeared every five hundred meters (Kwŏn Hyŏk-pŏm 2000, 50). The decades-long ubiquity of the impersonal surveillance mechanism has resulted in the internalization of anticommunism among a majority of South Koreans. A useful indicator of this public perception is the market dominance of three conservative newspapers which have maintained a fiercely anticommunist tone and have frequently engaged in accusing liberal politicians and government officials of having communist orientations. These newspapers together have enjoyed over 70 percent of the consumer market in the process of the progressive decline of repressive state control over the press (Yi Hyo-sŏng 2003, 148).

The legal and conventional practices that integrated military service into the organization of the industrializing economy started to unravel as a result of the transformation of the Korean economy and the acceleration of globalization. I will discuss this change in chapter 6 because it is directly relevant to the women's movements to challenge their marginalization in the economy.

THE RISE OF THE COUNTERHEGEMONIC DISCOURSE
OF SOCIOECONOMIC DEMOCRATIZATION: IMAGINING NEW
FORMS OF MEMBERSHIP IN THE BODY POLITIC

The growth of civil society in post-military-rule Korea, uneven as it might be, has enabled various social groups to articulate the discourse of socioeconomic democratization, emphasizing equality among members of the nation, their citizenship rights, and the building of a democratic community. This counterhegemonic discourse to militarized modernity reflects a popular desire for sharing the fruits of economic growth so far monopolized by the economic conglomerates and political elites. This common desire among grassroots women and men has also, to a limited degree, influenced the state's actions toward the adoption of this alternative discourse as part of the search for a new source of state legitimacy after the transition to procedural democracy. Institutionally, a state controlled by elected officials is more likely to be accountable for the well-being of the ruled, and to address issues of equality and social welfare, than is an authoritarian state. Along with this institutional change, the populace's relation to the nation-state has begun to shift from being the object of mass mobilization in the pursuit of militarized modernity to being citizens monitoring the state's actions and negotiating their demands for social welfare and equality.

There has also been a significant global factor contributing to the official concern with socioeconomic democratization, especially during Kim Young

Sam's administration. Throughout the 1990s, South Korea gained membership in a series of major international organizations: the United Nations,
the Organization of Economic Cooperation and Development, and the International Labor Organization. While membership in these organizations increased South Korea's national prestige, it also exposed the inferior quality
of life in the society in comparison with other middle-income countries, as
well as more-affluent Western ones. There is a huge gap between Korea's economic growth and the quality of life for its grassroots population. While South
Korea became the eleventh-largest trading nation and reached an annual per
capita income of $10,000 before the 1997 economic crisis, it showed a miserable
record in the development of the social welfare system, environmental pollution, and the frequency of various types of workplace accidents. Responding
to these discrepancies, the government directed its attention to improving the
quality of life in the name of "globalizing" it (Ch'oi Kyun 1998, 567).

To examine the spread of the counterhegemonic discourse of socioeconomic democratization that imagines citizenship as a new form of membership
in the nation or in a democratic community against militarized modernity, I
focus on four major social movement organizations that gained either a central status as an umbrella organization or a relatively large membership base:
the Korean Women's Associations United (KWAU: Yŏsŏngdanch'eyŏnhap), the
Citizens' Coalition for Economic Justice (CCEJ: Kyŏngjejŏngŭisilch'ŏnsimin-
yŏnhap), the Korean Federation for Environmental Movements (KFEM: Hwan-
kyŏngundongyŏnhap), and the People's Solidarity for Participatory Democracy (PSPD: Ch'amyŏyŏndae).

Korean Women's Associations United
Formed as an umbrella organization of twenty-one voluntary associations with
a feminist orientation in February 1987, the KWAU, the oldest of these four organizations, marked a shift in the character of social movements from militant
protests against ruling regimes to institutionalized efforts to reform society,
later known as "citizens' movements." The KWAU has played a central role
in pursuing the common goal of gender equality and articulating the specific
needs and interests of diverse groups of women such as factory workers, clerical workers, professionals, college students, urban housewives, rural women,
and the urban poor (Sin Yŏng-suk 1995; Yi Sŭng-hŭi 1991). The founding members of the KWAU included three main categories of women: women workers
who had participated in the struggle to form democratic unions in the 1970s,
college-educated intellectuals involved in the student movement against mili-

tary rule, and Christian women engaged in social activism (Yi Mi-kyŏng 1998, 18). Initially, reflecting its oppositional stance toward the repressive state, the KWAU maintained a conscious distance from the government, but as the relationship between civil society and the state began to shift, in 1995 the KWAU was granted legal status by the state. Faced with the challenge of expanding its membership base, the KWAU has maintained a democratic structure without hierarchical leadership (Yi Mi-kyŏng 1998, 38; Yi T'ae-ho 1996, chap. 8; Yi Sŭng-hŭi 1991). In a nutshell, the establishment of the KWAU symbolized women's entry into growing civil society. In 2003, it had thirty-three member organizations nationwide.[12]

The centrality of democratization to the KWAU's view of women's liberation and gender equality can be seen in the inaugural statement of *Minjuyŏsŏng* (Democratic Women), its house organ, first published in July 1987. Yi U-jŏng, the first president of the KWAU, described the objectives of women's movements as follows:

A genuine women's movement cannot confine its goal to the acquisition of equal rights with men. Rather, it should aim at the transformation of the social structures that oppress diverse groups of women. . . . To eliminate the oppressive reality, the women's movement needs to establish itself as an antiforeign struggle to accomplish national independence, a *democratization struggle to obtain democracy and gender equality*, and a *struggle for basic rights* to secure a humane life. (Yi Mi-kyŏng 1998, 18; translation and italics mine)

Approaching gender equality as an integral part of democracy, the women's movement focuses not only on women's equality with men but also on the democratic transformation of the entire society. This emphasis on democratization reflected the urgency to bring about a democratic government in the aftermath of massive popular protests in the first half of 1987. In linking gender equality to democracy, the inaugural statement recast women as the subjects of this transformative movement struggling for basic rights (as opposed to the object of the state's mass mobilization). While not using the notion of citizenship explicitly, this conception of membership in the democratic body politic points to an active and participatory notion of citizenship, distinguished from the formalistic view of citizenship as a political status conferred by the state.

Although the explicit reference to democratization appears less frequently in its discourse after Korea's transition to procedural democracy, the KWAU's discourse has used fundamental idioms of democracy such as women's human

rights, equality in the home, workplace and society, and participation in political, economic, and cultural areas. A decade later, co-representatives of the
KWAU summarized its ten-year history against the backdrop of the inauguration of Kim Dae Jung's government (1998–2002) and the 1997 Asian economic
crisis:

> For the first time in the fifty-year history of the Republic of Korea, we have
> accomplished the transfer of power between ruling and opposition parties.
> Women have raised their expectations about the new government. Yet the
> status of women as a socioeconomic minority has been regressing as a re-
> sult of the unexpected structural adjustment programs imposed by the IMF.
> Under this condition, the voice of reform has become more important than
> ever before. The KWAU intends to play an active role in supporting the new
> government to pursue comprehensive reform. At this juncture, it is signifi-
> cant for the KWAU to publish *Open Hope*, recording its movement for the
> past ten years, because the KWAU movement has been pursued within the
> large framework of *equality*, *peace*, *welfare*, and *human rights*, and these
> values can present alternatives to the contemporary values of limitless com-
> petition and materialism. (KWAU 1998, 4; translation and italics mine)

Recognizing women's position as a minority, the KWAU representatives continue to imagine women as active participants in building substantive democracy where the values of equality, peace, welfare, and human rights will be
the substance of daily life rather than merely political rhetoric. What distinguished this statement from the earlier one is the absence of any explicit reference to national independence, which has been in fact weakened in the process
of accelerated (economic) globalization. This difference is attributable to the
sense of hope stemming from the peaceful change of regime and the election
of an opposition politician to the presidency for the first time in contemporary Korean history. The softening of the KWAU's radical position vis-à-vis the
ruling regime affects its view of women as members of the body politic, changing from fighters against the state to collaborators with it.

Citizens' Coalition for Economic Justice
Founded in 1989 by around five hundred individuals as the first self-defined
citizens' movement organization, the CCEJ has addressed not only the issues
of economic justice, including big-business reform, the use of real names in
banking, and the reform of labor-employer relations, but also social and political issues ranging from health insurance and justice reform to peace and

unification. In 1999 its national membership grew to tens of thousands, but it still faces the common problem of civil society in Korea, which is the lack of active participation by grassroots members. Composed mainly of the educated middle class, who are university professors, lawyers, housewives, business owners, students, and white-collar workers, the coalition's leadership is dominated by male professors and lawyers.[13]

The wide spectrum of issues that the CCEJ has dealt with, parallel to those of the KWAU, reflects its emphasis on socioeconomic democratization beyond procedural democracy, highlighting the imperative to check powerful economic players such as big business, the rich, and employers, and to protect the weaker groups in society. The CCEJ's mission statement, as posted on its Web site, summarizes the dire consequences of militarized modernity, which have necessitated socioeconomic democratization through ordinary citizens' participation, as follows:

> The Citizens' Coalition for Economic Justice was formed in response to the extremely unjust structure of Korean economic life today. Rapid economic development over the past thirty-some years has brought wealth to the giant "chaebol" business groups singled out by the government for preferential treatment, and has raised the per capita GNP to more than $10,000. In this process, however, equitable distribution has been forgotten, the environment gravely damaged, and democratic development postponed. The priority on industrialization and urbanization has alienated large groups and areas and created wide structural gaps, even risking collapse of the economic system.
>
> Above all, the "chaebol" monopoly system has brought undeserved suffering to many citizens: small-business owners, workers, farmers, fishing people and all the others who were the main producers of the "economic miracle." Regardless of the impressive GNP, these ordinary citizens see their economic capacity shrinking day by day. (Citizens' Coalition for Economic Justice)

It is noteworthy that the CCEJ acknowledges economic differences among citizens but brings them together as willful agents who can correct the injustices generated by militarized modernity. In particular, stressing the participatory nature of democracy, the CCEJ imagines citizens as actors who can bring about economic justice through their collective power. It advocates the gradual transformation of society into a just community where those who labor for economic growth enjoy their fair shares.

In its efforts to influence state policy, however, the CCEJ has focused on public hearings, discussion meetings, and workshops led by professional experts on selected topics, as well as active lobbying of government officials and the use of the mass media to disseminate the organization's activities to the general public. Its leading members have occasionally been appointed to government office. These activities to promote and achieve socioeconomic and political reform reclaim citizens' rights to shape government policies, which had been monopolized by high-ranking government officials. At the same time, the professional nature of these activities tends to be less than inviting to lower-class and less-educated men and women.

Korean Federation for Environmental Movements
Established in 1993 as a federation of eight local environmental groups that sprang up in the second half of the 1980s, the KFEM has popularized how important clean water, clean air, waste reduction, the diversification of energy resources, and antinuclearism are to the quality of life. In particular, the federation has emphasized working closely with local communities victimized by environmental problems. This focus on the quality of everyday life under the rubric of environmental issues distinguishes the KFEM's discourse of social change from those of dissident groups and the authoritarian regimes, which emphasized regime change and economic expansion, respectively. The quotidian focus of the environmental movement intends to facilitate the democratization of a decent quality of living for grassroots women and men beyond procedural democracy and the capitalist logic of economic expansion. Hence it has also been concerned with other related social issues, ranging from poverty, human rights, and women's rights to peace. To disseminate environmentalist practices in local communities, the KFEM has reached out to the general public through membership expansion in local areas and educational programs for children. Multiplying to forty-seven local branches with a total of 85,000 members in 2002, the KFEM has become the largest citizens' movement organization.[14]

The KFEM's founding declaration explicitly connects the environmental movement to democratization and envisions itself as a collectivity of active citizens monitoring powerful actors such as big business and the government and putting pressure on them to alter the course of their actions. Responding to rampant environmental destruction and pollution caused by rapid industrialization, and to the lack of initiatives from the government, industry, and the populace to remedy the dire situation, the KFEM explains the reason for its foundation:

The previously separated segments of the antipollution civil organizations have today united and stand under a single flag. We intend to cooperate with the *citizens* of the areas where pollution has become a problem, and also to create a national network to cope systematically with the causes of pollution. We must go one step further from simply protesting and advance the environmental movement into a voluntary movement in which *citizens participate willingly*, based on scientific analysis of the causes of environmental destruction. . . . We will play a key role in keeping watchful eyes on the actions of industry, take a lead role in preserving the ecology, and pressure the government to have faith in its environmental policies. Moreover, we will form *a community* in which each and every individual has liberty and equality by breaking through short-sighted self-interest and bringing an order in which humans and nature live in harmony. (Korean Federation for Environmental Movements; italics mine)

The declaration imagines both the body politic and its members in a new light. The new community envisioned is a democratic and sustainable one where the basic natural resources necessary for human survival are preserved. As the KFEM manifesto articulates, it is also a community where wealth and development are equally distributed across different and autonomous regions. Individual members of such a community are free, equal, and proactive citizens who are able to transcend their narrowly defined self-interests and collaborate for the common good. They are citizens who work to protect "environmental rights" and participate in the process of formulating environmental policies.

People's Solidarity for Participatory Democracy
Formed in 1994 by around two hundred former political activists involved in the minjung movement and educated middle-class professionals, the PSPD concerns itself with substantive democratization beyond procedural democracy in various aspects of Korean society. This general objective, shared with the other three grassroots organizations I have discussed, is reflected in the PSPD's activities, ranging from "monitoring state power by citizens of diverse strata" to researching and discussing policy proposals and facilitating the formation of informed public opinion. Unlike the CCEJ, whose activities tend to focus on the state, the PSPD has developed both specialized centers to monitor the legislative body and the justice system and a set of member-based groups that encourage individual members to participate in activities of their own interests and concerns.[15] It has devised a focused annual campaign to encourage members' participation in monitoring the powerful institutions in society

and in building solidarity with social minorities to pursue public interests.[16] It also promotes human rights and public interests through the monitoring of business corporations and the mass media (Cho Tae-yŏp 2000, 253, 255, 258).

The PSPD's inaugural statement, read during its opening meeting in 1994, expressed the primacy of citizens' participation in establishing rights and justice in society and thereby building a genuinely democratic society.

> Until the 1980s, struggle for democracy took place on the streets filled with thick tear gas. But now the situation has changed. Our struggle to build genuine democracy in this new era needs to take place at the center of the social and political stage and citizens' daily lives. Democracy literally means that the kungmin [nationals or members of the nation-state] are the *masters of the nation*. Yet until now the anachronistic situation in which the masters have been treated like servants and the public servants of the kungmin have dominated the masters has perpetuated. Whoever has political power, they are not willing to correct this absurd situation. Therefore, it is necessary for the kungmin themselves to participate [in democratization] and monitor [the powerful]. It is not enough for the masters of the nation to cast their votes every few years. To be *masters worthy of the name*, we need to be watchpersons who monitor the process in which state power is being operated every day. . . . Approaching the new century, we are confronted with numerous social problems that require urgent solutions. It is a failure of sacred duty for *fellow citizens* to be indifferent to the alienated and oppressed. We must build social conditions that allow our neighbors faced with physical, mental and social difficulties to lead more humane lives. (People's Solidarity for Participatory Democracy; italics mine)

While interchangeably referring to kungmin and citizens as members of the nation, the inaugural statement recasts the nature of membership in the political community. Apart from this conceptual ambiguity, the PSPD places active participation and monitoring at the core of its new conception of the political subjectivity of grassroots men and women. Like the CCEJ, it recognizes inequalities among citizens but envisions solidarity among citizens of different power positions in establishing a humane society for the powerless.

STATE RESPONSES TO COUNTERHEGEMONIC DISCOURSE

To what extent has the counterhegemonic discourse of socioeconomic democratization affected the state's actions? While the state's expedient attention to social and political democratization can be seen as early as the beginning of

Chun Doo Hwan's rule, it was not until the period of Roh Tae Woo's rule (1988–92) that it became an integral part of the lexicon of the state's policies. Confronted with growing activism among previously marginalized sectors of civil society such as workers, farmers, women, and the middle class, Roh's regime was forced to respond to their demands for equality and social welfare. In response to the explosion of popular demands, the regime used the rhetoric of "social development," marking an apparent departure from the pursuit of militarized modernity. For the first time, the government paid attention to basic elements of a social security system such as national health insurance, a national pension, and a minimum wage. In 1988 it introduced a national pension system that would cover a majority of the employed. It apparently promoted a balanced distribution of income and regional development (Chang-hee Yu 1993, 129–30).

Continuing the rhetoric of social development, Kim Young Sam's civilian government promoted the image of the state as the provider of social welfare in an effort to establish a new identity separate from the preceding military regimes. During his rule, new social welfare laws were passed, and some old ones were substantially reformed. To give a few major examples, in 1993 the Employment Insurance Law (*koyongbohŏmbŏp*) was passed to protect workers from unemployment. In 1995 the Social Welfare Basic Law (*sahoebojanggi-bonbŏp*) was enacted, for the first time in South Korean history, to define the content and form of social welfare. The regime revised the Industrial Injury Compensation Law (*sanŏbjaehaebosangbohŏmbŏp*) in 1994 and the national pension law (*kungminyŏngŭmbŏp*) to include the self-employed in urban areas in 1995 (Ch'oi Kyun 1998, 572).

President Kim Dae Jung, a former political dissident who had struggled against military dictatorship, stressed socioeconomic democratization, starting with his election campaign. His government articulated the three major goals of its social policy as a democratic market economy, productive welfare, and the balance between economic growth and social welfare. At a meeting of the Association of Southeast Asian Nations (ASEAN), Mr. Kim reiterated the importance of democratizing the market, referring to fair competition among economic players, accountability and transparency of business management, the protection of small stockholders, equity in taxation, and the strengthening of the social welfare system. The notion of productive welfare was borrowed from the Swedish model, which emphasizes the improvement of human resources through continuous education and training (Yu Mun-mu 1999, 390, 391). As announced in 1999, Kim's government viewed socioeconomic democratization as a path to "the second foundation of the nation" (*che iŭi kŏn'guk*) (the first foundation of the nation being through economic growth) (Kim Ho-jin 1999).

Having mentioned a series of positive changes by the democratizing state, I should point out that their significance has been so far more symbolic and formalistic than substantive, in that the South Korean state has maintained a passive view of social welfare that expects individual families to be primarily responsible for health care, housing, education, child care, and care of the elderly. In other words, the state steps in to provide assistance and aid only when families fail to do so (Ch'oi Kyun 1998, 577; Chin Chae-mun 1999, 16). This underlying view is reflected in the budgetary allocations for the provision of social welfare and in the pervasive resistance to social welfare demands within the government bureaucracy and the legislature. As recently as 1997, total social welfare expenses represented roughly 10 percent of the government budget (Ch'oi Kyun 1998, 569). The Protection of Minimum Standards of Living Bill (kungmingich'osaenghwalbojangbŏban) was submitted to the National Assembly in 1998. What changed in the 1990s was the presence of progressive social movements willing to fight this difficult uphill battle. Indeed, the citizens' movement organizations played an instrumental role in revising the national pension act and the national health insurance system (Kim Yŏn-myŏng 1999).

Moreover, the state's interest in socioeconomic democratization lessened in the aftermath of the economic crisis. The dire problem of restructuring the economy in the face of resistance from powerful economic conglomerates has postponed the demise of the chaebol-centered model of economic development that sacrificed issues of socioeconomic democratization. The sweeping force of economic globalization has also undermined the state's capacity to implement progressive policy promoting equality and social welfare. Domestically, conservative forces are widespread in the state bureaucracy, economic conglomerates, and the mass media. Confronted by these domestic and global structural constraints, Kim Dae Jung's government retreated from its initial promise to pursue socioeconomic democratization as the second stage of nation building (Hong Tŏng-yul 1999).

Despite its limited impact on the state, the discourse of socioeconomic democratization has far-reaching implications for the long-term transformation of the nature of membership in the body politic. The category of citizen is crucial to forging a new political identity in the nation imagined as a democratic community. Although falling short of presenting a theoretically consistent view of the citizen, and at times conflating citizens with the old category of

kungmin, the counterhegemonic discourse has recast the nature of membership much closer to the active and participatory view of citizen. The discourse
of socioeconomic democratization repeatedly stresses rights and the struggle
to obtain and protect them, as well as the responsibility to monitor the powerful and participate in creating humane conditions of life. Such a notion of
membership is starkly different from the notion of kungmin, a subject position
"hailed" by the mobilizing state during the period of militarized modernity,
connoting a political subjectivity shrouded with state nationalism and defined
by its obligations rather than rights.

In the context of this question of the nature of membership in the body politic, I would now like to discuss briefly how gendered citizenship, as a conferred
status, has been practiced in South Korea, and to show the institutional context
in which women and men forge citizenship as a new form of membership in
the body politic and as an expression of human agency for self-transformation
and social change under the governance of the nation-state.

THE ECLIPSE AND REEMERGENCE OF GENDERED
CITIZENSHIP AS A CONFERRED STATUS

Despite their nominal presence in legal documents, citizenship rights for men
and women in South Korea were eclipsed in practice for decades. To give a brief
genealogy of men's citizenship as a status conferring a set of rights, I draw on
the discussion of citizenship rights by T. H. Marshall (1950) in his classic study,
without accepting his unilineal evolutionary and gender-blind approach. As
in many postcolonial societies, and in contrast to the West, men of different
classes in South Korea were simultaneously granted the formal political right
to vote and to run for office as a trapping of the modern polity in the context
of decolonization after World War II. Yet these political rights were in practice
severely curtailed for decades by civilian and military authoritarian regimes.
Unequal economic resources also prevented lower-class men from running for
office. During the Fourth Republic (1972–79) and the Fifth Republic (1981–87),
political rights were altogether suspended as a result of the elimination of direct elections. For men of different social classes, civil rights such as freedom
of thought and speech and equal treatment before the law, which are deemed
necessary for individual freedom, were grossly constrained by the National
Security Law and the Anticommunism Law from the dawn of the South Korean
state. The right to own property was irrelevant to a majority of propertyless
men, and the right to enter into contracts was irrelevant to the majority in the

absence of any protection by due process of law. The social right to basic welfare and economic security did not exist. The negative consequences of this absence were graver for lower-class men than for their upper-class counterparts who possessed property and other forms of power.

For decades, women's citizenship rights have been denied in ways parallel to men's. Noteworthy gender differences, however, did exist in the eclipse of citizenship. Patriarchal social relations within family and kinship further curtailed women's formal citizenship in South Korea. In particular, parts 4 and 5 of the civil code, which sanctioned conventional practices of the patriarchal family and patrilineal kinship groups until the code was substantially revised in 1989, contradicted the abstract principle of equal citizenship between women and men set forth in the constitution (S. Moon 2003). Women did not enjoy liberty of the person in marriage, because the law failed to address domestic violence and marital rape. The chasm between formal citizenship and the reality of women's daily lives, embedded in patriarchal domestic relations, reflected the extent to which women's relations to the nation-state were mediated by the family and kinship during military rule,[17] when citizenship, defined as a democratic relationship between the state and its individual members, virtually did not exist.

Since the political transition to procedural democracy in 1988 and then to civilian administration in 1993, political rights and some civil rights for men and women have been restored. National and local elections have been held to select public officials at various branches and levels of the state. The rights to the freedom of thought, expression, and assembly have been significantly expanded, along with the growth of civil society resulting from the collective struggle of a wide spectrum of social groups for a democratic government. Using political and civil rights in expanding civil society, different groups of social activists have fought for "social rights" to guarantee minimum standards for wages, economic justice, and a healthy environment free of pollution. The severe circumscription of women's right to paid work (due not only to patriarchal social conventions in the workplace but also to the specific paths of mobilization for women and men in the pursuit of militarized modernity) and women's resulting economic marginalization have been major issues for the autonomous women's associations revived in the transition to procedural democracy. Against the backdrop of the overall expansion of citizenship rights, the new citizens' movements have tended to be dominated by educated urban middle-class men, a relatively privileged social group among grassroots men and women.

The largely masculine and middle-class character of the CCEJ, for instance, can be read as a revealing commentary on the centrality of socioeconomic power to the emergence of the political subjectivity of citizen. It is noteworthy that while the KWAU has used the gender-specific term "women" (of different social strata) to identify the subject of its movement, the CCEJ has used the apparently gender-neutral term "citizen" as its subject. While (middle-class) women cannot but see themselves as gendered beings in the public sphere, (middle-class) men can apparently see themselves as gender-neutral citizens in the public sphere. It is useful here to consider an insight from the postmodern criticism of power and universalism, suggesting that it is often a dominant social group that attaches the mantle of universalism to its specific experiences, reducing subordinate groups' experiences to "special" ones.[18] Within this logic, a social movement organization dominated by men can claim the mantle of a gender-neutral citizens' organization, but a social movement organization dominated by women remains a women's organization. Hence some feminists reject the notion of citizen altogether as a masculinist category. However, I would argue that we need to reconceptualize the notion of citizen to make it a genuinely inclusive category; the justification for this reconceptualization is the importance of a political subjectivity to building a genuinely democratic society. The term "women" as the subject of the social movement envisioned by the KWAU connotes the subjectivity of citizens who struggle to obtain their rights and protect them. The contrast between these two grassroots organizations suggests that social groups in more-privileged positions have better access to citizenship when there is a political opening, as observed in post-1987 Korea. The unbalanced leadership composition of the CCEJ may be not so much a problem of undemocratic intention as it is a structural problem of organizational culture and accessibility to civil society, linked to class and gender, which will be explored further in chapters 5 and 6.

CONCLUSION

Despite differences in the composition of their membership, focal issues, and relationship to the state, the major social movement organizations have together produced a counterhegemonic discourse of democratization that re-envisions members of the nation as citizens. Yet the shifting nature of political membership is more prefigurative than actual for the majority of women and men in post-1987 South Korea. The transformation of women and men from duty-bound nationals subject to mass mobilization into active citizens who monitor the powerful and demand their rights requires collective struggle. The following two chapters will examine the ways in which men and women (of different social strata) wage such a struggle to be citizens, and how the trajectory of citizenship has been shaped by the gender-specific paths of mass mobilization in the period of militarized modernity.

5   THE TRAJECTORY OF MEN'S CITIZENSHIP
AS SHAPED BY MILITARY AND ECONOMIC
MOBILIZATION

Anticipating the violence of the state and the save-our-company corps, at each entrance and exit of our 220,000-*p'yŏng* company complex, our union members organized themselves into a vanguard and a counter-police corps, erected barricades, held steel pipes, and affirmed that "workers protect workers' sovereignty" and "we want to live like *human beings* and *masters.*" . . . Before the June 28 general strike, our labor was aimless toil reflecting alienation and inferiority that stemmed from our lack of power, capital, and education. Leading listless lives, we just accepted overtime and overnight work, low wages, and long working hours as our destiny. But through labor organizing, we overcame inferiority, despair, and alienation. Organizing made us realize the meaning and value of our lives that we were unaware of before. And finally, through this strike we changed into workers who can live the life of *masters*.

— statements by workers arrested at Kia Automobile Co. and their families, October 1991

The relation of both self-consciousnesses [of the master and of the slave] is in this way so constituted that they prove themselves and each other through a life-and-death struggle. They must enter into this struggle, for they must bring their certainty of themselves, the certainty of being for themselves, to the level of objective truth, and make this a fact both in the case of the other and in their own case as well. And it is solely by risking life that freedom is obtained. . . . The individual, who has not staked his life, may, no doubt, be recognized as a Person; but he has not attained the truth of this recognition as an independent self-consciousness.

— G. W. F. Hegel, *The Phenomenology of Mind*

The words of the male workers and their families quoted here depict the transformation of powerless Korean workers into masterly subjects through militant struggle against their employer and the state. Evoking Hegel's discussion of the master-slave dialectic (1807/1967, 228–40), the workers' empowerment through their collective struggle accentuates the process by which workers emerge as citizens who demand their rights. To examine the ways in which, and the extent to which, men of different social classes forge citizenship, I focus on two arenas in which South Korean men were mobilized as undifferentiated nationals: compulsory military service and employment in heavy and chemical industries. I argue that men's military mobilization functioned as a constraint in the trajectory of men's citizenship because it did not generate collective struggle to challenge the continued use of men as dutiful nationals in the process of democratization. In contrast, economic mobilization produced an enabling condition for the citizenship trajectory because it entailed the meteoric growth of the labor movement led by male workers in heavy and chemical industries that transformed powerless workers into rights-bearing members of the democratic body politic imagined by the social movement organizations discussed in chapter 4.

The first section of this chapter discusses how the hegemony of military service as men's national duty continues to prevent men's emergence as citizens through collective struggle. Given that military service as men's national duty contradicts citizens' rights to freedom of the body and thought, the paucity of the public debate on the place of military service in democratizing Korea suggests the persistence of the anticommunist national identity and of the political identity of dutiful nationals. The second section focuses on the emergence of working-class men — employed by large companies in heavy and chemical industries — as citizens, through their collective struggle to create and sustain autonomous labor unions. The positive affirmation of workers as "masters" in the labor movement's discourse approximates the active and participatory view of citizens imagined by the social movement organizations discussed in chapter 4. The last section discusses the significance, for middle- and lower-class men, of the citizenship trajectory of the upper segment of working-class men.

PROBLEMS OF MILITARY SERVICE AS MEN'S NATIONAL DUTY AND THE TRUNCATED EMERGENCE OF MEN'S CITIZENSHIP

The Civic Republican View of Martial Citizenship versus
Military Service as Men's National Duty

To begin with, the relationship between military service and citizenship is neither uniform nor static. The civic republicanism in the West that defines military service as a (male) citizen's duty constructs military service as a precondition for full citizenship (Brubaker 1992). By implication, women, who are neither required to perform military service nor prevented from serving, are not deemed full citizens. Adopting this view, some feminists in the United States have used the notion of military service as a citizenship rite in their support for "gender equality" in military service (Feinman 2000; Stiehm 1989). Although this position assumes a gender-neutral and essentialist link between military service and citizenship, the civic republican construction of martial citizenship is deeply gendered and historically specific. After all, compulsory military service has been largely masculinized by the common organizational culture of the contemporary military in many societies. The masculinization of conscription enabled certain groups of subordinated men to obtain full citizenship through military service in some societies. In contrast, there are several historical cases showing that women's participation in national militaries and nationalist struggles in guerrilla units does not necessarily guarantee their full citizenship, measured in terms of equal participation in all areas of collective life of a national community (Yuval-Davis 1997, 103).[1]

Women's inclusion in the military in some Western countries since the early 1970s has coincided with the decoupling of military service from citizenship, resulting from the end of conscription and the professionalization of the military (Isacsson 1988). This recent decline of (male) conscription in the West suggests that the civic republican view of martial citizenship is a relic of a specific historical era, when women's participation in the public sphere of politics and paid employment was severely circumscribed. In Western societies, women's integration into the postconscription military resulted from an imperative to solve the practical problem of recruitment: the end of male conscription had led to a paucity of qualified men in the recruitment pool.[2] The preconditions for citizenship shifted when it was expanded to include marginalized social groups. Civic republicanism constructed military service as a precondition for full citizenship when women were categorically excluded or exempted from military service, and women were allowed to perform military service when military service was no longer tied to citizenship.

In South Korea, where there is no such tradition, the nation-state has conceived military service as a male national's duty rather than a citizen's duty. The political subjectivity of national is different from that of citizen in that it is a type of membership in a nation ruled by an authoritarian state that disregards or suspends citizenship rights and imposes obligations in the name of patriotism. Therefore, in the absence of a balance between rights and obligations, men's performance of compulsory military service did not necessarily guarantee full citizenship even for men. Rather, compulsory military service in South Korea was predicated on the denial of the freedom of the person, particularly freedom of thought and the body, in that men as martial nationals were not allowed the option of conscientious objection to military service or alternative national service to military service. Instead, as discussed in chapter 2, the modernizing state reciprocated men's military service with certain economic advantages in paid employment and thereby contributed to men's position as family providers in the militarized economy of the 1970s and 1980s. Confirming the argument that the link between citizenship and military service is ideological rather than empirical (Yuval-Davis 1997, 89), the experience of Korean women soldiers integrated into the army as professional officers in the name of gender equality in the 1990s shows that the performance of military service does not guarantee full and equal citizenship for social minorities when military service remains tied to men's national duty (S. Moon 2002b).

While the hegemonic construction of military service as men's national duty in South Korea conjures up a unified body of men, a close reading of the categories of military service exclusion and exemption reveals a hierarchy among men justified by class and social status, as well as sexual orientation and race. That is, practices of military service generate not only a hierarchy that separates women and men but also a hierarchy among men, which contradicts the very ideal of equality implied in the subjectivity of citizen. The contradiction becomes visible when we look at the categories of men excluded from men's duty. The Korean military has employed multiple categories to separate men fit to protect the nation from those who are not. According to my chronological survey of *Pyŏngmu*, a quarterly magazine published by the Office of Military Manpower since 1988, the contents of the categories of exclusion changed over time. For example, according to a historical survey, level of education was not a criterion for exclusion until the beginning of the 1970s, but as the level of education among the population soared, a minimum level of education was required and has now been raised, so that the completion of high school is now a requirement for regular military service. In the mid-1990s, the Korean military excluded the following categories of men from martial duty: the undereducated, felons, orphans, and "those of mixed blood" (Han Sangt'ae 1995, 21).

The reasons given for these exclusions disclose much about what sort of men are considered trustworthy nationals and therefore desirable to the military. The undereducated are considered "low-quality" manpower, which the military wants to avoid as long as the supply of manpower is sufficient. The National Assembly debates on conscription in the National Defense Committee offer revealing exchanges of questions and answers among legislators and the director of the Office of Military Manpower concerning the other categories of the "unfit." According to these discussions, orphans who grow up in state institutions from a very early age and for more than five years are likely to develop "personality problems" that can disrupt the collective life and security of the military barracks. "Those of mixed blood," who do not look quite like other Koreans, are likely to feel alienated from other Koreans and can thereby be driven to abuse firearms (KNA 1993, 28; 1994, 28, 37). In South Korea, with its history of a U.S. military presence, this group is usually understood to mean the children of American soldiers and Korean sex workers, a group that is heavily stigmatized. While these two categories are numerically insignificant, their very existence in the categories of exemption reveals hidden assumptions concerning who constitutes the body of male nationals. The concern about differences in terms of physical features, in particular, as a source of potential danger alludes to the racialized boundary of the nation. It implies that those who look different from the majority of Korean men cannot be trusted to bear arms.

There are also categories of exemption, meaning categories of men who are not compelled to serve in the military (these are technically different from the excluded, who do not have the choice to serve). One category of exemption involves gender and sexual identity. The transgendered and transsexuals can request exemption from military service. (While these terms do not exist in Korean society, this group is described as those who have changed their sex through surgical operations and/or those who cross-dress [Chang Min-sŏ and Yi Yeha 1998, 19, 29].) The fact that they are allowed to request exemption conveys a strong sense of their stigmatization. This group is treated as a category of "physical handicap," along with serious mental illness and mental retardation, dwarfism, epilepsy, and other forms of "physical abnormalities." This practice in military recruitment suggests that individuals with fluid sexual and gender identities, who therefore do not have a definitely sexed body that fits into the normative sex dichotomy, are not "normal" males suitable for military service: in other words, that unequivocal biological maleness, considered to be a fixed anchor of masculinity, is crucial to fitness for military service.[3] The convoluted logic of men's exclusion and exemption from military service reveals the extent to which the state continues to treat individual men as objects of mobilization for the state's own interest while disregarding them as citizens who possess basic rights. Men's subjectivity as nationals entrenched in the practices of military service hampers the emergence of men as citizens.

Public Discontent over Military Service:
Class and Male Conscription

In contrast to the unity of men assumed in the hegemonic construction of military service as men's national duty, men of different social classes have different relationships to military service. Since the end of the Cold War elsewhere and the transition to procedural democracy in the early 1990s, sons of affluent middle-class families in South Korea have displayed a growing distaste for military service, which deprives them of their comfortable lifestyle and of time to prepare for a middle-class career. In December 1997, the Office of Military Manpower commissioned Media Research, a private polling company, to conduct a nationwide survey on the changing public attitudes toward military service. According to this survey, there was a significant gap in public perception of men's martial duty between the younger generation of prospective conscripts and the rest of the population. This national poll illustrated that the younger and the more educated a respondent was, the more critical of military service that respondent was, and the less accepting of its imperative (Pyŏngmu 1998a).[4] According to a 2002 Internet survey of the popular perception of compulsory military service among high school students in Seoul, only 34 percent of the students responded that "they would have to perform military service" (Hangyŏre Newspaper, November 19, 2002). This implies that the majority of the young respondents are willing to avoid military service if they can.

Middle-class men have dealt with their distaste for military service by attempting to avoid regular service in favor of less-onerous forms of service. Although the categories of military service were modified in the 1990s in response to growing popular discontent, the general categories can be summarized in the following ways. First, there has been a secondary form of military service involving a lesser burden than that of regular military service. Between 1968 and 1994, conscripts performing this "supplementary service" were called "defense soldiers" (pangwibyŏng). This group of conscripts commuted from their homes to local military units or government offices, as opposed to living in remote military barracks. Their service was shorter (eighteen months), and their tasks usually involved office work. (In 1995, this service was replaced by "commuting reservists" [sangkŭn yebiyŏk] and "public interest service members" [kongikgŭnmuyowŏn].)[5] Second, as discussed in chapter 2, there have been substitutes for military service altogether since 1973, when Park's regime created the "military service special cases" to deal not only with the oversupply of prospective conscripts but also with the undersupply of skilled labor in strategic heavy industries.[6] The initial subcategories included under the military service special cases were skilled industrial workers, researchers, and medical doctors serving in remote areas. (In 1993, farmers with technical licenses to operate farming machines were added to cope with the problem of a labor shortage in rural areas.)[7] Consequently, while some conscripts perform regular military service in remote barracks with little pay, others are paid by civilian firms and research centers designated by the Office of Military Manpower.

The existence of the supplementary service and the substitutes for military service has induced affluent families to use connections and money to get their sons into the less-onerous forms of military service. In addition, the wealthy or powerful can use loopholes in the military service exemption system, based on physical and psychological criteria. These unfair practices in the mandatory military service have fomented popular discontent, which grew into vociferous public criticism under Kim Young Sam's civilian administration. During this period, by disseminating statistical information on the completion of military service by region and socioeconomic status, the mass media confirmed the widespread public suspicion that the burden of military service had been borne unequally by sons of lower-class families.[8] The mass media also revealed similar class differences in military service during Kim Dae Jung's government (1998–2002).[9]

The middle-class coping mechanism to avoid or reduce the burden of military service has directly generated the problem faced by the sons of lower-class families throughout the 1990s and beyond. According to researchers in the KIDA, slightly over half of prospective conscripts perform regular military service.[10] In the democratizing polity of the post–Cold War era, it would be difficult for the military or the state to convince a young man to bear "men's national duty" when "universal" conscription in practice means that the physically fit and educated among the lower-class population are recruited for regular military service, while a disproportionate number of the elite population enjoy exemption or supplementary service, under whatever name the military adopts.

In the relative absence of money and social connections to deal with the problem of inequity in military service, the lower class accepted symbolic recognition and material rewards for military service, both of which have been in decline in the period of globalization and post Cold War. (As I have discussed elsewhere in detail [S. Moon 2002a], this popular desire for symbolic recognition for military service was poignantly revealed in the exceptionally strong reaction, largely among lower-class men [and women], against the 1999 Constitutional Court ruling that the extra-points system was illegal, and against the system's subsequent elimination.)

As a result of the middle class's ability to avoid service and the lower classes' acceptance of recognition and rewards for service, the simmering popular discontent with military service among middle- and lower-class men has not developed into an organized effort to demilitarize men's membership in the nation. It is noteworthy that the citizens' movement organizations, largely led and participated in by educated urban middle-class men (see chapter 4), have not paid attention to the issue of military service and citizenship. As Cynthia Enloe argues, militarization as a social process in which military values and practices spread to various aspects of civilian society is neither linear nor incremental (2000, 3). Similarly, the demilitarization of men's political subjectivity, when it is to be transformed from the national into the citizen, is neither linear nor incremental. In democratizing South Korea, this specific outcome, which requires the decoupling of men's citizenship from military service, is contingent on the combination of various factors. The presence of perceived or real threats to national security, the fair distribution of the burden of military service across social groups, high societal recognition and prestige given to military service, and the lack of considerable financial reward in the civilian labor market will facilitate the militarization of men's citizenship in the process of its making. South Korea is moving in the opposite direction from these conditions promoting men's martial citizenship, and the issue of men's conscription is therefore potentially explosive in democratizing Korea.[11]

THE EMERGENCE OF MALE WORKERS AS
CITIZENS IN THE LABOR MOVEMENT

The Contours of the Labor Movement

As discussed in chapter 1, militarized modernity constructed workers as useful and docile nationals through discipline and violent punishment, resulting in the suspension of workers' civil rights and the virtual absence of autonomous labor unions during the period of rapid industrialization. Against this harsh political situation, the organizing of democratic labor unions persisted, growing into a powerful wave of militant labor disputes during the summer of 1987, shortly after the June 29 Democratization Declaration by Roh Tae Woo. During this period, the frequency of labor disputes rose to 3,749 in 1987 from 276 in 1986 (Koo 2001, 158, 159). The unprecedented upsurge of labor disputes during the summer of 1987, known as the "great workers' struggle" (*nodongja taet'ujaeng*), erupted first in Ulsan, the heartland of the Hyundai conglomerate, the largest *chaebol* group in South Korea. The first wave of labor conflicts soon spread to other major industrial cities: Pusan, Masan, and Ch'angwŏn in the South, where heavy and chemical industries were concentrated. By mid-August the labor strikes reached the Seoul and Inch'ŏn area, where smaller light-manufacturing industries were clustered (Ch'oi Yŏng-gi et al. 2001, chap. 4). The spread of labor disputes led to the multiplication of "democratic labor unions" (*minjunojo*), new autonomous labor unions, involving the participation of hundreds of thousands of workers throughout the country.

In the post-1987 labor movement, semiskilled and skilled male workers employed by large companies in the heavy and chemical industries became a visibly leading force. Their dominance in the labor movement was both numerical and symbolic. The total number of labor unions and their membership had increased during the late 1980s. Between June 1987, before the great workers' struggle, and 1990, total union membership grew from 1.05 million to 1.88 million, and the aggregate rate of union membership among the entire body of employees increased from 11.7 percent to 17.2 percent. During the same period, the rate of union membership among the entire body of male workers grew from 13.0 percent to 20.5 percent, whereas that of female workers increased from 9.5 percent to 12.0 percent (KWDI 1999, 260, 261). Yet Robert P. Kearney points out that, despite the explosion of labor strikes in 1987, 1988, and 1989, labor activism was limited to the large companies with better working conditions. While 70 percent of the 374 largest firms (hiring more than one thousand employees) were struck by the upsurge of labor strikes, 99.4 percent of the smaller firms (hiring fewer than fifty employees) were not affected by it (Kearney 1991, 25). In 1986, although the corporate structure in the Korean economy was dominated by a handful of economic conglomerates hiring hundreds of thousands of workers, 64 percent of the entire workforce was employed by over 200,000 small and medium-size firms hiring fewer than three hundred employees each (Kearney 1991, 20, 55). In 1989, 73.7 percent of all male workers were employed in small firms hiring fewer than fifty employees, and 47.4 percent of all male workers were employed in very small firms hiring fewer than five employees. The concentration of women workers in small firms was even higher than that of their male counterparts in 1989, reaching 83.5 percent and 64.6 percent, respectively (KWDI 1991, 147). Despite the dramatic growth of the labor struggle in the late 1980s, by 1989 the majority of workers were not organized. Instead of organized collective struggle, the silent majority of workers used job change to deal with discontent with their working conditions. The turnover rate among Korean workers was 4.3 percent, higher than that in either the United States or Japan (Kearney 1991, 25).

As discussed in chapter 2, hundreds of thousands of male workers in heavy and chemical industries had been recruited and trained in lieu of mandatory military service since 1973. This path of mass mobilization accentuated the masculinization of semiskilled and skilled labor and the workforce employed in the strategic and foundational industries. Although they were unquestionably exploited, male workers employed by large companies occupied a relatively privileged position among the working-class population (in relation to working-class women and men employed in smaller companies or in informal sectors). Numerically a minority among the entire body of working men and women in South Korea, these most privileged working-class men played the major role in the post-1987 labor movement and emerged as citizens in the process of their collective struggle. The dominance of semiskilled and skilled male workers in heavy and chemical industries in the labor struggles of the late 1980s was visible from the beginning. A close reading of the growth of labor unions and their membership reveals the centrality of male workers in heavy and chemical industries to the post-1987 labor movement. During the great workers' struggle of 1987, metalworkers' unions and chemical workers' unions showed the largest membership increases, reinforcing the numerical dominance they had already had in the state-sponsored labor unions of the pre-1987 period (Kang In-sun 2001, 22).[12]

Throughout the 1990s, despite the decline in the overall rate of unionization among workers, caused by aggressive crackdowns on the democratic union movement by the state and management and by economic restructuring linked to globalization, the democratic unions' dominance relative to other industry-based unions in terms of membership numbers was largely maintained. In 1992, the two largest groups of unions were the metalworkers' unions (400,482 members) and the chemical workers' unions (178,668 members). Even while achieving comparably large membership in 1992, unions of the banking industry (145,663 members), taxi drivers (115,950), and the textile industry (105,082) did not carry the symbolic significance of workers in the heavy industries (KWDI 1995, 222). In 1998, the metalworkers' unions and chemical workers' unions remained the two largest, with memberships of 291,867 and 122,146, respectively (KWDI 1999, 261). After the establishment of the Federation of Korean Metalworkers' Unions (Chŏn'gukkŭmsoksanŏbnojoyŏn-maeng) in 1998, metalworkers consolidated their core position in the Korean Confederation of Trade Unions (Minjunoch'ong), the national body of democratic labor unions (Ch'oi Yŏng-gi et al. 2001, 540, 542). In 2000, the total memberships of the metalworkers' unions and chemical workers' unions were 294,135 and 117,597, respectively (KWDI 2001, 267).[13]

The dominance of male workers from the heavy and chemical industries in labor unions continued in the early 1990s, when the labor movement was in decline as a result of the state's return to its previous pattern of labor repression (Song Chae-bok 1994). Throughout the 1990s, men dominated the metalworkers' and chemical workers' unions. In 1992, men represented 81 percent of the membership of the metalworkers' unions and 75 percent of the membership of the chemical workers' unions. Male dominance in the leadership structure of these unions was even higher, reaching 93.8 percent in the metalworkers' unions and 96.8 percent in the chemical workers' unions (KWDI 1995, 222). In 1998, while men represented 76.5 percent of the membership of both unions under the rubric of the Federation of Korean Trade Unions (FKTU), formerly controlled by the state and management, men represented 94.3 percent of the membership of the metalworkers' unions and 94.1 percent of the chemical workers' unions under the rubric of the Korean Confederation of Trade Unions (KWDI 1999, 261, 262). It is noteworthy that women's membership was far lower in the KCTU, the national body of democratic labor unions, than in the FKTU. In 2000, these gender ratios in membership remained roughly the same, with a slight decrease in the men's ratio in the metalworkers' unions (73 percent) under the FKTU and, likewise, a slight decrease in the men's ratio in the chemical workers' unions (88.8 percent) under the KCTU (KWDI 2001, 267).

The extent to which middle-class intellectuals were involved in the post-1987 labor movement led by male workers remains ambiguous in the absence of substantial studies. Some scholars point out that male college-educated labor activists were present in the heavy industrial estates in South and North Kyŏngsang Provinces as late as the early 1990s.[14] However, in comparison with the role of middle-class women in the women's labor movement, the role of middle-class men in the men's labor movement seems relatively limited. As indicated hereafter, publications in the late 1980s and early 1990s reflected the inter-class aspect of the post-1987 men's labor movement. Nevertheless, as the labor movement grew and the transition to procedural democracy took place in the 1990s, the movement's interclass nature was further weakened.

The Forging of Citizens in the Process of Labor Struggle

The discourse of the post-1987 labor movement led by male workers in heavy and chemical industries reveals their emergence as citizens, entitled to rights and therefore willing to fight to obtain them if those rights were denied. The writings that I examine here include *Labor and the World*, the house organ of the KCTU, published since March 1997, as well as observations and reflections by Gramscian "organic intellectuals" of the working class and middle-class intellectuals identified with the labor movement.[15] Interpreting the meanings of the great 1987 workers' struggle and the subsequent development of the labor struggle to form and sustain labor unions, these writings thematically constructed workers as "human beings" and "masters." Not explicitly employ-ing the notion of citizens (because that term had customarily been used in the 1990s to refer to middle-class people who were not manual workers),[16] the discourse as a whole highlighted the ultimate goal of the labor movement as the transformation of workers into rights-bearing subjects who were to be the masters of democratic society (Hŏ Yŏng-gu 2003; KCTU 2003; An 2002; KCTU 1999).[17] My insistence on using the notion of citizen is not to impose the exoge-nous category on workers but to capture the essentially political nature of the transformation of workers' identity and its possibility for reconstructing a new form of membership in the body politic.

According to the discourse of the labor movement articulated in the afore-mentioned writings, a democratic labor union was an essential vehicle, within a capitalist economy that reduced workers to an instrument of production, for those workers to become human beings. Echoing the voices of individual workers yearning for humane treatment, but also moving beyond their indi-vidual pleas,[18] the discourse highlighted the importance of collective struggle in obtaining workers' rights. Pak Dong-su, a chief of the organizing division of the National Council of Labor Unions (NCLU: Chŏnnohyŏp), formed as a national body of the democratic labor unions in January 1990, viewed the great 1987 workers' struggle as powerful proof that workers were not merely obedient beings who would accept what was given to them and follow what they were told to do (1990, 71). Most importantly, the great workers' struggle altered workers' consciousness by compelling them to confront state power with their own solidarity and by changing the perception that the state could easily pulverize labor unions anytime it wanted to; workers began to see themselves as deserving of the labor rights that would give them their humanity. During the late 1980s, workers obtained real wage increases as a result of collective struggle, and this improvement gave the government and management a pretext to delegitimize the workers' collective struggle. Rejecting the merely economic view of the labor movement, Pak Dong-su wrote:

> Workers are neither a machine that runs when the switch is on, nor are we animals satisfied with a full stomach. As the fruit of high-speed economic growth becomes abundant, we want accordingly just treatment for our hard work of blood and sweat. The common response, "Aren't you eating and living O.K.?," reveals the social trend to look down upon workers. The more despised we are, the more workers desire to overcome this social contempt. . . . We have to unite and struggle to restore our rights. (1990, 70–71)

The centrality of the concept of rights in the discussion of what constitutes a human being strongly suggests that such workers are making themselves into citizens. The pivotal significance of the active struggle to obtain rights as workers indicates that workers' citizenship is not a formal status conferred by the state but a result of participatory membership in the "authentic world" (*ch'amsesang*), the community envisioned by the labor movement.

Crucial to workers' transformation into citizens is their actual engagement in large-scale public meetings and marches involving tens of thousands of workers and their supporters in the late 1980s and early 1990s. Kwŏn Yong-mok, chairperson of the Hyundai Group Labor Unions Council, described a massive street protest by around forty thousand workers and their families during the Hyundai Group's general strike in August 1987, and the workers' empowerment through the collective struggle:

> A four-kilometer throng, a sixteen-kilometer march! It was an orderly march during which numerous cars, various fixtures on the street, and glass windows [of buildings] remained intact in the midst of the explosive energy of the marchers. It was a heartfelt expression of the workers' will to break the chains of the past and march for a new day. It was a powerful wave that destroyed an invincible fortress in one moment. It was workers' power that brought the immensely powerful [companies] to their knees by putting their hearts together. It was a great march. (Quoted in Ch'oi Yŏng-gi et al. 2001, 103; translation mine)

In the process of this type of transformative collective effervescence, workers were able to forge a new identity as citizens whose relationship to the state shifted from being the objects of mobilization to being rights-bearing subjects. Since the first workers' conference was held in Seoul in November 1988 (see figure 10), drawing some fifty thousand workers from all over the country, annual workers' conferences have not only energized workers but also pulled them into violent clashes with armed agents of the state deployed to block these large-scale meetings.

The discourse of the labor movement revealed the emergence of workers as citizens in its recurring discussion of workers' transformation from "slaves" into "masters." According to this view of workers' liberation, the ultimate goal of the labor movement would be "to build the truthful world where workers become masters" (Kim In-ok 1990, 142). From this perspective, the great workers' struggle signified that "workers rejected their slavish labor and dared to resist the capitalists who were their masters" (An 2002, 103), and the Hyundai Heavy Industry strike in April and May 1990 symbolized the "fierce struggle between the minority of haves trying to secure the status quo and the power to build a nation where workers become masters" (Yi Jin-p'yŏng 1990, 241). Raising consciousness among workers, a newsletter of the Masan-Ch'angwŏn labor unions federation (Mach'angnoryŏn), one of the leading forces of the labor movement, also emphasized that "true workers desire to live like human beings in the world without exploitation rather than working more to earn more wages like a slave" (Pak Kyŏng-nam 1990, 153). A play entitled "March forward! Forward!" performed in 1990, conveyed this recurring theme in the following lines spoken by a worker:

> We carried out a strike to become laboring human beings, not working machines. We did it to become genuine masters of the future. The principle of no labor, no wages [referring to the rule that workers during a strike will not be paid their wages because they did not work], reflects the power struggle. . . . It is a theory that cannot but be broken if workers unite. But if we are weak, we will be reduced to a flock of swallows chased away by a scarecrow. We need to unite.[19]

These lines interpret a labor strike as a vehicle for workers to become masters rather than a vehicle for a wage increase. What transforms them into masters is the sobering awareness that "no one will protect workers' interests and well-being except workers themselves" (Pak Kyŏng-nam 1990, 149), and therefore workers use their collective power to solve their problem for themselves.

10. The first National Workers' Conference held at Yonsei University, 1988.
Photograph by Yonhap News Agency.

From this point of view, the labor movement as a whole symbolizes workers' challenge to the brutal reality of the capitalist economy that reduces them to a passive element in the entire process from production planning to the distribution of products; in this challenge, the workers forge their new identity as a "subject" (*chuch'e*) (Hŏ Yŏng-gu 2003, 87). Such an active subject resembles the active and participatory category of the citizen who takes matters into his or her hands.

The transformation of workers into human beings and masters was accompanied by the collective affirmation of the formerly stigmatized identity of manual workers (*nodongja*). The labor movement discourse profusely used *nodongja* as a positive self-referential term that honored their hard work and productive labor. For decades, Korean workers had been not only exploited but also subjected to contemptuous and humiliating treatment in the workplace, stemming from a disdain for manual labor that is deeply rooted in Confucian culture. Reflecting this social custom, (male) factory workers were derogatorily called *kongdori* (factory hand). Hence, in many large companies, management exercised varying degrees of surveillance over workers' appearance to highlight and maintain their inferior status, including the imposition of color-coded uniforms to distinguish manual workers from white-collar workers and managers, the use of separate entrances and dining halls, and the regulation of workers' hairstyles, resembling the tactics of the military government of the 1970s (Kang In-sun 2001, 25). Documenting a history of the labor movement at the Hyundai conglomerate, Yi Su-wŏn, a worker at the Hyundai Group, describes its militaristic and paternalistic labor control as follows:

> A company guard at the entrance gate cut a worker's hair right on the spot if his hair slightly touched the back collar of his jacket. Instructions related to work were considered commands to be obeyed, and obedience marked an entire working day. The atmosphere in the workplace was saturated with the Chung Ju Young [the founder of the Hyundai Groups] style, which subjected even a high-ranking manager to a kick at the knee by his boss in front of his subordinates. There was also a distinction between managers and production workers in their residential lives. There were two separate worlds, just like those observed in a mining town. (Quoted in Ch'oi Yŏng-gi et al. 2001, 94; translation mine)

As kongdori, workers were understood to be subhuman beings encumbered with obligations without rights, who should therefore be grateful to their exploitative employers for their jobs. As nodongja, workers understood themselves not only as manual laborers, with a positive self-affirmation of this previously stigmatized category, but also as citizens. As nodongja, workers rejected their state-imposed identity as *sanŏpyŏkgun* (industrial soldiers) or *kŭloja* (workers), who were merely dutiful objects of the mobilization to build the national economy and therefore supposed to forgo basic rights for the sake of the nation.

The discourse of the labor movement frequently linked the workers' struggle to democracy and democratization. It viewed humane treatment for workers as necessary not only for the development of the national economy but also for the development of democratic society (*World of Living Together* 1989, 181). From the outset of the great workers' struggle, workers called their autonomous unions "democratic labor unions" (minjunojo) because the humane treatment of workers would be constitutive of the democratization of Korean society; the workers' collective struggle aimed ultimately to build a democratic society that would allow them to be human beings and masters (Pak Dong-su 1990, 78). Indeed, workers' collective struggle since 1987 has emphasized the creation of democratic labor unions free from the intervention of the state and management as well as the democratization of the already existing unions that had been controlled by these powerful actors and their collaborators. During the great workers' struggle in the summer of 1987, the establishment of democratic labor unions was one of the major demands articulated by workers. While wage increases were the most frequently mentioned issue during labor disputes, workers made a consistent demand for the recognition of autonomous unions as a means to improve their working conditions and inhumane treatment by management (An 2002, 102; Kang In-sun 2001, 21; Ch'oi Yŏng-gi et al. 2001, 152). Roughly half of the labor disputes during the great workers' struggle took place in companies without labor unions; workers formed unions as a result of their struggle against management (Kang In-sun 2001, 22). In 1990, over 4,000 unions (out of the total of roughly 7,800 unions) held elections, and approximately 70 percent of elected leaders were considered democratic leaders who would protect autonomous unions (Ch'oi Yŏng-gi et al. 2001, 311). Until 1995, when the KCTU was established as a national body of newly formed democratic labor unions, the workers' struggle to establish and protect autonomous unions in the face of violent repression by the state and management constituted a major aspect of the labor movement. Autonomous labor unions stood for, and would guarantee, workers' civil rights to form an association, to strike, and to engage in collective bargaining.

Distinguishing "people's democracy" for workers and the oppressed from "liberal democracy" for the haves, the labor movement discourse criticized the repression of the workers' movement as the repression of workers' demands for democracy (Yi Jin-p'yŏng 1990, 244) and affirmed that a democracy that did not guarantee basic labor rights would be false (Hŏ Yŏng-gu 2003, 42). This insistence on the link between the labor movement and democracy envisions workers as members of a democratic body politic.

However, the culture of the labor movement was largely masculinized as a result of the exigency of militant struggle against the (historically violently antilabor) state and management (see figure 11). Frequently calling on the state to use organized violence to defeat workers' strikes and break demo- cratic unions, management also used its own physical force, organizing the save-our-company corps (kusadae), composed of managers, pro-company workers, professional thugs, security police, and special paramilitary forces (Ch'oi Yŏng-gi et al. 2001, 253). During the first three years after the great workers' struggle, in particular, workers and the state were often drawn into combative clashes.[20] The discourse of the labor movement was profuse in its use of military metaphors to describe workers' collective struggle, especially during the late 1980s and early 1990s, when the labor movement was heavily in- fluenced by Marxism-Leninism (An 2002, chap. 7). The discourse of the labor movement depicted workers as warriors and soldiers involved in combat, and described large-scale marches as "battle lines" (chŏnt'udaeyŏl). Viewing art and literature as "weapons" to arm the working class with the consciousness of labor liberation,[21] even workers' culture groups, performing music, dance, and plays, were commonly described as a vanguard to build the "workers' army for labor liberation" (Kim In-ok 1990, 141).

The militarized trajectory of male workers' citizenship allows us to discern an important aspect of the gendered trajectory of citizenship connected to physical violence. Violence, ranging from the beating of union workers with wooden bars and metal pipes to the destruction of union offices, was so perva- sive that many workers were deterred from joining labor unions or withdrew from them (Ch'oi Yŏng-gi et al. 2001, 253, 254). Elsewhere I have examined the violent androcentric civil society in South Korea and its implications for women as political subjects (S. Moon 2002c). Feminist scholars have argued that women's primary responsibilities for care work and housework in house- holds and their subsequent position as secondary workers in the labor market undermine their ability to participate in civil society and therefore emerge as full citizens (Leblanc 1998; Lister 1990). I would argue that in addition to the

11. Militant confrontation between riot police and unionized workers of
Daewoo Automobile Co., 2001. Photograph by Yonhap News Agency.

gender division of labor in households, pervasive violence in civil society prevents women more than men from participating in it owing to their gender-differentiated socialization and to certain physical differences between sexes. It is telling that the democratic union movement of young female factory workers in the 1980s was devastated by the physical force used by the repressive state apparatuses and the save-our-company corps (Kang In-sun 2001, chap. 9). The symbolic power of male workers in the heavy and chemical industries sprang not only from their large numbers but also from the heavy machinery and equipment they could use as weapons against the state and management. The following portrayal of a street protest waged by some 40,000 Hyundai workers, responding to Hyundai founder Chung Ju Young's adamant refusal to negotiate with unions, conveys the significance of physical force and the threat of such force in establishing a new political subjectivity against the powers that be:

> In the first row of the protest march, a union leader carrying an armband with a sign reading "Democratic Union Chief Guard" was riding on a fire-truck followed by about ten automobiles. In the next row, a motorcycle unit equipped with antidust masks and helmets followed like a mobile troop, and in the next row, four-hundred-some workers armed with anti-dust masks, helmets, wooden bars, and metal pipes followed like a special-forces unit. Some forty thousand workers, including their families, staged an organized and systematic protest like a military march. (*Chosŏn Daily*, August 20, 1987, quoted in Ch'oi Yŏng-gi et al. 2001, 103; translation mine)

There is an irony in the paradoxical relationship between physical force and the subjectivity of citizens. Military service as men's national duty, in the absence of alternative forms of service or the recognition of conscientious objection to military service, tends to discourage the emergence of men as citizens. That is, men's compulsory access to the institutionalized use of organized violence encapsulates men in the subjectivity of dutiful nationals to be mobilized for the sake of a nation. At the same time, male workers' privileged access to heavy machinery and equipment that can be used as weapons in armed conflict with the police and the military enables them to sustain their will to be citizens. After this kind of armed protest and warlike clash with the powers that be, as Hegel theorized in his master-slave dialectic (1807/1967, 234–38), the male workers became rights-bearing subjects.

The emergence of the most privileged group of male workers as citizens is not a linear evolutionary process. Nor is there a teleological or ineluctable path in the development of citizenship. Some students of the labor movement in South Korea have expressed concerns about the economic focus on wage increases and the indifference to larger issues of social justice and democratization among unionized workers. These critics of allegedly depoliticized workers argued that by the mid-1990s, unionized workers, able to afford a car, a modest apartment, and occasional leisure time outside cities as a result of relative improvement in the material standards of living, became individualistic and reluctant to take an active part in union activities beyond wage negotiation (Ch'oi Yŏng-gi et al. 2001, 362, 363). It can be argued that this image of the worker is closer to that of the consumer than to that of the citizen. Although this irony may well suggest a powerful trend in the trajectory of citizenship in (postmodern) consumer society, it is still too early to reach such a conclusion. Against incredible odds, these workers have struggled to obtain their rights. Even their economic focus on wage increase has been simultaneously political in that this demand challenged the so-called Korean model of industrialization based on "cheap" unorganized labor. The first national strike collaboratively led by the KCTU and the FKTU (in response to the National Assembly's passing in December 1996 of a labor law reform bill that would further undermine employment security) illustrates the possibility that organized labor can alter state policy. The combination of apparently apolitical union members and politically inclined union leadership seems to suggest a diversification as well as fissure within unions. With the growing institutional acceptance of labor unions, the labor movement, like other types of social movements in procedurally democratic societies, tends to become professionalized; grassroots union members, in the absence of urgent threats to their employment, tend to become distanced from dealings with the state and other actors in civil society for broad issues beyond wage increases.

Yet the largely negative consequences of globalization for blue-collar workers do pose a growing threat to workers, including those who are positioned at the highest level of the labor market. Articulating the experiences of male workers in heavy industry, organic intellectuals of the working class point out that the problem is not so much workers' loss of interest in collective struggle beyond the issue of wages as it is the lack of vision and deeper meaning in the collective struggle led by elected union officers. After a few years of collective struggle for wage increases, workers yearn for a deeper meaning in their struggle because they have learned that their strikes will result in just a little more income, not worth the risk of violence, severe injury, and, worse, the permanent loss of employment after joining a strike (An 2002, chap. 8). It remains to be seen how this current problem will affect the labor movement in South Korea, particularly the attitudes of the relatively privileged male workers in the heavy and chemical industries.

THE SIGNIFICANCE OF THE MALE WORKER'S CITIZENSHIP TRAJECTORY

Arguing that the collective struggle to form autonomous labor unions and to sustain them against the state and management was the crucial way for the upper segment of working-class men to obtain citizenship, in this section I relate this trajectory to men of other classes, as the employed in general. The discussion of class difference in the forging of citizenship in South Korea requires caution; it is rather like shooting at a moving target. Because the country has only recently become industrialized (during the past decade or so), the boundaries of class structure are still fluid and ambiguous. The specific definitions of the middle class in Korean society vary depending on the theoretical orientation of those who are doing the categorizing (Ham et al. 2001, 22–32). Yet most researchers tend to agree on a distinction between the new middle class (professional, managerial, and clerical workers) and the old middle class (small shop owners and sometimes landowning farmers). The official criteria for the middle class used by the Economic Planning Board since 1993 include a household income at least 2.5 times higher than minimum living expenses, ownership of a residential house or an exclusive rental, stable employment, and a high school degree or above (Mun et al. 2000, 47). A subjective definition of the middle class expressed among Seoulites similarly stressed stable employment and sufficient income to enjoy leisure and cultural activities (Ham et al. 2001, 221–22). Adopting these common criteria, I use "middle class" loosely as a descriptive term to encompass urban residents who meet the common criteria in terms of occupation, level of education, and household income.

First, the working-class trajectory of citizenship has served as a model for middle-class employees in both public and private sectors. Newly affirming their identity as "workers," sizable minorities of white-collar employees of banking and finance industries and research centers, along with schoolteachers, legal and medical professionals, and clerical workers, have fought for the fundamental labor rights to form unions, bargain collectively, and carry out strikes. Although the constitution guarantees these basic labor rights, labor-related laws, subordinate to the constitution, have undermined them in practice (Hŏ Yŏng-gu 2003, chap. 1).[22] Hence middle-class men and the upper segment of working-class men have both continued to struggle for such basic rights, even under Kim Dae Jung's "people's government." In the first decade of the twenty-first century, state employees, having been mobilized by the state for decades as its instruments, have been at the center of this labor struggle. In the face of the postmilitary governments' persistent denial of basic labor rights among all state employees, including policemen, firefighters, soldiers,

prison guards, judges, and prosecutors (36, 40), this recent change is significant because state employees represent a large segment of the new middle class
of white-collar professional, managerial, and clerical workers.[23]

Second, the labor union movement as the avenue to citizenship is also relevant to the lower classes in the period of the post-1997 economic crisis, characterized by the acceleration of globalization that has increased insecure employment in the name of a "flexible labor supply" to maximize international
competitiveness. Almost 60 percent of the employed in South Korea in 2000
were working as "irregular" workers in temporary, part-time, day labor, and
outsourced positions (Hŏ Yŏng-gu 2003, 131). Often working as much as, or
more than, regular workers for a prolonged period of time, these irregular
workers are denied their basic labor rights. This precarious condition of employment has compelled them to organize labor unions as a vehicle to obtain
their rights. And their ability to organize to protect their rights as workers
is crucial to their democratic membership in Korean society because, echoing the mobilizing rhetoric of militarized modernity, the state and the conservative mass media have criticized the labor union movement in the name
of saving and strengthening the national economy. Exhorting the employed
to work hard despite layoffs, wage decreases, and the intensification of the
labor process, the hegemonic discourse during Kim Dae Jung's government
attempted to keep men of various social groups as docile and useful nationals
(Hŏ Yŏng-gu 2003, chap. 2; An 2002, chaps. 12 and 13).

Third, the focus on the working-class trajectory of men's citizenship in this
chapter does not mean that this has been the only avenue to men's citizenship. As discussed in chapter 4, a sizable minority of urban, college-educated,
middle-class men have affirmed their identity as rights-bearing subjects in
the "citizens' movement." Equally significant for the emergence of men (and
women in principle) as citizens in the long run, the citizens' movement has not
propelled the transformation of nationals into citizens as much as the labor
movement did. Empirical studies of the urban middle class in contemporary
South Korea indicate that, while relatively more supportive of the labor movement and social change than were their counterparts in other East Asian countries (Koo 1999), the new middle class in South Korea as a whole showed little
interest in active participation in civil society except for formal elections, and
is in fact deeply distrustful of civil society (Ham et al. 2001; Mun et al. 2000;
Kim Yŏng-mo 1997).

Against this backdrop, the relationship between the citizens' movement and
the labor movement has altered over time. In the 1970s, the labor movement
stood apart from the democracy movement led by middle-class intellectuals

and students. In the 1980s, when the radicalized democracy movement against military rule became the people's movement, the labor movement became its pivotal element because the people's movement relied on Marxism-Leninism for its vision and analysis of society (see chapter 4). Procedural democratization since 1987 has resulted in the growing independence of the labor movement and the emergence of citizens' movements aiming at gradual reform of society through institutional channels. Since this divergence, the two, while at times collaborating, have maintained separate identities along lines of class and of the methods chosen to effect social change.

CONCLUSION

The military and economic mobilization of men during the period of militarized modernity shaped the emergence of men as citizens and the obstacles to that emergence in post-1987 South Korea. Generating the problem of inequity across classes, men's military mobilization did not lead to the development of the citizens' movement to redefine the relationship between military service and men's citizenship during the process of procedural democratization. The demand for basic rights has been collectively articulated through the labor movement, dominated by (relatively privileged) male workers employed by large companies in the heavy and chemical industries. In their militant collective struggle to form autonomous unions in the face of violent opposition from the state and management, these male workers shattered their subjectivity as dutiful nationals and became rights-bearing subjects. Yet despite its significance to men and women as the employed in principle, the labor movement was deeply masculinized by the pervasiveness of militarized violence and the patriarchal culture of the labor union. It was not until the beginning of the twenty-first century that *Labor and the World*, the house organ of the KCTU, featured substantial articles about women workers' issues. It is not accidental that the family members of the Kia Automobile Co., often women and children, remained invisible behind the militant workers, despite their participation in the labor movement. The perception of women as male workers' family members rather than as workers in their own right suggests the ambivalent relationship between women and the "democratic" labor unions. In the next chapter, I will analyze this relationship in the trajectory of women's citizenship as shaped by the mass mobilization of women as reproducers that marginalized their subjectivity as productive workers in the industrializing economy.

6 THE TRAJECTORY OF WOMEN'S CITIZENSHIP AS SHAPED BY THEIR ECONOMIC MARGINALIZATION AS REPRODUCERS

I've known that it's not easy to live as a confident woman and worker in this society, but can it be this hard? . . . At least to survive, we have to eat, don't we? When the most basic right to survive is denied, what's the use of "globalization" and "national competitiveness"? We've never ruined the nation. We've only worked hard. But now in the name of "the second building of the nation" we're exhorted to erect the nation again. We're told to remain unemployed for the sake of "the second nation building." . . . If the revival of the nation requires the killing of so many workers, this nation is not our nation. Perhaps the nation belongs to those who need to make us workers jobless for their own prosperity.

—*Seoul Women Workers' Association Newsletter*, September 1989

Responding to the massive layoffs in labor-intensive manufacturing in the late 1980s, the woman worker quoted in the epigraph refused to remain a docile and useful national and rejected the nation that demanded of workers like her that they forgo their basic right to earn a living to rescue the economy in crisis. How did women of different social classes forge their new political subjectivity as citizens after being mobilized as unmarried workers and then, after marriage, as reproducers? How is the trajectory of women's citizenship similar to, and different from, that of men's citizenship, as exemplified by the militant struggle to form, protect, and use autonomous labor unions and the "citizens' movement"? To address these questions, I examine two major paths to women's citizenship: the women workers' labor movement in the manufacturing industries, and the autonomous women's movements that fought for women's equal employment in the period of postmilitary rule. I argue that the women's labor movement was actively supported by autonomous women's associations formed outside labor unions, especially during the late 1980s and early 1990s. With the drastic decline of the women's labor movement in the 1990s, the focus of women's movements moved to the issue of equal employment. In comparison with the trajectory of men's citizenship, the women's movements for advocating labor struggle and equal employment often worked in the form of interclass coalition in their challenge to women's economic marginalization, but the movement to challenge the militarized economy was carried out mainly by middle-class women.

The first section of this chapter discusses the women factory workers' movement within and outside labor unions, focusing on the difference between the trajectory of the women's movement and that of the working-class men's labor movement. To the extent to which labor unions were patriarchal, autonomous women's organizations played an instrumental role in creating space for women in the male-dominated labor movement of the post-1987 period. The second section explores the ways in which the interclass women's movement fought to obtain an equal right to employment for women as a whole. The third section discusses the middle-class women's movement in the late 1990s to eliminate the military service extra-points system, a component of the militarized economy described in chapter 1. Despite its middle-class orientation, this movement made both symbolic and practical progress in equal employment for women as a whole, challenging one of the most sensitive issues of the militarized economy in post-military-rule Korea. The last section examines how the interclass movement's support for the factory workers' labor struggle and for equal employment for women as a whole redefined the substance of citizenship beyond liberal and Marxist notions, illuminating the relational nature of citizenship situated in the family and thereby challenging the gender hierarchy predicated on the division of labor between women and men (see chapter 2).

WOMEN FACTORY WORKERS: FORGING CITIZENSHIP
THROUGH THE LABOR MOVEMENT

After the eruption of the great workers' struggle in 1987, the women workers' labor movement spread nationally, ranging from major industrial regions such as Seoul-Inch'ŏn-Puch'ŏn, Masan-Ch'angwŏn, Taegu-Gumi, and Pusan to minor industrial areas in the Chŏlla and Ch'ungch'ŏng provinces (see figure 12). The women's labor movement to form unions to protect their rights as

3·8세계여성의날기념
여성노동자큰잔치
주최:한국여성노동자회
일시·1988.3.6

12. The first Women Workers' Festival in Seoul, 1988. Photograph by Yonhap News Agency.

workers encompassed women not only in manufacturing sectors but also in clerical and other service sectors, including banking, health care, publishing, mass media, education, and research institutes (Chŏng Kang-ja 1998, 49). I focus on women factory workers here for two reasons. First, they were the group massively mobilized to fuel the industrializing economy in the period of militarized modernity and therefore became a leading force in the women workers' movement of the late 1980s. Second, the women workers' movement in other sectors is much less documented during this period in which the women's labor movement was revitalized. Women's involvement in the labor struggle became most visible in labor-intensive manufacturing, numerically dominated by women, but women also played a leading role in some male-dominated factories. Both as workers without unions and as union members and leaders, women demanded not only wage increases and the improvement of abject working conditions but also the legalization of an autonomous labor union to obtain and protect a set of basic rights, including freedom from sexual harassment (Kang In-sun 2001, 11, 25, 27).

Overshadowed by the labor movement led by the upper section of working-class men, discussed in chapter 5, the women's labor movement served as a crucial path to citizenship among women workers. Pivotal to the transformation of women workers into citizens was the collective struggle (in a process parallel to the emergence of male workers as citizens) to form and protect "democratic labor unions" and to practice collective bargaining in the face of blackmail and brutal violence from the state and management. A woman worker at Hanyŏng Aluminum, a large corporation in Kyŏnggi Province manufacturing a refrigerator cooling device for Gold Star, Samsung, and Daewoo (the three major home-appliance companies), described the violence she encountered during a union strike in September 1987:

> Around four o'clock in the afternoon, several dozen unidentified and well-built men entered, followed by the save-our-company corps. They were accompanied by two troops of riot police armed with helmets, shields, and steel pipes. Until then we had thought that the police would protect us from the corps, and we just prepared ourselves for defense. . . . Suddenly, a fire broke out in the storage area, and at the same time the electricity went out. . . . Then the police started fusillading tear gas bombs, and the factory turned into a hell. . . . We resisted to the end in the midst of that hellish situation. *Ajumŏni* [married women workers] produced the stones they had carried, and male workers fought against the police and the corps. . . . These ajumŏni were dragged by their hair to the union office by young policemen and corps members and severely beaten up. Calling ajumŏni reds, and pouring red paint on their heads, some of those young men poked their breasts and genitalia with steel pipes, leaving them so injured that they had to be hospitalized. The police were present at the union office, but directed the violence rather than anything else, saying: "Don't kill them, but it's okay if these women become disabled. We'll take care of it." (Kang In-sun 2001, 82–83; translation mine)

This kind of violence was quite prevalent at the scenes of labor struggle, especially before the transition to civilian government in 1993, but it has not disappeared altogether even under civilian rule. While severe violence such as that described here deterred many women workers from participating in the labor movement, it also enabled those who were involved to realize that no one but themselves would care about their well-being, and the only way to take care of themselves would be to unite to fight for their rights.

Apart from the violent nature of labor struggles commonly experienced by men and women workers, the trajectory of women's citizenship through the labor movement reveals the instrumental role of autonomous women's associations, formed outside labor unions, in forging women workers' citizenship. In the late 1980s, women workers' associations (*yŏsŏngnodongjahoe*) and the labor council (*nodongwiwŏnhoe*) of the KWAU concentrated on advocacy work for women workers who were involved in the emerging labor unions. The Seoul Women Workers' Association (SWWA) was the first women workers' association serving blue-collar women, established in 1987 by women factory workers who had been involved in the democratic labor union movement of the 1970s and 1980s and by former student activists who had been engaged in the anti-military-regime movement in the 1980s (Sin Illyŏng 1988, 323). After the great 1987 workers' struggle, the SWWA organized small-group meetings on women's issues to raise consciousness among women workers, and these educated workers formed local women workers' associations in the late 1980s and early 1990s. In 1992, six local women workers' associations formed the Korean Women Workers Associations Council (KWWAC: Yŏsŏng nodongjahoehyŏbŭihoe) as its national body.[1] The labor council was formed as a permanent component to the KWAU in 1988 (Kang In-sun 2001, 473). Through consciousness-raising in small-group activities and training programs for women unionists, as well as solidarity protests and visits to women workers on strike and the use of the mass media to publicize women's labor struggle, the women's associations actively supported women workers in organizing autonomous labor unions, carrying out their collective struggle against the repression of labor unions and massive layoffs, and becoming union leaders (Kang In-sun 2001, 325; KWWAC 1997, 41–54).

The founding statement of the SWWA allows us to appreciate the urgency of advocating for women workers, who confronted distinct problems, and to appreciate as well the major obstacles to overcoming those problems. The statement described the situation as follows:

> Under these conditions [i.e., military rule, which represented only the interests of a small number of monopolistic capitalists and foreign powers], our women workers earn less than half what men workers earn and are forced to work the longest hours in the world. Hence women workers' livelihood and maternity are endangered. In addition, they bear the double burden of housework and suffer from beating, sexual violence and harassment, and even sexual torture. Continuous ideological manipulation aimed at taming them into obedience finally leads to the destruction of their *subjectivity*. . . . Our workers are growing as a leading political force in carrying out the historical mission to build a society where all oppressed people [*minjung*] are to be liberated. . . . Observing many of our coworkers who left the labor struggle front after marriage and childbirth to stay within their families,

we realized that women workers cannot become the *subject* of the labor movement without eliminating the exploitation and discrimination they experience as women. (Quoted in Sin Illyŏng 1988, 326; translation and italics mine)

It is noteworthy that this founding statement identifies the problem that women workers face not so much in terms of labor exploitation as in terms of the destruction of women's subjectivity in the workplace, and identifies marriage, childbirth, and the confinement to domestic life as a hindrance to the establishment of women as the subject of the labor movement. Labor exploitation, combined with the additional burden of housework, endangers women's very basic survival and their distinct capacity to give birth. Physical, sexual, and ideological assaults further undermine their entire being, including agency. Participation in the labor movement is a way to recover their subjectivity.

The SWWA advocated the women workers' struggle to eliminate discriminatory wages. It organized educational classes and cultural events to raise consciousness among women and men unionists. It also disseminated "guidelines for the wage increase struggle to resolve discriminatory wages between women and men" and "women workers and wages." A successful example of such a struggle can be seen in the case of Taehan Optics, located in the Kuro Industrial Complex in Seoul. Actively engaged in the women's school and the speech contest developed by the SWWA, the Taehan Optics labor union conducted a survey to identify the state of wage discrimination against women and was able to construct a logic for equal wages between women and men. Arguing that women also provided for their families and that women's lower wages also damaged male workers, in 1989 the union obtained differential wage increases for women and men in order to reduce the gender-based earnings gap. The Samsung Pharmaceutical labor union also obtained gender differential wage increase rates in 1989 (because a uniform fixed wage increase rate was disadvantageous for women) and, in 1990, a uniform wage and promotion system for women and men in the categories of family wages and children's educational expenses. Even when collective struggle for equal wages did not succeed, women workers' active involvement in such struggles altered their consciousness (KWWAC 1997, 75–76).

The massive layoffs of women workers, undermining the base of union organizing, became, ironically, an important cause of the revitalization of the women's labor movement in the late 1980s and early 1990s. In 1991 alone, some 6,100 small- and medium-sized companies went bankrupt; during the first three months of 1992, 1,794 companies went bankrupt. As a result, numerous women workers in the Seoul-Inch'ŏn region and the Masan-Ch'angwŏn region were laid off. The drastic change aggravated women's economic marginalization, increasing the number of women working part-time and on a temporary basis. The number of temporary women workers grew to 370,000 in 1993, from 106,000 in 1980, and the ratio of these temporary women workers to the total number of women wageworkers grew to 8.4 percent in 1993, from 5.2 percent in 1980. Women represented 64.7 percent of the total body of temporary workers in 1993, compared with 45.9 percent in 1980 (KWWAC 1997, 60–61). From 1989 until the mid-1990s, the local Women Workers' Associations, which were precursors of the KWWAC, and the KWAU actively supported women workers' struggle to protect their work within and outside the unions (61–64).

In the absence of training programs and educational centers for union leaders, the SWWA provided a crucial source of education not only for women but also for men. Emerging labor unions in 1987 asked the SWWA to provide their members with educational programs to raise their consciousness, which it did, offering leadership training, including instruction in, and group discussion of, labor unions' routine activities, how to strengthen labor unions and cope with their repression, union leaders' attitudes, the Labor Standard Law, and case studies of small-group activities in labor unions.[2]

To increase women's participation in emerging labor unions nationwide, in the late 1980s and early 1990s, the women workers' associations and the KWAU labor council collaborated to create women's divisions in new labor unions and to energize those that already existed (which were often nominal), identifying women workers' issues such as maternity, child care, sexual harassment, and employment discrimination, and supporting women workers in dealing with these and other issues (Kang In-sun 2001, 475). (In the last section of this chapter, I return to a detailed discussion of the significance of these issues in redrawing the boundaries of citizenship.) The SWWA invited union leaders to meetings to educate them on women's issues and published guidelines for labor union women's divisions (KWWAC 1997, 55). In collaboration with the KWAU and the National Council of Labor Movement Organizations, SWWA members launched a movement to eliminate the violence perpetrated by the save-our-company corps (46). The SWWA played a crucial role in creating the women's division of the National Concil of Labor Unions (Chŏnnohyŏp), the first national body of "democratic" labor unions (Kang In-sun 2001, 477). In the process of creating space for women within labor unions, women workers began to see themselves as rights-bearing subjects. A unionist at Insŏng Corporation, a medium-size business manufacturing consumer electronics and toys in Inch'ŏn, expressed such a view of workers in commenting on protest visits organized by the union, newly formed in response to the company's sudden closing after bankruptcy in 1991:

> The first time we visited the ministry of labor to protest, we had no idea about what it did and how it could empower us. But as we carried out our protest visits and encountered the labor supervision officer, who was disconcerted by our collective action and began shouting at us, we began to wonder whether "the labor ministry is for workers." . . . For whom does the labor ministry exist? How can the officer threaten us with imprisonment for exercising collective action this way, calling us "the reds, impure force, regime-overthrowing force," etc.? . . . We got into a physical fight with him, as he cursed us and said, "I'll kill you, xxx," and in the process two of our coworkers got arrested for the obstruction of duty. We just want to find workers' rights, and the labor ministry and the police locked us up. (Quoted in Kang In-sun 2001, 399; translation mine)

However, even labor unions, including the "democratic" ones formed by workers themselves, were patriarchal in many ways. Many individual male unionists strongly believed that men as family providers deserved higher wages than women. This perception was still so pervasive in the late 1980s that the women's associations organized a "family struggle" involving male workers' wives and established a "family struggle committee" to broaden the base of the women's labor movement. While the family struggle contributed to softening the militant image of the labor movement and gaining more sympathy for the workers' struggle from the conservative public, the workers' wives did not remain in the labor movement after the family struggle ended (KWWAC 1997, 53–54). Male unionists were often reluctant to accept women as coworkers. A woman unionist commented on her male colleagues:

> Male union members often say, "What's the matter with this union office, without a flower, where a woman is a division chief? Why did we make her the chief? The office atmosphere is very bleak because women put on pants when we're not on strike. Miss Lee, why don't you wear a skirt and put on some makeup to look pretty?" These comments made me think that there is no difference between unionists and other men when it comes to women. (Quoted in O-jang 2003, 128; translation mine)

In the absence of the awareness of sexism and in the face of violent repression by the state and management aimed at destroying autonomous unions, union leadership tended to perceive women workers' issues as secondary or distracting, paralleling the patriarchal orientations of many other leftist organizations fighting for workers' liberation elsewhere. Men's dominance in labor unions was particularly evident in their leadership structures. In 1992, although women represented 64.4 percent of the membership in textile workers' unions, they represented only 12.2 percent of union leaders. Similarly, women represented 36.5 percent of the membership of the banking, financial, and clerical workers' unions, but only 8.3 percent of its leadership. The worst example was the rubber workers' unions, in which women represented 56.5 percent of the membership, but only 4.8 percent of leadership (KWDI 1995, 222).

Initiating and carrying out activities to deal with issues such as maternity, child care, sexual violence and harassment, and discriminatory employment practices, the women workers' associations and the KWAU modified their initial emphasis on working within labor unions. While still continuing their collaboration with labor unions, they began to concentrate on building their own organizational base outside labor unions (KWWAC 2003a, 29; Kang In-sun 2001, 322). This change is directly related to the development of the interclass women's movement to obtain equal employment for women, discussed in the next section. While the collaboration between women's associations (the KWWAC and the KWAU) and labor unions (the KCTU and the FKTU) was positive, it did not make women's issues an integral part of union activities. Rather, women's issues remained something for women's associations to specialize in, while labor unions, at best, showed their support for them (Kang In-sun 2001, 478). Therefore the active support from the autonomous women's associations for the revitalization of women's participation in democratic labor unions was crucial to women workers' emergence as citizens.[3]

Despite its significance to the trajectory of women's citizenship, the women factory workers' movement weakened in the process of the economic restructuring linked to globalization, characterized by increasing employment insecurity among women workers and the growth of new service sectors. Peaking at 12 percent in 1990,[4] the unionization rate among women workers dropped to 5.4 percent in 1998, which was sharper than that of male workers, which dropped from 20.5 percent to 15.3 percent (KWDI 1999, 260). Rebounding to 7.5 percent in 2000, women workers' unionization rate still remained very low (KWDI 2001, 260). A close reading of the decline of women workers' unionization reveals a shift in its main composition from manufacturing workers in labor-intensive industries to white-collar workers in education, health care, banking, financial, and clerical sectors. Women's union membership in 1992

Table 7. Women Workers in Labor Unions in Manufacturing Industries in the 1990s

Type of Union	1992	1998*	2000*
Metal workers	77,653 (19.4)	39,064 (13.4)	42,394 (14.4)
Textile workers	67,618 (64.4)	22,302 (49.8)	** (NA)
Chemical workers	44,291 (24.8)	26,048 (21.3)	** (NA)
Rubber workers	23,951 (56.5)	1,628 (16.7)	1,812 (19.7)
Total***	411,077 (23.4)	346,682 (18.1)	305,878 (20.0)

Sources: Korean Women's Development Institute (KWDI), *Statistical Yearbook on Women* (1995), 222; KWDI, *Statistical Yearbook on Women* (1999), 261, 262; KWDI, *Statistical Yearbook on Women* (2001), 267, 268.

Note: Unions are listed in which the percentage of women members is more than 30%, or women's membership is larger than 10,000; percentage of women members is indicated in parentheses.

*Numbers and percentages for 1998 and 2000 are based on the combined subtotals of union members of the FKTU and the KCTU.

**These numbers are not available because the categories of industry-based unions have changed over time. The FKTU created a category that combines textile workers and distribution workers, and the KCTU created a category that combines textile workers with chemical workers.

***Total women in all unions (including unions not listed here).

was sizable within the metal, textile, chemical, and rubber manufacturing industries (see table 7) and in the banking, financial, and clerical sectors of the service industry. By 1998, women union members in manufacturing industries had dropped drastically. Women union members in textiles dropped to a third of the 1992 number (from 67,618 to 22,302); those in metals and chemicals dropped by almost half; those in rubber dropped most dramatically of all, from 23,951 to 1,628. Reflecting the recovery from the Asian economic crisis, women's membership in these manufacturing unions increased somewhat in 2000. Yet the overall shrinkage in women's union membership in the metal, textile, chemical, and rubber industries is unequivocal. While women union members in the banking, financial, and clerical sectors dropped from 67,448 in 1992 to 51,351 in 2000, these sectors had the largest number of women union members throughout the 1990s, except for those in the textile and metal industries in 1992 (see table 8). In 2000 there were sizable numbers of women in the newly established teachers' and public workers' unions. Women dominated teachers' unions in their absolute number (63,700) and relative size (60.1

Table 8. Women Workers in White-Collar Labor Unions in the 1990s

Type of Union	1992	1998	2000
Banking, financial, and clerical workers	67,448 (36.8)	53,768 (31.5)	51,351 (34.4)
Teachers	*	*	63,700 (60.1)
Public service workers	*	*	20,270 (17.9)
Health care workers	*	25,001 (62.4)	5,757 (12.7)
Tourism workers	11,362 (44.0)	6,825 (39.7)	7,136 (40.96)
Foreign organization employees	7,279 (25.8)	6,823 (33.0)	6,826 (31.6)
University and college workers	*	2,947 (26.1)	2,597 (34.2)

Sources: Korean Women's Development Institute (KWDI), *Statistical Yearbook on Women* (1995), 222; KWDI, *Statistical Yearbook on Women* (1999), 261, 262; KWDI, *Statistical Yearbook on Women* (2001), 267, 268.

Note: Unions are listed in which the percentage of women members is more than 30%, or women's membership is larger than 10,000; percentage of women members is indicated in parentheses.

*Unions in these categories were not formed yet.

percent). Among small labor unions (with a women's membership of less than 10,000), women represented a critical mass of 30 percent or more in tourism, foreign organizations, universities and colleges, and sales (KWDI 2001, 267, 268).

The women factory workers' labor struggle in the late 1980s and early 1990s, actively supported by the autonomous women's associations, provided a valuable model for the women workers' movement in the clerical and service sectors in the 1990s and beyond. This continuity is reflected in the content of *Samujikyŏsŏng* (Clerical Women), a quarterly magazine published between 1990 and 1995 by the People's Friends Society (Minuhoe). The quarterly has featured several established sections on the activities and struggle of local labor unions for women workers' empowerment, including the work of male chiefs of women's divisions, along with specific guidelines for collective bargaining to obtain women workers' rights.[5]

THE INTERCLASS WOMEN'S MOVEMENT FOR EQUAL EMPLOYMENT

The women's movement for equal employment with men sprang from the advocacy work of autonomous women's associations for individual women workers legally disputing discriminatory employment practices in the 1980s. The equal employment movement can be seen as being interclass in terms of the clients it served and the composition of the women's associations involved. In 1983, Kim Yŏng-hŭi, a telephone operator employed by the Korean Electricity and Communications Public Corporation, filed a civil lawsuit against the company's early retirement practice, according to which women workers were forced to retire at the age of forty-three.[6] In 1985, after a car accident, Yi Kyŏng-suk, a factory worker hired by Pangil Corporation, received a court ruling that ordered monetary compensation for her injury calculated under the assumption that unmarried factory workers like her would retire at the age of twenty-five. Appealing her case, in the following year she won a court ruling that the retirement age for unmarried women, like that for men, would be fifty-five. In 1987, Chu So-nyŏ, a clerical worker at a private bank, was forced to quit her work upon her marriage. In the same year, Kim Kŭn-hwa, a nurse employed by a private hospital, was forced to retire at the age of fifty-five although the retirement age for medical professionals was sixty-five (Sin Yŏng-suk 2000, 408; KWDI 1991, 481–85). It is notable that these collective struggles against employment discrimination took place in female-dominated occupational sectors such as banking, communications, textile manufacturing, and health care. The individual workers, supported by the autonomous women's associations, challenged the conventional view that women's paid employment would end with marriage or pregnancy, or if it did not, that it would at any rate not last throughout their adult life. An underlying assumption of that view was that women's employment would be at best supplementary to men's. Using the legal means available and organized support from women's associations, these individual women affirmed their political subjectivity as citizens entitled to equal rights in employment.

The interclass women's movement to promote equal employment was galvanized by the passage of the Equal Employment Law (EEL) in the late 1980s.[7] Because the EEL was inadequate,[8] its reform became a focal point that brought various women's associations together in 1989, resulting in the institution of equal pay for equal work, equal treatment in recruitment, hiring, training, and promotion, and the recognition of (unpaid) child-care leave of up to one year as an employment period to be considered in the calculation of employment benefits. Throughout the 1990s, the coalition of women's associations achieved incremental reform of the EEL, including the regulation of indirect forms of sex discrimination and sexual harassment in the workplace (Sin Yŏng-suk 2000, 407; Minuhoe 1997, 31).

In particular, the Korean Women's Associations United played a central role in initiating and directing various projects to achieve women's "right to equal labor for lifetime" (p'yŏngsaeng p'yŏngdŭng nodongkwŏn). In the early 1990s, making this issue its central project, the KWAU focused on legal reform and public relations, ranging from organizing a discussion meeting to contacting the mass media. Throughout the 1990s, organizing public hearings, campaigns, and discussion meetings and using the mass media, the KWAU focused on the passage of laws promoting equal lifetime employment for women, including a child-care law and a sexual harassment law (Yi Mi-kyŏng 1998, 30, 31). Meanwhile, local branches of the KWAU member organizations provided counseling services for working women affected by employment discrimination (Chŏng Kang-ja 1998, 52, 54). In 1995, in response to pervasive discriminatory employment practices continuing even after the 1989 EEL reform,[9] and to the government's announcement of the "Year of Equal Employment," this counseling activity developed into the establishment of two mechanisms by KWAU member organizations: the equal employment promotion headquarters (koyongp'yŏngdŭng ch'ujinbonbu) of the Korean Women People's Friends Society (PFS),[10] and the equality hotline (p'yŏngdŭngŭi chŏnhwa) of the Korean Women Workers' Associations Council (KWWAC).

The equal employment promotion headquarters started a grassroots movement to achieve equal employment between women and men (Minuhoe 1996, 14). To build and maintain this movement, it relied on its members as volunteer "equal employment watchpersons," who monitored compliance with the EEL by corporations, labor unions, the government, political parties, and the mass media in terms of their representation of women and men. In 1996, women and men workers, prospective employees, students, and other activists monitored the employment practices of the national government and the thirty largest economic conglomerates (4, 5). In the same year, the headquarters published a report based on a study of 168 companies in the public employment sector and in banking industries. In 1997, local members again monitored women's employment conditions at the five largest economic conglomerates (Minuhoe 1997, 24, 26). Although the headquarters ceased functioning, the monitoring activities have been carried out by the Minuhoe members to promote equal employment.[11] This continuity suggests a positive model for the transformation of women (and men) into citizens, participating in civil society to obtain rights.

In its organizational guidelines, the PFS lists the major components of a humane society as the protection of basic standards of living based on a self-reliant national economy, genuine equality between women and men, women's right to equal labor, maternity protection and child-care provisions to guarantee women's participation in society, and the elimination of sexual violence and sexist culture. Diverse groups of women are part of the "people" (minjung) who are oppressed by unjust social structures (see chapter 4). Women who struggle for their own empowerment and liberation become willful agents and acquire the political subjectivity of citizens. While the PFS does not explicitly use the seemingly gender-neutral term "citizen" to refer to women as active agents, its emphatic reference to democratic society as a vision of the good society for which women must fight implies the emergence of women's political subjectivity as citizens.

Unlike the equal employment promotion headquarters located in Seoul but monitoring employers nationally, the equality hotline had local branches run by local women workers' associations to serve employed women from the beginning. In 2003 there were eight branches nationwide, serving diverse groups of women workers. Avoiding one-shot counseling in favor of sustained support, the local hotlines worked closely with individual women who contacted them by telephone, e-mail, and at times personal visits. The KWWAC provided training for counselors twice a year and published an annual collection of counseling cases. It also consulted with other organizations interested in instituting an equality hotline to expand the locally based movement to achieve equal employment. The local branches divided women's employment problems into categories of employment conditions, sex discrimination, maternity protection, sexual harassment and violent behavior in the workplace, occupational illness, and other unjust labor practices (KWWAC 2003b). The survey of the annual collections of counseling cases suggests that women workers have become more conscious of their rights and seek to protect them. The total number of counseling cases doubled from 1,273 in 1999 to 2,494 in 2002. The nature of the employment problems that women face changed; for instance, the counseling cases involving maternity protection tended to be a question of the protection itself (i.e., granting maternity leave) in the beginning, but later such cases gradually came to focus on specific problems of return to work and pressure to quit after using maternity leave (see figure 13).

Serving women of various classes in local communities, these institutional-

13. Pregnant women workers' rally to support the establishment of maternity leave, 2001. Photograph by Segye Daily Co.

ized mechanisms for obtaining women's right to equal employment raised consciousness among women (and men) and thereby facilitated women's emergence as citizens. In the following section, I discuss the women's movement to eliminate the military service extra-points system, which directly challenged women's marginalization in the militarized economy and at the same time revealed the contradiction between equal citizenship and the construction of men as dutiful nationals in mandatory military service.

CHALLENGING THE MILITARIZED ECONOMY: THE MIDDLE-CLASS WOMEN'S MOVEMENT TO ELIMINATE THE MILITARY SERVICE EXTRA-POINTS SYSTEM

Instituted in 1961, the military service extra-points system had existed without drawing public scrutiny for over three decades (see chapter 1). The women's movement, in addressing the extra-points system in the 1990s, viewed it as an old practice, from the period of military rule, that discriminated against women in the labor market. Women's organizations began attempting to abolish the extra-points system starting with the inauguration of the first civilian government in 1993,[12] but it was not until 1998 that economic and political conditions shifted in their favor. The process of globalization, particularly after the 1997 economic crisis, accelerated economic liberalization, leading to the reduction of the influence of extraeconomic factors such as military service in the labor market. In the name of increasing the "flexibility of the labor market," a large number of businesses in South Korea have replaced the established system of stable employment based on seniority of employees with a "merit-based system" or "contract system." Although these carefully worded phrases may conjure up the image of a rational and fair system of employment, these systems are in fact designed to enable employers to increase labor intensity and hire temporary workers (Yong Cheol Kim and Moon 2000, 57; Kim T'ae-hong 1998, 19–20). The legally based practice of honoring military service in employment had come to be unmistakably at odds with rational economic calculation and the management of workers to increase flexibility in the labor market. According to a 1994 study of eighty-one private and public corporations of large size (300 employees or more) and of medium and small size (fewer than 300 employees), 100 percent of eleven banking firms and 80 percent of thirty-one public corporations complied with the extra-points system. In contrast, only 9 percent of eleven large private firms and 0 percent of twenty-three medium and small private firms did (KIDA 1995a, 36). Similarly, a 1998 study of companies of five major economic conglomerates showed that these private firms did not observe the extra-points system (Kim T'ae-hong 1998, 17, 18).[13] Compared with the 1980s (see chapter 1), these studies suggest the decline of the extra-points system in private employment in the 1990s.[14]

Politically, Kim Dae Jung's government was relatively accommodating to demands from women's organizations to remake its image as a "people's government."[15] Immediately after the outbreak of the 1997 economic crisis and in the face of growing popular discontent with the fairness of conscription (see chapter 5), the Office of Military Manpower (OMM) attempted to reinforce the extra-points system through the Military Service Law reform, the Veterans Assistance Act, and its Enforcement Ordinance. On October 19, 1998, however, the Regulation Reform Committee (Kyujegaehyŏk'wiwŏnhoe), formed by Kim Dae Jung's government to democratize domestic politics, declared the draft of the Military Service Act revision to be a "countertrend to economic liberalization" and a "violation of equal employment between women and men" (*Seoul Newspaper*, October 20, 1998). Interpreting this decision as a positive signal, on October 19, 1998, the Korean Women's Associations Council, in coalition with the Center for Rights of Friends with Disability (Chang'aeukwŏnikmunjeyŏn'guso), sponsored five women and one disabled man, who were all preparing for civil service examinations, in filing a constitutional lawsuit (*Nyuspipŭl*, October 23, 1998).[16] In late December 1999, to many people's surprise, the Constitutional Court ruled that the extra-points system described in the Veterans Assistance Act (Clause 1 of Article 8) and its Enforcement Ordinance (Article 9) were unconstitutional. Despite visceral criticism from the conservative public, generating a heated national controversy that lasted for several months (S. Moon 2002a), the extra-points system was finally abolished.

The legal battle added to the success of the women's movement, largely led by educated middle-class women using institutional avenues to achieve equal employment for women. Major events that generated momentum and sustained it throughout the movement were initiated and carried out by middle-class women. The collective petition against the extra-points system was delivered by a large group of college students and professors from Ewha, the elite women's university in South Korea (KIDA 1995a, 39). Representatives of the two major umbrella women's organizations involved in the movement were generally educated middle-class women. In particular, the KWAC, which sponsored the constitutional lawsuit, is an umbrella body of mostly middle-class women's associations, focusing on consumer protection, charity work, education of housewives and brides-to-be, and job training in feminized occupations. The six individuals who filed the lawsuit were college-educated women, with the exception of the man with a disability, who was also a college student at the time.[17]

The largely middle-class makeup of the movement appears to reflect the extra-points system's uneven burden on middle-class women as the employed in the aftermath of the 1997 economic crisis.[18] The number of women in the "economically inactive population" grew by roughly one million, from 9,023,000 in 1997 to 10,029,000 in 1999. Between June 1997 (before the Asian economic crisis) and March 1999 (after the crisis), the ratio of women employed in full-time, regular positions, as opposed to part-time or temporary positions, shrank from 38.1 percent to 30.8 percent of the total number of women gainfully employed (Ŏm 1999, 37, 38). Confronting highly circumscribed opportunities in the gender-segregated labor market and growing employment insecurity, women considered public employment as a secure source of income, relatively free of discrimination against women and sudden layoffs. Hence women with high school or even college degrees (in the absence of better options) tended to consider lower-level government positions (to which the extra-points system was applied) as a secure employment option.

Even before the economic crisis, the extra-points system was a serious obstacle to the public employment of women. In 1993, women represented 62 percent of successful applicants nationwide for the ninth-grade civil service examination. Were it not for the extra-points system, they would have represented 76 percent of the successful applicants (KIDA 1995a, 40). (In one local example, the proportion of women among successful applicants at the same level of civil service examination in South Kyŏngsang Province would have increased from 44 to 55 percent without the application of the extra-points system.) A similar trend was also observed in the case of the 1993 seventh-grade public service examinations. Without the extra-points system, women would have accounted for 9 percent of successful examinees, but the actual percentage was 4 percent (40). The minimum score required to pass the 1993 seventh-grade civil service examination in the Seoul area was an average of 85 points. Since men are usually eligible to add 5 percent of the full score to their scores, they could pass the exam with an average of 80 points. While only 42 applicants scored 85 points or above, 431 applicants scored between 80 and 84 points (Yŏsŏng 1994, 17). Another telling example after the economic crisis is the 1998 ninth-grade chemical engineering test, for which the required minimum passing score was 95.6 points. One thousand sixty applicants had scores between 95 and 90 points, which means that the women among them could not pass, while their male counterparts, with the help of their extra points, could (Nuspipŭl, October 23, 1998).

The problem that the extra-points system posed to women's public employment was as much a matter of principle as it was a matter of practical consequence. The women's movement to eliminate the extra-points system was a contest over the principle of equal citizenship. The class action suit (filed by five women and one man) claimed that the extra-points system violated the plaintiffs' constitutional right to equality, to be elected or appointed to public office, and to choose their occupation. It recognized the legitimacy of compensation for former conscripts but questioned the appropriateness of the extra-points system as such a method. Responding to a pervasive conservative argument that the extra-points system was intended to punish conscription evaders, the class action petition pointed out that women and disabled men, who were not involved in evading conscription, were unduly penalized by it.[19] In other words, their petition demanded the equal right to employment regardless of military service; it argued implicitly that military service should not be a basis for economic benefits to the point of violating the fundamental right to equal employment. The class action suit also implicitly questioned the hierarchy of membership in the nation justified by the exigency of military service and national defense. As the presence of a disabled man among the plaintiffs suggests, the hierarchy of membership in the nation cannot be reduced to the dichotomous gender line. Nevertheless, gender was the major factor in drawing the hierarchy, in that almost 90 percent of Korean men perform mandatory military service, including regular services and other supplementary and special services, whereas there are only around 2,700 women soldiers, who all serve as professional officers (Chŏng-Pak 2003, 95).

If one focuses on the number of women directly affected by the extra-points system, the problem it posed for women's employment was not the most serious one. The total numbers of state employees in the seventh- and ninth-grade positions, to which the extra-points system was applied, were 84,243 and 33,513, respectively, in 1998. Women represented 18.9 percent (15,936) of the seventh-grade public employees and 39.8 percent (13,345) of the ninth-grade public employees (Presidential Commission on Women's Affairs 1999, 318). Although hiring practices for these positions affected employment opportunities for thousands of (middle-class) women annually, the total threat to women's employment posed by the extra-points system, operating within this subsection of public employment, was in no way as grave as the massive shrinkage of positions for women in manufacturing industries throughout the 1990s, involving tens of thousands of (working-class) women. The total number of women in manufacturing industries decreased from 2,050,000 (41.7 percent of the total workforce in manufacturing) in 1990 to 1,526,000 (35.9 percent of the total workforce) in 2000 (KWDI 2001 176, 177).

The problem of public employment discrimination against women caused by the extra-points system is also not as large as the problem of the persistent marginalization of women in public vocational training programs. As table 9 shows, in 1998 women made up 17.2 percent of the total number of trainees. In comparison with the percentage of women trainees in public programs during the 1980s (less than 5 percent; see table 2) this figure appears to indicate a significant increase. Yet a close examination of the content of vocational training programs reveals a less rosy picture of this apparent improvement. According to table 10, the largest vocational training field in 1998 was "miscellaneous office skills" that were heavily feminized. Although table 10 does not provide a breakdown of public, private, and state-sponsored programs, it suggests that the increase in the percentage of women trainees is likely to come from women's massive influx into clerical skills training programs.

In light of these larger problems of women's employment, the significance

Table 9. Vocational Training by Agent in 1998

Agent	Women	Men
Public	31,409 (17.2)	151,444 (82.8)
Private	29,955 (11.6)	228,082 (88.4)
State-approved	2,713 (6.7)	37,992 (93.3)

Source: Presidential Commission on Women's Affairs, *Yŏsŏngpaeksŏ* [White Paper on Women] (Seoul, 1999), 305.
Note: Percentage of total is indicated in parentheses.

of the military service extra-points system is as symbolic as it is practical. The militarized economy that boosted male veterans' employment functioned smoothly as long as women accepted their position as the secondary labor force in the economy and the man's position as family provider (modern patriarch) was sustained by economic security. Yet local and global factors worked against maintaining these two conditions. On the one hand, rising standards of living in the midst of industrialization and urbanization resulted in growing numbers of young educated women who were willing to pursue long-term employment but faced discrimination in the job market, starting with recruitment and hiring. On the other hand, the restructuring of the global economy in the early and mid-1990s took a heavy toll, particularly on middle-class men, many of whom were laid off even before the 1997 economic crisis. One of the most urgent social issues in South Korea in the mid-1990s was the problem of the "laid-off family head" (*siljikdoen kajang*) (J. Lee 2001). Although it may appear gender neutral, the term for family head in the Korean context usually means the husband and father. While this was not an accurate portrayal of the reality of laid-off workers, since women workers were more vulnerable to layoffs (precisely because of a pervasive assumption that women were supported by their husbands or other male family providers), this type of mass-media representation of the problem did reflect the underlying assumption that only men as family providers were entitled to secure employment. The 1997 economic crisis triggered a sense of urgency among conservative forces in the state and society to protect men's employment prospects and thereby to secure their subjectivity as dutiful nationals willing to perform military service. This attempt to reinforce the martial duty of male nationals in conjunction with men's patriarchal prerogative to be first-class workers clashed with the emerging view of women and other nonmartial members of the nation as citizens. The women's

Table 10. Five Major Fields of Vocational Training

1987		1998	
Field	Number of Trainees	Field	Number of Trainees
Metal processing and manufacturing	14,679	Miscellaneous office skills	290,388
Machine manufacturing	6,366	Machine manufacturing	63,229
Wood processing and construction	5,611	Information processing	17,051
Electronics and communication	4,076	Electricity	16,592
Textiles	2,714	Construction	15,003
Total for these 5 fields	33,446	Total for these 5 fields	402,263
Total for all fields	46,059	Total for all fields	481,595

Sources: Ministry of Labor, *White Paper on Labor* (1989), 193; Ministry of Labor, *Yearbook of Labor Statistics* (1999), 421.

movement as an organized response shows that political transition in the context of sociopolitical democratization enables middle-class women to employ their civil and political citizenship to fight for the equal right to work.

REDEFINING THE SUBSTANCE OF CITIZENSHIP AND CHALLENGING GENDER HIERARCHY

Contesting women's economic marginalization through their active support for factory workers' labor struggles and their fight for equal employment for all women, the autonomous women's associations redefined what constitutes citizens. Essentially, moving beyond the liberal notion of the individualized boundary of the citizen and the Marxist notion of the uniformly collective boundary of the citizen, the interclass women's movements illuminated the intersubjectivity of citizens situated in the web of social relations and articulated new rights necessary to women's equal employment. The relational nature of a woman's self as a citizen was implicit in the founding statement of the PFS. Discussing the remedy for women's oppression, the 1987 statement read:

The root of women's suffering lies in the undemocratic and antipeople [*pan-minjung*] structures of this society, which also allow competition, materialism, and dehumanization to proliferate like poisonous mushrooms. In order for women to be liberated, this society, including the family, must be transformed into a genuinely democratic society where human dignity is actualized. . . . Our movement needs the participation of urban and rural working women, housewives, young women, and all other suffering women. Although women's suffering differs from one social stratum to another, problems that all these women face can be solved only through building a truly democratic society. (Minuhoe 1997, 6, 7; translation mine)

In linking women's liberation to the genuine democratization of society, the PFS envisioned liberated women as members of a democratic society. In line with my definition of citizenship as membership in the democratic body politic, women as such would be citizens. To democratize the family, considered a precondition for women to become citizens, major activities carried out in the family such as reproduction and the nurturing of children need to be democratized. According to the interclass women's movements discussed earlier, this means that pregnancy, childbirth, and child care need to be understood as public concerns rather than as individual women's private burden, because they are necessary phases of human life crucial to the reproduction of the body politic. Therefore the state and business need to share responsibilities for the sustenance of the body politic.

Within this framework, the interclass women's movements insisted on women's rights to maternity protection and child-care facilities outside the family. Viewing these rights as integral to women's equal employment, the women's associations began with the passage and revision of laws concerning these issues, including protests against inadequate bills and the proactive submission of alternative bills and policy proposals. On this basis, advocating for the women factory workers' labor struggle, the women's associations pushed for the adoption of the two issues (maternity protection and child care) by labor unions and raised women workers' awareness of them over time through training programs and small-group activities. In their national and local activities to promote women's lifetime equal employment, while the equality hotlines counseled women workers on the violation of maternity protection, the equal employment promotion headquarters monitored employers' compliance with legal regulations on maternity protection and child-care facilities.

Yet the collective battle to redefine women's right to equal employment is only a decade old. Conservative resistance to women's demands to incorporate maternity protection and public child-care facilities into a set of rights to equal employment has been quite persistent. According to a 1994 survey of women workers' attitudes published by the National Council of Labor Unions, an absolute majority of its forty-six member labor unions were unable to obtain any maternity protection clauses beyond a "menstruation leave" (one day per month) and a maternity leave in their collective agreement. In practice, the respondents took an average of 5.4 days of menstruation leave per year; only 12.3 percent of married women workers surveyed used their maternity leaves. A 1995 analysis, prepared by the KCTU, of the collective agreement bills of 213 labor unions indicated that only twenty-five unions had secured maternity leave of sixty days, and only eleven unions had secured paid paternity leave for a husband (KWWAC 1998, 87). A 2002 review of equality hotline counseling cases revealed that women workers' use of maternity leave in the sales and service sectors (in which women were heavily concentrated) was very low, and that maternity leave was even more difficult to obtain in small businesses (employing ten or fewer workers) than in businesses employing one hundred or more (KWWAC 2003b, 7, 8).

The movement to institute public child-care facilities had mixed results. The coalition movement of the women's associations and labor unions to obtain child-care facilities in the workplace began after the passage of the Infant and Child Care Law and its Enforcement Ordinance in 1990 and 1991, respectively. The encouraging cases that resulted were like an oasis in the middle of the desert;[20] overall, the coalition movement met with a cold to lukewarm reception, at best. At the same time, for-profit and public child-care facilities with varying degrees of adequacy multiplied throughout the 1990s. In this milieu, responding to working women's urgent need for child-care facilities, the women's associations maintained their activities to establish and manage community-based child-care facilities in low-income neighborhoods.[21]

In 1999, after the third revision of the EEL (for which the women's associations had persistently pressed throughout the 1990s), sexual harassment was legally recognized as an obstacle to women's equal employment. The revised EEL requires businesses to provide employees with education to prevent sexual harassment and with mechanisms to prevent it and to deal with it when it is perpetrated. The legal change generated fierce criticism from the conservative public, especially employers. Reflecting the common male perception that touching or groping a woman's body, ogling it, and commenting on it are just a "little lubricant" that makes the competitive and rationalized world of paid work bearable, the sexual harassment of women in the workplace has been pervasive ever since women entered it. According to a 1998 survey of 1,314 women and men conducted by the PFS, 84 percent of 673 women replied that they had experienced sexual harassment in the workplace, and 85 percent of 613 men replied that they had done what is defined as sexual harassment in the workplace (Minuhoe 2000, 14). Suggesting a growing awareness among women, the reporting of sexual harassment to the equality hotlines had rapidly escalated. The number of sexual harassment cases among those who used the hotline counseling service (not counting repeated counseling for the same individual) multiplied from 28 in 1998 to 237 in 2002 (KWWAC 2003b, 6; KWWAC 1999, 6).

The formal recognition of sexual harassment as an obstacle to women's equal employment radically redefines the boundary between private and public and the meaning of sexuality for women and men. It affirms that women are entitled to their bodily integrity in the workplace and separates them from their sexuality. It also illuminates the apparently intimate interaction between men and women in the workplace as a matter of power difference. The strong criticism of this legal recognition reveals underlying assumptions that women belong to the family as the realm of sexual intimacy and that men's sexual desire is uncontrollably strong. Within this framework, women who step outside the family unattended by men are supposed to be available for sexual advances.

The ramifications of redrawing the boundary between private and public for the substance of citizenship are twofold. First, the recognition of maternity protection and child-care facilities as matters of equal employment reveals that the reproduction of the body politic depends on privatized pregnancy, childbirth, and caring work asymmetrically performed by women. The recognition of this fact allows us to reconceptualize a citizen as an interdependent being who needs to take care of others and be taken care of, rather than as an atomized individual. Second, equality among citizens does not mean sameness among members of the body politic, which often translates into identical treatment of members who are in fact located in different social and economic positions. Such an application of equality tends to disregard actual power differences among citizens. Rather, equal citizenship would mean democratic membership that guarantees the right to eliminate obstacles to self-determination. Hence the practice of equal employment between women and men needs to include mechanisms to eliminate or mitigate obstacles to women's equal employment beyond identical treatment between women and men. Within this framework, the recognition of sexual harassment as an obstacle to equal employment becomes compelling.

Finally, the interclass and middle-class women's movements to contest women's economic marginalization have undermined the gender hierarchy that hinges on the division of labor between man the provider and woman the dependent housewife that was instituted in the process of the mass mobilization of women and men as dutiful nationals. Replacing women's economic marginalization with women's equal employment, these movements opened a path that remakes gender relations.

CONCLUSION

Women in South Korea emerged as citizens in the process of contesting the economic marginalization stemming from their mass mobilization during the period of militarized modernity. In comparison with the trajectory of men's citizenship, which showed the division between the working-class labor movement and the middle-class citizens' movement, the trajectory of women's citizenship demonstrated the centrality of autonomous women's associations and the relatively interclass orientation in struggling for labor unions and equal employment for all women. The interclass women's movements reflect the ambiguous class positions of women in Korean society. Marginalized in the industrializing economy as the secondary labor force, a majority of women have structurally occupied less definite class positions than men. Social scientists tend to subsume a woman's class position under that of the husband or male household head. Women's emergence as citizens, however, is a process in the making and by no means indicates a fixed path. In the book's conclusion, I will reflect on this gender difference to elaborate on the trajectory of gendered citizenship.

CONCLUSION

Modernity, Gender, and Citizenship

THE CULTURAL POLITICS OF MODERNITY AND THE
DECOLONIZATION OF THE PRODUCTION OF KNOWLEDGE

In this book I have examined the making and remaking of political subjectivities of grassroots women and men against the backdrop of the rise and decline of militarized modernity in South Korea. I have approached the notion of modernity not so much as a fixed set of normative values and social conditions as a keyword that has produced competing claims, commitments, and knowledge about what a desirable (or undesirable) society looks like and how to build it (or avoid it). The pursuit of modernity (or outright rejection of it) depends on specific local interpretations of modernity shaped by unequal national and transnational encounters among social groups in the past and present. Such local interpretations are by no means isolated from the theoretical and empirical discourse of modernity in the West that has circulated globally since the period of colonialism. Rather, local leaders and grassroots women and men reinterpret and reinvent the discourse of modernity in their specific cultural and political context. In South Korea during the late nineteenth century and most of the twentieth, nationalist leaders imagined modernity primarily in terms of economic and political conditions, embodied in the nation that possessed an industrial economy and a strong military. The counterhegemonic discourse of democratization and grassroots social movements in contemporary Korea have challenged such a meaning of modernity with alternative views of the body politic and membership in it. While not all social groups contributing to the counterhegemonic discourse employed the notion of citizens explicitly, the recurring themes of people as "masters" and "subjects" and the centrality of rights to these new identities warrant the use of the active and participatory view of citizen to refer to them. Highlighting the politics of meanings, I hope to contribute to the decolonization of the production of knowledge about social change in the non-Western world.

THE DIALECTIC OF MASS MOBILIZATION AND
THE EMERGENCE OF CITIZENSHIP

As much as militarized modernity was a product of a peculiar historical and social context in South Korea, the mass mobilization of women and men by the state in the process of nation building has historical and contemporary parallels in East Asia and elsewhere. The significance of mass mobilization to the formation of political subjectivity lies in the possibility that it opens up for remaking the membership in the nation (or beyond it). While such a mobilization is intended to use the grassroots population as an instrument of the state in carrying out its project, the powerful imaginary perception of a shared destiny between rulers and the ruled, a hallmark of a nation distinguishing itself from earlier forms of the state, can turn the top-down mobilization, to varying degrees, into grassroots participation in pursuing a nationalist project. Despite the repressive rule by military regimes, which did incite dissident protests and movements, the project of "national modernization" in South Korea gained acceptance and acquiescence from a majority of those who were objects of mobilization. For example, as chapters 2 and 3 demonstrated, the disciplinary power of the modernizing state meticulously regulated the populace to alter their perceptions of military service and contraception. Under the nationalist spell, mass mobilization for industrialization and military security can turn into the willing participation of the mobilized, rather than being merely coercion.

The peculiar combination of coercion and discipline in South Korea's militarized modernity provides us with some insights on Foucault's view of the (modern) subject as the product of disciplinary power. In South Korea, the disciplinary power of the modernizing state did not encourage individuals to see themselves as rights-bearing subjects. Yet the discipline to mold individuals into dutiful nationals cannot contain human beings merely as efficient instruments. The road is quite slippery between the dutiful national called to contribute to the project of nation building and the citizen who demands his or her rights. Nevertheless, Foucault's "useful and docile" subject is not merely a body to be disciplined but a human being with agency.

Another important insight from South Korea's militarized modernity is the coexistence of discipline and coercion in reality. As much as disciplinary power is efficient in minimizing the political and economic cost of exercising power over women and men, it cannot function without the ultimate backing of force, or at least the threat of using force in real political situations. The violent punishment of women and men who defied discipline was intended to deter others from doing so, but it inevitably generated resistance. In South Korea, the pervasiveness of violent punishment of those who did not conform to the norm of dutiful nationals, including factory workers and political activists, during the military rule ensured the vibrancy of the counterhegemonic discourse and grassroots social movements for democratization.

REFLECTIONS ON THE TRAJECTORY OF GENDERED CITIZENSHIP

The South Korean experience of militarized modernity and the emergence of gendered citizenship in the midst of its uneven decline provide some useful insights for understanding the tortuous trajectory of citizenship as a democratic form of membership in the body politic.

First, despite legal references to individual rights as trappings of modernity, the exigency of nation building in postcolonial Korea, as a latecomer to the pantheon of modern nations, constructed women and men as dutiful nationals expected to work and sacrifice for the nation. Hence, citizenship formally defined as the membership in the modern body politic has been an ideal to be strived for, not an actual status for a majority of people in the society. Reflecting the gender division of labor in the modern family, the making of dutiful nationals through mass mobilization was fundamentally gendered and entailed the asymmetrical incorporation of women and men into the nation. The South Korean case in this regard resembles the experience of militarized nation building in prewar Japan, except that there was no formal political exclusion against women in contemporary Korea. In her study of Japan's empire building in the 1930s, Louise Young (1998) documents the ways in which ordinary women and men were mobilized to support the invasion of Manchuria and the extent to which gender shaped their incorporation into the project of imperial nation building. Reflecting the Meiji leadership's view of women's place in modern Japan, wartime and interwar mobilization of women from the Sino-Japanese War (1895) through the Russo-Japanese War (1905) to the Manchurian incident (1931) was characterized by the expansion of their domestic role as reproducers and caretakers in public. The lack of the distinct boundary between public and private, which has been so central to the state-society relation in the West, resonated in the nationalist call for Korean women to practice the rational management of their households. Organized into numerous neighborhood residential associations, Japanese women of different social strata embraced their role as "military mothers" responsible for helping soldiers' families in their local villages, raising funds to purchase military supplies and weapons, and sending comfort items to soldiers on the battlefield (L. Young 1998, 171, 172). This gendered mobilization took place against the backdrop of the official exclusion of women from a range of political activities at the end of the nineteenth century.[1] In the absence of other opportunities for public participation, many women embraced militaristic mobilization, and some feminists attempted to use it as leverage to improve women's position in society (167, 168). While providing individual women with an elevated sense of belonging and purpose in their lives, such wartime mobilization and participation did not immediately yield any substantial alteration in women's marginalized membership in the nation.

Second, however, mass mobilization of women and men by a nation-state (or theoretically any other form of centralizing political authority) can lead to the transformation of dutiful nationals into rights-bearing citizens in the context of procedural democratization generated by a demand from grassroots social movements, top-down reform to contain popular discontent, or a combination of the two. While procedural democratization can facilitate the emergence of citizenship rights to varying degrees, socially structured inequalities such as gender and class continue to circumscribe individual access to, and practices of, citizenship.[2] In this sense, although citizenship refers to the democratic membership in the body politic, its trajectory is affected by differences in social power, which function as a powerful mechanism of "social closure" both within the boundaries of the nation and outside it as well (Brubaker 1992, 21). Hence different social groups acquire new political subjectivity as citizens through different paths. In the self-consciously named "citizens' movement" in South Korea after 1987, educated middle-class men have emerged as citizens through autonomous associations that aim to monitor powerful political and economic actors such as the state and business (see chapter 4). The upper segment of working-class men employed in the heavy and chemical industries have forged their new political subjectivity as citizens through the militant labor movement (see chapter 5). In contrast, middle-class and working-class women have obtained their new membership in the nation as citizens through relatively interclass women's movements to contest economic marginalization predicated on their essentialized role as reproducers (see chapter 6). It is ironic that the homogenization of women as such by the modernizing state and their secondary position as workers in almost all levels of employment generated the possibility for an interclass movement. Men were also homogenized by the state, but their position as the primary labor force in the industrializing economy seems to have made class difference more visible.

Third, apart from the unintended consequence of fostering women's inter-class movements, economic marginalization in capitalist society is an obstacle to the emergence of women as citizens. Historically, citizenship as a formal status in the West was conditioned by property ownership, and therefore the universal duty of a citizen was to pay taxes. With the expansion of citizenship to the propertyless classes, this duty has been conditioned by the amount of a person's earnings. Hence paid employment became the enabling condition that made one have to pay taxes. It is noteworthy that in the West, employment as an element of citizenship rights was introduced at a time when architects of the welfare state were constructing men as breadwinners and workers and women as dependent housewives (Yuval-Davis 1997, 90). As we have seen, mass mobilization of women and men in South Korea hinged on this model of the gender division of labor. In postwar Japan, women's integration into the project of national reconstruction continued to be conditioned by their role as reproducers. Similar to Korean women, Japanese women were marginalized in the androcentric employment system "which was *not* a natural outgrowth of either preindustrial or early industrial employment relations" but a product of deliberate design in the postwar decades (Brinton 1993, 115). The system of lifetime employment often praised as the hallmark of the prosperous Japanese economy (before the chronic recession that has lingered since the beginning of the 1990s) did not develop until the motor of industrialization shifted from the feminized textile industry to masculinized heavy industries. During the earlier stage of light industrialization, employers were reluctant to train workers, who were predominantly young, unmarried women, and secure them as skilled workers, even though this could increase productivity. In contrast, employers in heavy industries attempted to secure skilled workers by instituting incentives such as wage increases based on seniority, and family wages. By the 1920s, a few large companies started recruiting young male workers as lifetime employees, a practice that became widespread by the 1960s and 1970s. Emerging as a central actor in wartime industrialization during the 1930s, the Japanese state also played a crucial role in establishing the permanent employment system by regulating and promoting a reliable system of family wages for male workers (Brinton 1993).

In this gendered making of the industrial economy, women's access to paid employment, necessary for their citizenship in capitalist society, is truncated in two ways. Individually, the lack of full-time and stable employment as a source of economic independence erodes women's ability to pay taxes and thereby keeps women's membership in the body politic mediated by family and kinship. Women's subjectivity as reproducers immersed in family and kinship is not conducive to the political subjectivity of citizens entitled to rights and willing to fight to give substance to such rights. Collectively, the lack of full-time and stable employment deprives women of interaction with other workers in the workplace that can develop into collective struggle for obtaining rights and protecting them. As Robin Leblanc (1998) argues in her study of housewives' citizenship in urban Japan, women's economic marginalization and their continuing relegation to unpaid reproductive labor in the domestic sphere does not allow women to participate in running for public office. According to her study, although these urban housewives carve out their own public sphere through volunteer activities in their local communities, these activities tied to their role as caretakers lack continuity because they are secondary to the women's primary role as mothers and housewives. While I caution against equating citizenship with the narrow definition of political participation in running for public office, Leblanc's study illuminates the fundamental connection between the formation of citizenship and economic positions.

Fourth, the equal integration of women and men into the modernizing nation does not guarantee women's transformation into citizens as long as equality with men is conceived as conformity with what is normative for men. The experience of mass mobilization in the People's Republic of China can further illuminate the enduring effect of gender on the trajectory of citizenship, even in a revolutionary context in which the state consciously addressed problems concerning gender inequality. In contrast to South Korea and postwar Japan, mass mobilization of women and men in postrevolutionary China was accompanied by the state's professed interest in eliminating gender hierarchy. Viewing women's emancipation as a significant objective of the revolutionary transformation of China, the communist state granted equal rights to women and men in access to farmland through land reform, and in marriage and kinship through the Marriage Law (1950). During the Great Leap Forward, promoting women's participation in the productive workforce outside households, the party state experimented with the collectivization of housework and child care. During the later years of the Cultural Revolution, women increasingly entered the fields of work conventionally reserved for men. Yet this line of promoting equality between women and men resulted in the masculinization of women, forcing women to conform to masculinity as the underlying norm for workers and members of the nation.

Focusing on the problem of normalizing masculinity as seeming gender neutrality, Chizuko Ueno (2000) argues that women cannot obtain full membership in a modern nation that is deeply masculinist in its conception and practices of membership, regardless of whether they are constructed as dutiful nationals through gender-differentiated integration into the nation or as citizens through seemingly gender-neutral integration. In doing so, Ueno does not consider the differences in the specific nature of a nation-state. According to her, Japanese women were reduced to instruments of the state in and after their gender-specific integration into the project of imperial nation building in modern Japan, and contemporary American women remain second-class citizens even after their "gender-neutral integration" into the nation.

Recognizing a kernel of valid insight in Ueno's feminist criticism of the nation-state, I nevertheless find that her analysis falls into the trap of over-generalization. I would argue that the changing nature of a specific nation-state matters because it will affect the strategies formulated by women and men to forge citizenship in the aftermath of mass mobilization and in the context of political opening. While it is valid to imagine the ultimate transcendence of nation as the hegemonic political unit, such a transformation will not be possible without a specific struggle to renegotiate the nature of membership in the current form of political community. Beyond the too-rosy view of citizenship in liberalism and the dark view of it in Marxism and radical or cultural feminism,[3] it is important to analyze the specific ways in which the state and society interact.

Fifth, military service in the form of male-only conscription is incompatible with citizenship as the democratic form of membership in the body politic. Men's military service in South Korea continues to deny civil rights because men cannot opt for alternative national service to military service, and military service involves a period during which a wide range of citizenship rights are suspended. In exchange for men's military service, the state gave men the symbolic and material recognition to bolster their position as providers for their families in the militarized economy of the 1970s and 1980s. This (unequal) exchange between the state and martial members had uneven ramifications for women and men. As discussed in chapters 1 and 2, women were marginalized in the industrializing economy in part through conventional and legal practices that honored military service in recruitment and employment. The absence of military service further curtailed women's access to citizenship rights by reducing their possibilities of economic independence and reinforcing men's patriarchal prerogative to rule the family on the basis of their role as providers. While military service denied men fundamental civil rights at a more basic level, it contributed to the maintenance of their position as modern patriarchs.

The tension between military service and citizenship observed in South Korea goes against the civic republicanism in the West that defines military service as a (male) citizen's duty and constructs military service as a precondition for full citizenship. Some feminists in the United States have used the notion of military service as a citizenship rite in their support for gender equality in military service (Feinman 2000). Yet it is crucial to recognize that women's integration into the military in the West began after male conscription ended. As a result, the social meaning of military service shifted from "citizenship duty" to an occupational choice. In South Korea, where male conscription still exists, women soldiers have been integrated into the Korean army since 1990. Although women's military service as officers can expand women's career options if equality in employment is guaranteed, women's integration into the military has functioned as a token of gender equality without substantially altering the masculinist construction of soldiering in the continuing presence of the institution of male conscription (S. Moon 2002b). These two cases from the United States and Korea suggest that military service for women is not so much a precondition for full citizenship as an arena where women struggle to obtain their equal right to employment as citizens.

Sixth, the expansion and intensification of capitalism observed in the process of globalization has generated contradictory conditions to promote and undermine women's access to, and practices of, citizenship. Korean women, particularly working-class women, have been hit hardest by globalization; their employment in manufacturing industries has been worsened in the midst of economic restructuring. This negative consequence of globalization echoes the experience of Chinese peasants migrating into urban centers after the economic reform. Dorothy J. Solinger (1999) argues that the logic of the market undermines citizenship because the market tends to minimize a government's power to administer the distribution of resources in the process of commercial exchange for the maximization of profit. Although Solinger defines citizenship only as a formal status conferred by the state that enables one's access to resources of a given community, her analysis can apply to the active and participatory dimension of citizenship I have emphasized in this book. I would argue that the negative consequences of increasing marketization involve not only the reduction of social benefits granted to citizens by the state but also the decrease of secure employment and collective action as the enabling conditions for forging citizenship. These findings suggest that a majority of women and men marginalized by the expansion and intensification of the market mechanism will not be able to forge citizenship. At the same time, globalization has some positive effect on the middle-class women's movement to eliminate the military service extra-points system in South Korea. As discussed in chapter 6, were it not for the tide of globalization that has reduced the influence of extra-economic factors such as military service on the labor market, the middle-class women's movement to abolish the extra-points system as a marker of the militarized economy that discriminated against women would not have been successful.

The checkered struggle by which women and men in South Korea determine who they are and who they will become as members of the body politic has begun. For both women and men, the civil rights deemed by liberal thinkers to be necessary for individual freedom (that is, liberty of the person, freedom of thought and speech, and the right to defend and assert one's rights on terms of equality with others and by due process of law) have been severely curtailed by the National Security Law and Anticommunism Law from the beginning of the South Korean state. Since the political transition to electoral democracy in 1988 and then to civilian administration in 1993, citizenship for women and men has been formally and substantially expanded, along with the growth of civil society. Women and men have obtained substantive political and civil rights through their popular struggle against military authoritarian rule. Using political and civil rights in revived civil society, different social groups have fought for "social rights" to guarantee minimum standards of social security for the old, the infirm, the unemployed, mothers, and children. Although members of these social groups represent a very small minority of Koreans and have been waging an uphill battle, their presence bodes well for the future of citizenship in South Korea.

CHRONOLOGY OF POLITICAL EVENTS

1884	Kabo reform
1894	Tonghak peasant war
1895	Sino-Japanese War in the Korean Peninsula
1905	Annexation of the Chosŏn Dynasty (1392–1910) to Japan as a protectorate
1910–45	Japanese colonization
1945–48	Rule of the U.S. Army military government
1947	Establishment of the People's Democratic Republic of Korea (North Korea)
1948	Establishment of the Republic of Korea (South Korea)
1948–60	First Republic (President Syngman Rhee)
April 19, 1960	Student uprising and the overthrow of Rhee's regime
1960–61	Second Republic (Prime Minister Chang Myŏn)
May 16, 1961	Military coup led by General Park Chung Hee
1961–63	Military junta rule
1963–72	Third Republic (President Park Chung Hee)
October 1971	Declaration of Yushin Constitution
1972–79	Fourth Republic (President Park Chung Hee)
October 26, 1979	Assassination of Park by his KCIA chief
1979–80	Interregnum (President Choi Kyu-ha)
December 12, 1979	Military coup led by General Chun Doo Hwan

May 18–28, 1980	Kwangju citizens' democracy movement and their massacre by the military
1980–87	Fifth Republic (President Chun Doo Hwan)
June 29, 1987	Declaration of Democratization
1988–92	Sixth Republic (President Roh Tae Woo)
1993–97	President Kim Young Sam
1998–2002	President Kim Dae Jung

NOTES

INTRODUCTION

1 Williams explains keywords as "words which, beginning in particular specialized contexts, have become quite common in descriptions of wider areas of thought and experience." They are the vocabularies "we share with others, often imperfectly, when we wish to discuss many of the central processes of our common life" (1976, 12).

2 Kim Eun Mee 1997; Rhee 1994; Wade 1990; Bello and Rosenfeld 1990; Haggard 1990; Amsden 1989; Deyo 1987.

3 Kil and Moon 2001; Diamond and Kim 2000; Doh C. Shin 1999; Weiner, Huntington, and Almond 1994.

4 For discourse on Confucianism and East Asian economic development, see Tu 1996; Berger and Hsiao 1988; Dore 1987; and Morishima 1982.

5 Building on Edward Said's seminal work *Orientalism* (1978), scholars of diverse disciplines have examined the relationship between the economic, political, and cultural power of the West and knowledge about non-Western societies produced in the West and elsewhere. See Escobar 1995; Marchand and Parpart 1995; and Mohanty 1987.

6 While the specific tradition (in the form of, say, religion or cosmology) that generated a given gender ideology is crucial to our understanding of contemporary gender politics in a specific social context, we need to treat tradition not as the fixed repository of values and practices but as a major site of cultural contestation among various social actors (Hobsbawm and Ranger 1983). In a careful examination of contemporary discourses on sati and dowry murders, for example, Uma Narayan (1997) argues for "restoring history and politics to 'Third-world traditions.'" This means that we need to pay attention to economic and political interests of different social groups that inform the construction of a specific cultural practice as an element of tradition. As studies of the cultural politics of tradition and collective identity often note, women and the family tend to occupy both a privileged and a constrained position for maintaining tradition as the essentialized core of cultural and national identity (Yuval-Davis and Anthias 1989).

7　A streak of relativism can be seen in postmodernism's radical rejection of man, history, and metaphysics as the totalizing metanarrative of the Enlightenment and modernity. For example, see Flax 1990 and Lyotard 1984. See I. Young 1990 for ironic essentialism in the politics of identity and difference.

8　See Frank 1998 for the role of Asian economies in developing modern capitalism in western Europe. See Amin 1989 for the contribution of Arab culture to the making of Western culture, once believed to be rooted in ancient Greek and Roman cultures. For a pathbreaking study of the cultural politics of hybrid modernity, see Rofel (1999), who examined the Post-Mao Chinese encounter with modernity through the experiences of three generations of women workers in a silk factory in Hangzhou.

9　Lydia Liu (1993) explores this kind of translingual practice in her study of the "Western" concept of individualism introduced to China in the second decade of the twentieth century. She traces how the meaning of individualism was reinterpreted and reinvented by different groups of Chinese intellectuals in relation to their agendas to reform ailing Chinese society in the face of imperialist powers. Hence individualism becomes a concept neither purely Western nor purely indigenous.

10　For an example of such work, see Shin and Robinson 1999.

11　An example of this would be the stereotypical image of the Japanese as imitators of Western things. The literature on East Asian development emphasizes the formula of "borrowed technology," educated but cheap labor, and the organization of a semiskilled workforce. This kind of description often connotes a lack of the ability to create and invent.

12　Current examples of this type of discourse can be observed in the discussion of globalization and Islam. See Barber 2001.

13　The focus on the making and remaking of political subjectivities of women and men in this book intends to highlight the paradoxical duality of the human subject who is both an actor and the subjected. Althusser (1971) explores this duality in his discussion of the "ideological state apparatus." Critiquing the Enlightenment ideal of the human subject as an autonomous and free individual, Foucault points out the subjection of that individual to "disciplinary power" in modern society (Foucault 1979, 1984). He argues that the human subject is constituted by the disciplinary power that operates meticulously through numerous institutions and quotidian practices. While I do not discard such normative values of empowerment and freedom as merely discursive constructs or alibis for the individual's subjection to disciplinary power, I recognize the paradoxical coexistence of subjection and subjectivities in the human subject as a way to understand the deeply contradictory nature of domination in the process of modern nation building in South Korea.

14　For such gender studies of East Asia, see Chow 2002; Brinton 2001; and Horton

1996. For South Korea, see Seung-Kyung Kim 1997 and Nam 1996. For Japan, see Ogasawara 1998 and Brinton 1993. For China and Taiwan, see Ching-kwan Lee 1998 and Hsiung 1996.

15 Focusing on women workers who worked in the Pusan-Masan export-processing zone before their marriages, Seung-Kyung Kim (1997) documents the experiences of exploitation and economic marginalization among women factory workers in South Korea. Observing the highly gender-segregated labor market in postwar Japan, Mary Brinton (1993) argues that women are socialized to be inferior human capital by family, school, and workplace. That is, the interplay of specific institutional arrangements has facilitated women's secondary position in the labor market (222). Examining the satellite factory system, the backbone of the export-oriented economy in Taiwan, Ping-chun Hsiung (1996) shows that under the slogan of "living rooms as factories," the Taiwanese state has promoted the use of married women as cheap and expendable workers to perform assembly work at home for the satellite factories. Focusing on factories in South China, Ching Kwan Lee (1998) examines the significance of gender ideology for the organization of labor processes in industrialization in post-Mao China.

16 The class and gender approach within Women and Development studies also avoids reductionism by examining the interplay between production and reproduction that determines women's position in the economy. See Beneria and Roldan 1987; Afshar 1985; and Elson and Pearson 1981.

17 This body of studies of gender and industrialization tends to build on Louise Tilly and Joan W. Scott's pioneering study of industrialization in England and France between the eighteenth and twentieth centuries (1978). They demonstrate that the shift in the site of production from households to workshops and then industrial factories was accompanied by married women's gradual separation from paid employment outside the home. During the initial stage of industrialization marked by textile manufacturing, families adapted to the changing economy by sending wives and children out for wage work. In this transitional stage, families continued to function as economic units where all members were involved in productive tasks. Married women managed to combine wage work with housework and child rearing. However, as industrialization proceeded, women's domestic responsibilities could not coexist with full-time employment. Similarly, Judy Lown (1990) argues that relations between women and men in households before industrialization shaped the way in which industrialization took place in nineteenth-century England.

18 See Escobar (1995) for the historical emergence of the development establishment, characterized by the discovery of poverty in the postwar world. It is also noteworthy that Rostow's classical text on economic development (1960) is subtitled "A Non-communist Manifesto."

19 As I am finishing this book manuscript in mid-2003, the Korean peninsula is

again embroiled in a nuclear weapons crisis at the intersection of North Korea's withdrawal from the International Atomic Energy Agency and the escalation of tension between the United States and North Korea.

20 Some scholars in South Korea besides myself have begun to investigate various aspects of militarization in that society. *Tangdaebipy'ŏng* (Contemporary Critique), a quarterly published in Korea, focused on "fascism within us" in two issues. See vol. 8 (fall 1999) and vol. 9 (winter 1999).

21 Janoski 1998; Lister 1997; Yuval-Davis 1997; Walby 1994; Dietz 1993; Somers 1993.

22 By associating military service with the gender division of labor, I do not mean to presume that gender is the only criterion for inclusion in, or exclusion or exemption from, military service. As historical and current examples of the organization of military service in various societies illustrate, race, ethnicity, and sexual orientation have also been employed to demarcate the boundary of the military (Zürcher 1999; Zeeland 1996; Enloe 1980). Class further complicates the composition of the military. Although the civic republican principle of mandatory military service as a male citizen's duty has connoted a sense of prestige, conscription in practice has often resulted in mass armies disproportionately manned by conscripts of lower classes, especially during the early days of conscription systems. Even in France, the birthplace of the modern mass-conscription army, the middle class was almost entirely exempted from conscription during Napoleon's rule, and the standing army relied heavily on men from the poorest sections of society (Lucassen and Zürcher 1999, 9). In the South Korean military, likewise, sons of lower-class families are disproportionately represented in regular military service (as opposed to supplementary service and exemption). Nevertheless, gender has been employed as the salient principle of the organization of the military in that modern nation-states commonly require men as a group to perform military service, whereas few states require women as a group to do so.

To appreciate the depth of the masculinization of military service, it is useful here to address two polar examples of the military service system: Israel, with universal conscription for both men and women in principle, and the United States in the post-Vietnam era, with all-volunteer forces recruited from both men and women for most military tasks (Herbert 1998). While conscription of women in Israel appears to be an exception to the general rule, it is noteworthy that even in Israel, women's military obligation differs considerably from men's. Almost half of young Israeli women are exempted from conscription on religious grounds. Women's military service is shorter (a year and nine months) than men's (three years). Labor is also divided by gender in the Israeli Defense Force (IDF), which assigns women conscripts to office work. Moreover, only 15 percent of female conscripts finish the required length of service, whereas an absolute majority of male conscripts do. While women can be mustered for reserve service only up to the age of twenty-four, men serve in the reserve forces until they reach forty-five (in the case of combat units) or fifty-one (in all other units). In addition, women do not serve in reserve forces when they become pregnant or mother children (Klein 1999, 52, 54, 55).

The institutionalized coupling of masculinity with military service does not necessarily end altogether with the passing of the mass conscription system. In the United States, where the all-volunteer forces have the highest percentage of women soldiers in the world (approximately 15 percent), all male citizens and male immigrant aliens between the ages of eighteen and twenty-five who reside in the United States and its territories are required to register with the Selective Service System, designed for the likelihood of a draft "only in the event of war or national emergency." Women are exempted from this registration requirement. This suggests that women are never obliged to serve in the military, whereas men potentially are.

These examples from two poles of the continuum of military service systems suggest that the actual and symbolic link between masculinity and soldiering is pervasive and profound across different societies. While the specific relationship of women to military service varies over time within a given national society, as well as from one society to another within a given time, compulsory military service is defined predominantly as men's work, just as housework and child rearing continue to be defined primarily as women's work. It is noteworthy that women's incorporation into the military in the West has developed in tandem with the end of the mass-conscription army, which is accompanied by the qualitative and quantitative shortage of manpower (Ilnari 1994, 150–51). This normative dichotomy of gender identities organized around mandatory military service observed in many societies suggests that a study of gender and the modern nation needs to pay attention to the institution of male conscription.

23 I contacted an official in charge of information and publications at the OMM, briefly explained my project, and asked for help. This young official was very helpful and friendly, but two of his older colleagues came to ask, in an aggressive tone, who I was and what I was doing. The three of them and I ended up engaging in a heated conversation on the military service extra-points system controversy during their lunch hour. This was rather unusual; one would not expect government officials to get involved in such a discussion with a visitor and stranger like me. Throughout this encounter, I could feel their fervor over this current social issue. One of them explicitly criticized women's organizations for advocating the elimination of the system. Meanwhile the younger official tried to present neutral information about the possibility of a constitutional lawsuit (my meeting with the three officials took place after the Korean Women's Associations Council assisted a group of individuals in challenging the military service extra-points system in the Supreme Court in October 1999).

1. HISTORICAL ROOTS

1 I use the notion of trajectory here to stress the following points identified by current feminist theories of the state. First, this term captures the relational nature
   of the state, as opposed to its being an entity with a fixed nature. This means that
   the boundary of the state vis-à-vis civil society is fluid; hence, studying the state
   inevitably implies also studying its relation to society. Second, it conveys the his-
   toricity of the state as a heterogeneous set of institutions, agencies, and discourses
   shaped by specific social relations, an idea which implies that contradictions and
   inconsistencies will be an integral part of the state's imagining of modernity.

2 The radical faction carried out a coup d'état against the Confucian monarchy in
   1884 but failed after three days.

3 According to Kang Man-gil, this notion can be traced to Pak Kyu-su, a Confucian
   bureaucrat and forerunner of the Enlightenment Faction, whose view on the West
   changed from rejection to selective adoption over time. Yet his understanding of
   the Eastern way did not mention the issue of the form of polity in reforming the
   society. Rather, he seemed to define the Eastern way as morality and everyday
   culture (1985, 159).

4 The radical reformists addressed a cursory but broad range of issues to change
   political, economic, and social conditions. For example, the Enlightenment Faction's policy proposals, announced during its three-day reign, included the end
   of Korea's dependence on China, the selection of government officials based on
   merit, the increase of the cabinet's decision-making power and the decrease of the
   monarch's power, financial reforms to secure the state's revenue, and the establishment of a modern police force (Jae-Hyeon Choi 1986, 228).

5 Gregory Kasza summarizes the similarities between the AMOS and a conscription army in five points. First, both are instruments to implement public policy.
   Second, their membership includes entire categories of people—women, youths,
   factory workers, et cetera. Third, their membership is overtly or covertly coerced
   and exists in the absence of competing organizations. Fourth, their leaders are appointed by regimes. Fifth, their activities and goals are also determined by regimes
   (1995, 74).

6 Militarized "national security" is not unique to South Korea but rather a common
   view of collective security, to varying degrees, shared by modern nation-states
   with standing armed forces. According to Michael Mann, militarism, defined as a
   set of ideas and practices that promote militarization, is a central aspect of modern society and derives from the geopolitical nature of human society, far older
   than capitalism or industrialism (1984/1992, 127). Therefore militarization is pro-
   foundly interwoven with the very survival of the state, which historically rises,
   expands, and falls through warfare (Porter 1994).

7 In this attempt the United States was not alone. The Soviet Union also manipu-

lated the Korean People's Republic by increasing the representation of selected communist candidates at the expense of local representatives. See Gills 1996, 37.

8 However, Rhee's overt anticommunism stemmed from more than ideological zealotry. It also reflected adroit political calculation aimed at securing his power base by maximizing military and economic aid from the United States during the poverty-stricken postwar decade (Hong Yong-p'yo 1997). Anticipating the withdrawal of U.S. troops after the Korean War, he used his compliance with the armistice agreement as leverage in bargaining to gain U.S. commitment to South Korean military security. Initially reluctant to commit to long-term direct military involvement in South Korea, the United States came to see a bilateral defense treaty as a useful mechanism for keeping defiant Rhee and the South Korean military under its direct control (Gills 1996, 79). Consequently, throughout the 1950s, the various forms of U.S. military aid accumulated to a value of approximately $2 billion (Se Jin Kim 1971, 66), making the military the most advanced and well-funded sector of Korean society and contributing to the rise of military regimes that lasted for a quarter century.

9 Forming the Supreme Council for National Reconstruction (SCNR) after his coup in May 1961, Park's military junta proclaimed its project of "national reconstruction" by pursuing anticommunism and "administered democracy," as well as "guided capitalism" (Se Jin Kim 1971, 109).

10 Deeply alarmed by the Islamic revolution and the establishment of the "hostile" government in Iran, the United States perceived the explosion of popular protests for sociopolitical democratization in South Korea after Park's assassination as a dangerous sign. In the midst of mounting student demonstrations, on May 9, 1980, William J. Gleysteen, the U.S. ambassador to South Korea, informed Chun and Choi Kyu-ha, prime minister under Park who served as interim president, that the United States would not oppose the use of military force necessary to maintain order. Furthermore, after the initial crackdown on the Kwangju uprising, "Gleysteen actually told the South Korean foreign minister that the U.S. military would, if need be, directly assist South Korean 'army efforts to restore order in Kwangju and deter trouble elsewhere' " (Hart-Landsberg 1998, 192). Before the Kwangju massacre, many Koreans had tended to believe that the United States was defending democracy against communists. Even after the event, citizens of Kwangju expected the United States to support their democracy movement, expediently represented by the military regime as communist insurgency. A letter sent to Gleysteen by the Group of the Arrested after the Kwangju struggle on December 22, 1980, suggests this. See Han Sang-jin 1998, 71.

11 According to an official estimate based on the prosecutors' investigation in 1995, 193 people were killed by the military during the civil war in May 1980. See Kim Sŏng-guk 1998, 147.

12 Regarding the rise of modern discipline, Foucault qualifies that "the formation of

a disciplinary society" does not mean the complete replacement of all other modalities of power by the disciplinary modality of power, but rather the disciplinary power's infiltrating other modalities of power, undermining them, serving as an intermediary between them, linking them together, extending them, and above all making it possible to bring the effects of power to the most minute and distant elements (Foucault 1979, 216).

13 Internal pacification refers to the progressive reduction of the use of armed forces for internal ruling, the eradication of physical force from the labor contract, and the formal separation of the military from politics. See Giddens 1987, 181–92.

14 In 1969, following the strategy of export promotion, Park's regime started expanding the nation's industries by enacting the Regional Industrial Development Law. Under this law, it fostered at least one industrial estate in each provincial capital by means of a series of special incentives. The regime began to establish Export Industrial Estates and Free Export Zones in the late 1960s, expanding them throughout the 1970s. It offered industrial sites at significantly below-market prices; kept utility, transportation, and communication costs under control; and gave out generous credit to businessmen at virtually zero or even negative interest rates. Moreover, it exempted export firms — both domestic and foreign — from taxes on imports of raw material and from corporate income taxes (Ogle 1990, 39; Byung-nak Song 1990, 95–97). This kind of privilege was legitimized by Law 1656, Provisions of the Export Industry Estates Development and Formation Law (Korean Women Voters' League 1980, 132).

15 See Seungsook Moon 1997 for a detailed analysis of official nationalism constructed around the issues of national ethics and history under the Park and Chun regimes.

16 The Korean encounter under Japanese colonial rule (1910–45) with Japanese militarism, which was also an essential component of empire building, left lasting marks on the trajectory of South Korean militarism in later decades. Japanese colonial rule provided the precedent for the modern military administration in postcolonial Korea, including models of authoritarian control of society and mass mobilization for war preparation. While Japanese colonial policy on Korea changed over time, Japan maintained an overtly repressive military administration throughout its entire period of colonial rule over Korea (Peattie 1984b, 104–6), relying not only on the effective modern police forces but also on the traditional network in a local community for surveillance and control over colonized Koreans (Peattie 1984a, 27). Using these methods of social control, Japan was able to mobilize the masses of Koreans during the decades of heightened militarism in the 1930s and the early 1940s.

   As the Japanese war effort escalated during this period, the colonial administration launched aggressive propaganda to instill a sense of duty to the Japanese emperor by resorting to Confucian values such as loyalty (Peattie 1984b, 121).

Resembling the Nazi administration halfway across the globe, it also sponsored various types of mass movements by exploiting what Kasza (1995) calls the "administered mass organizations" of women, youth, workers, and local residents. Louise Young's study (1998) of the participation of ordinary Japanese in wartime imperialism and their mobilization during this period demonstrates the extent to which the use of voluntary mass organizations by the central power became pervasive in both Japan proper and its colonies. As early as 1910, the Japanese army unified numerous local organizations of veterans and reservists in Japan into a national association, and by 1915 it had completed the same kind of consolidation of thousands of youth organizations (132–33). More interestingly, national and local mass media in Japan launched and facilitated "war relief" campaigns by urging ordinary Japanese to raise funds and send "comfort goods" to Japanese troops on the battlefield.

17 When I was growing up in South Korea in the 1960s and 1970s, like many other schoolchildren, I was exposed to numerous trappings of the preparation for an impending war. We regularly practiced civil defense exercises in classrooms and outdoor shelters, including instructions on how to protect our faces and bodies and where to hide during a sudden air raid from the north.

18 According to Kim Chin-gyun, this tax lasted until 1991 (1996, 298).

19 This law was merely replaced by the "security supervision law" in 1989. The conversion system was abolished as late as 1998 but was followed by the establishment of the law-abiding oath (chunbŏpsŏyakchedo) that still requires individuals to accept the state's ideologies (Cho Yŏng-min 2001, 125).

20 For examples during military rule, see Catholic Human Rights Council 2001; Han Sŭng-hŏn 1997; and Kim Ch'ung-sik 1992.

21 This information is based on the abstract of the Fourteenth Regular Meeting of the Supreme Council for the National Reconstruction, June–July 1961. See Korean National Assembly 1998.

22 Specifications of business firms that fall under this category have changed over time. According to the Honorable Treatment of Persons of National Merit Act, the "organizations practicing employment protection" included private firms employing sixteen employees or more, exclusive of special manufacturing companies employing under fifty workers. See Clause 2 of Article 30 of the Honorable Treatment Act.

23 See Article 89 of the Enforcement Ordinance.

24 It is worth noting that the Korean version differs from the American version in three ways. First, as discussed earlier, the Korean system primarily benefits former conscripts, whereas the American system primarily serves professional soldiers. Second, the Korean version guarantees extra points indiscriminately to all honorably discharged soldiers, while the American system specifies that only those who earn certain minimum scores on the tests qualify for the extra points (Yi

Uk-han 1998, 13). Finally, the Korean system can be accused of promoting sex discrimination because of its military system based on the principle of universal male conscription. The American system, by contrast, is less susceptible to this problem because the U.S. military since 1973 has relied on professional soldiering open to both sexes.

25 This militarized corporate culture, persisting today, appears to be more pronounced in blue-collar factories than white-collar offices. Choong Soon Kim observed that "when an executive goes to a subordinate, the subordinate stands up much as an enlisted soldier faces a general in the army. When an executive walks into the shop of the plant, the rank-and-file workers stand at attention as if to a general. When I visited a steel plant, the plant workers saluted the plant manager" (1992, 152).

2. MOBILIZED TO BE MARTIAL

1 This feminist approach to military service departs from the existing body of literature on military service in South Korea. Many of the studies of military service in this society can be categorized into two groups: internal policy-related studies conducted by state-sponsored research centers or individual scholars, and social-science studies of military service that focus on civil-military relations. For classical examples of this literature on civil-military relations, see Johnson 1964, 1962; and Janowitz 1964. Jan Lucassen and Erik Jan Zürcher point out that while military historians have generated a sizable literature on conscription, they have focused almost exclusively on North America and Europe (1999, 16). Moreover, these historians have rarely concerned themselves with gender issues as related to conscription. A few exceptions to this lack of interest in military service as a site of gender politics include Anne-Marie Hilsdon's study of military service in the Philippines. See Hilsdon 1995.

2 According to a 1997 report by the United Nations high commissioner for human rights, 89 countries used conscription, and 77 of them were non-Western societies; 48 of the 89 countries used conscription without any alternative forms of service, and 47 of those 48 (Greece was the exception) were non-Western societies. Thirty countries used conscription with alternative services such as civilian or unarmed military service; 19 of them were non-Western societies. There were 11 countries in which military service was voluntary in principle but selective conscription existed; all these countries were non-Western societies. According to the same report, there were 70 countries without conscription; 57 of them were non-Western societies.

3 See Chŏng Kyŏng-hyŏn 1990a, 1990b, 1990c, 1991a, 1991b, 1992.

4 This structure of the military resulted from two factors. First, the United States did not want South Korea to possess mobile offensive power to attack North Korea.

Second, the dominance of the army in the South Korean military reflects the division of labor between South Korea and the United States, in which the former was to supply military manpower, and the latter to supply weapons and strategy. See Sŏ Chin-t'ae 1998.

5   Throughout this period, there have been numerous changes in the specific details regarding the length of military service, the minimum educational requirement, and the age limits for taking the conscription test (*chingbyŏng kŏmsa*) and receiving exemption (*Pyŏngmu* 1995, 16–22; Cho Sŏng-lyul 1996; Kang Kyŏng-hwan 1996; Kim Chin-dae 1996; Yi T'ae-ho 1996; Yi Yŏ-song 1996).

6   The length of yearly reserve training was reduced in 1994 to three days from the twenty-eight-day obligation established in 1957 (Chŏng Hwan-sik 1995, 29). This change reflects the ascendancy of economic activities over nonproductive military training during the decades of economic expansion, as well as the increasing significance of high technology in warfare.

7   For example, during the 152nd session of the National Assembly, a legislator associated the problem of using conscripts in private industries under "military service special cases" with the forceful mass mobilization of Koreans by Japanese colonial authorities during World War II. See KNA 1991, 11.

8   In fact, reflecting this legacy, the universal conscription system did indeed exempt only sons whose fathers were either also only sons or sixty years old and above. This special treatment of only sons was abolished by the end of 1993. See Kim Chin-dae 1996.

9   This information is based on the author's interview, in November 1998, with Kim Nak-chung, who has been a peace activist ever since he staged an antiwar protest in 1950 during the Korean War.

10 For a discussion of military service and citizenship in France and Germany, for example, see Brubaker 1992.

11 This sense of military service as a coercive burden is partly reminiscent of the structure of military service in premodern Korea. As the history of conscription in traditional Korea suggests, military service was always a heavy burden levied on the powerless commoners by the political elite, without any political or socio-economic entitlement in exchange. See Chŏng Kyŏng-hyŏn 1990a, 1990b, 1990c, 1991a, 1991b, 1992.

12 It is instructive here to discuss briefly the historical experience of conscription in the postwar United States. Thanks to unprecedented economic expansion and prosperity during the postwar decades, veterans were granted "broad readjustment benefits" as an extension of Franklin D. Roosevelt's Depression-era social welfare policies. These benefits allowed them to attend colleges, secure jobs, and purchase a family house. In other words, military service during wartime provided veterans and their families with the economic resources necessary to achieve upward social mobility. Furthermore, veterans of the "good war" received social

recognition and enjoyed high esteem. As a result, from World War II until the Vietnam War, the social meanings of military service in the United States were largely positive (Karner 1998, 206, 207).

13 See Kwŏn Sŏn-jin 1997; Kim Nam-guk 1995, chap. 2; Kim Hwan-t'ae 1993; Ch'a Chae-ik 1989; Pak Ki-yŏl 1989; Yang Hŭi-wŏn 1988.

14 These negative aspects of military culture are described in several books written by former officers and in numerous articles written by military experts and journalists in recent years. See, for example, Kim Tŏk-han 1996; Sŏ Hyo-il 1995; Kim Nam-guk 1995; and Kim Hwan-t'ae 1993.

15 Evaders were subject to one- to three-year imprisonment, depending on the specifics of their violation. Collaborators in evasion were penalized with varying degrees of imprisonment and fines, as well as the suspension of medical licenses for up to eight years (OMM 1986, 800, 810).

16 For instance, the term of imprisonment increased, to three to ten years (OMM 1986, 807, 810).

17 It is important to note that South Korean official statistics in general were still not very reliable in the 1980s. The statistics on the number of evaders collected by the OMM might be particularly inaccurate for at least two reasons. First, the nature of evasion does not allow for its precise identification and measurement. It is not clear how the office obtained the specific numbers printed on page 799 of OMM 1986, Pyŏngmuhaengjŏng (A History of Military Service Administration). Second, influenced by the authoritarian nature of ruling regimes, government offices during the military rule for decades tended to emphasize the visible achievement of specific policy and programs to impress their superiors and the grassroots population.

18 The amount of the fine ranged from 1,000,000 won to 10,000,000 won in 1973 (roughly from $2,500 to $25,000 at the 1973 exchange rate). See OMM 1986, 810.

19 This page range is not a mistake but an original in the report.

20 This information is based on the author's interview of a senior research fellow at KIDA in early December 1998.

21 The theme of the military as an instrument of nation building survives into the 1990s, with a historical twist. Later studies of the military as a modernizer tend to emphasize the educational role of military service in giving lower-class men from rural areas basic literary and technical skills, as well as "time orientation" and "subjugation to formal authority" (Koo 1990, 677; Paek 1985). Choong Soon Kim, an anthropologist in the United States, echoes this view when he identifies wartime mobilization through a mandatory military draft system as a "noneconomic variable" to account for the rapid industrialization of South Korea (1992, 214). In her study of universal conscription in Singapore, Elizabeth Nair argues that in a broader view of national security, it is a security issue to enhance the lives of underprivileged youths through military service (1994, 109).

22 According to researchers at KIDA whom I interviewed in December 1998, no reliable statistics on their numbers are available. This is plausible because government statistics in general were not well recorded until the late 1980s.

23 Jeanne Pyle's study of Irish industrialization, for instance, documents how Catholic gender ideology shaped the state's exclusion of women from paid employment in export-oriented factories. See Pyle 1990.

24 Due to its boldness, recklessness, and lack of practical calculation, the Heavy and Chemical Industrial (HCI) Plan was initially disregarded by most Western experts, including those at the World Bank, who later acknowledged the "successful" transformation of the Korean economy. President Park also ignored Western advice, including that of the Economic Planning Board technocrats educated in the West. The military elite, on the other hand, was directly involved in implementing the HCI Plan (Hart-Landsberg 1993, 60–61).

25 In the 1980s, Chun's regime reduced the government's direct involvement in the management of defense industries, in part because of the economic liberalization aggressively pursued by the Reagan administration. Chun's regime virtually abandoned a long-term research plan to develop advanced weapons, instead purchasing them from the United States. See Kim Chin-gyun 1996, 300

26 An exception to these fields is licensed workers in the field of textile manufacturing, which consisted predominantly of women. Yet their numbers were far smaller than those in heavy and chemical industries. See ML 1989, 193, 199.

27 Interview by the author, December 1998.

28 Major research institutes include the Korea Institute of Science and Technology (KIST), established in 1966, as well as the Korea Institute of Machinery and Metals, the Korea Research Institute of Chemical Technology, the Korea Institute of Electronics Technology, the Korea Research Institute of Ships, and the Korea Standards Research Institute. These last five institutes were established in the 1970s to "absorb some of the KIST's R & D functions" (UNESCO 1985, 18, 34, 45).

29 These statistics were given to me by a Ph.D. student at KAIST.

30 This information on financial support and military service was also obtained from a Ph.D. student at KAIST. Female students have been admitted since 1981 to the Ph.D. program and since 1973 to the master's program, according to information provided by the admissions office at KAIST in early January, 2005. However, according to earlier information I obtained from the school, the admission of female students to the Ph.D. program began in 1992 and to the master's program in 1996. The total number of female graduate students more than doubled in one year, from 50 in 1997 to 120 in 1998.

31 Chun's regime almost doubled the number of college students by simplifying college entrance exams and establishing standards for graduation in 1981.

32 I was told by an official of the Ministry of Labor that the number of women with engineering licenses during the 1970s and 1980s was so small that statistics on

them did not exist. This information is based on a conversation with an officer in the Ministry of Labor in March 1992.

33 This somewhat odd page number (155–48) is what appears on the page of the report cited here.

34 The practice of using surplus (male) conscripts to fuel the industrializing economy continued in the 1990s, with three modifications. First, in 1994, the several categories of military service special cases were streamlined into researchers and industrial workers (*Dong-A Daily*, December 2, 1994). Comprehensive statistics on the numbers of "industrial workers" and "special researchers" exempted from mandatory military service in the 1990s are not available to the public. However, their total numbers can be estimated on the basis of statistical information published in the mass media and related government documents. While there have been some fluctuations, the total number of military service special cases has gradually increased in the 1990s, due to the ascendancy of economic logic over military logic in the period of economic globalization and the post–Cold War. During the mid-1990s, between 3,000 and 3,500 conscripts served annually as special researchers (*Dong-A Daily*, December 2, 1994). During the same period, between 35,000 and 40,000 conscripts served annually as industrial workers (*Segye Daily*, June 18, 1997). The total number of special researchers increased from 12,145 in 1997 to 14,101 in 1998, while the total number of industrial workers decreased somewhat, from 55,214 to 52,296, during the same period (MND 1998, 186; MND 1997, 221). Overall these numbers are larger than those in the mid-1990s. These increases took place against the demographic decrease in the total pool of prospective conscripts as a result of declining birthrates in preceding decades. Second, the number of researchers employed in lieu of military service was increased, in an effort to promote advanced technology and natural sciences, deemed to be crucial to continued economic growth. From 1994 to 1995, for example, their numbers grew from 2,620 to 3,250 (*Segye Daily*, December 2, 1994). Third, the state has rechanneled economic conscripts into small- and medium-size manufacturing firms facing an acute labor shortage caused by the restructuring of the domestic and global economies. This initiative came from the Ministry of Commerce and Industry as early as 1990 (*Chungang Daily*, June 27, 1990). Consequently, the number of firms allowed to hire conscripts under the Military Service Special Cases Law rose from 4,030 in 1993 to 5,122 in 1994, with roughly 35,000 conscripts working in those firms in lieu of military service in 1994 (*Chungang Daily*, January 10, 1994).

3. MOBILIZED TO BE DOMESTIC

1 The picture of a labor market rigidly segregated by gender emerges from both the aggregate and the detailed labor statistics of the period of rapid industrialization. The growth in female workers over a thirty-year period was greatest in

secondary industry (manufacturing and mining), quadrupling from 6.4 percent before industrialization to 28 percent by 1990. Their absolute numbers grew more than ten times, from roughly 187,000 in 1960 to 2,000,000 in 1990. The dramatic increase in the number of women employed in manufacturing results from the expansion of light industries during the second half of the 1960s and the first half of the 1970s. Yet the largest number of women worked in primary industry— agriculture, forestry, and fishing—in 1980, and in the service sectors of the tertiary industry in 1990. Throughout the 1980s, a decade of heavy industrialization, the number of women working in the tertiary sector expanded the most rapidly (Economic Planning Board 1960, 1970, 1980, 1991).

2 In 1972, women workers employed in manufacturing firms represented 81.4 percent of the total female workforce in firms with ten or more employees (Bureau of Labor 1972, 46–47). In 1983, they accounted for 73.7 percent of the female workforce in firms with five or more workers (ML 1983, 12). By 1991, this ratio was further reduced to 65.6 percent (ML 1992a, 97). But this decrease is not entirely attributable to the masculinization of the skilled workforce in the heavy and chemical industries. By the late 1980s, the explosion of the militant labor movement had raised labor costs in South Korea. Consequently, labor-intensive manufacturing had begun to be relocated overseas in search of cheaper labor costs. Another factor was a growing avoidance of factory work among the younger generation of the working class.

3 No official statistics on women were compiled over the decade until 1978. This absence itself is a telling indication of the marginality of women workers in vocational training programs.

4 Applicants needed to have completed two years of a vocational high school or 1,800 hours of vocational training after regular high school education. In comparison with this, the test for the first-class craftsman license required additional qualifications such as three years of practical experience, a vocational college degree, or a record of winning in the International Vocational Training Competition.

5 During the 1970s, over 80 percent of employees in the textile industry were women (Ogle 1990, 80; Kim Yong-su and Lee Yong-ok 1976, 92). In 1983, when light industry (which had had the lion's share of Korean exports) had been declining for some time, women still represented 42.6 percent of the total workers hired in manufacturing firms (ML 1984, 60–61). When this rate is broken down into areas of manufacturing by gender, women represent 56.7 percent of the total workforce in textiles, whereas they account for only 15.6 percent in mechanical equipment assembly (KWDI 1984, 4). The percentage is even higher (92 percent) in production jobs in textiles in the same year (Shim 1988, 124). As recently as 1991, 52.1 percent of all paid women workers were concentrated in simple and labor-intensive production jobs (ML 1992a, 98).

6 See Yŏsŏng, March 1973, 32; Kim Ok-yŏl and Kim T'ae-hŭi 1973, 12; Bureau of Labor 1972, 46–47. The currency rate has fluctuated over time. In February 1973,

200 Notes to Chapter 3

the exchange rate was roughly four hundred won to one U.S. dollar. In 1999 the rate was 1,200 won to the dollar.

7 In 1972 women workers earned about 45 percent of men's income; this rate decreased to 42.3 percent in 1979. In 1984 it rose to 45.9 percent (KWDI 1985a, 533; Yu Yŏng-ju 1982, 172; Kim Ok-yŏl and Kim T'ae-hŭi 1973, 12). By 1990, women's average income rose to slightly more than half that of their male counterparts (KWDI 1991, 467; Chŏng Hye-sŏn et al. 1989).

8 See Kim Seung-kyung (1997) for a valuable ethnographic study of South Korean female factory workers which focuses on their lives after marriage.

9 One of the earliest women's AMOs specifically targeted to rural women was the Clubs for Improving the Conditions of Living (Saenghwalhyangsangcŭlŏp), formed by the Office of Agricultural Promotion in 1958. After years of neglect of agriculture, this office was established to cope with the problem of rural poverty aggravated by the reduction of free U.S. agricultural aid toward the end of the 1950s. The office organized rural women on the basis of a basic administrative unit. In 1962 the local clubs were hierarchically integrated into larger administrative units to form federations for the effective control of rural women (KWDI 1990c, 149).

10 Slogans from the 1960s included "Let's have a small number of children and raise them well," "Affluence in our home starts from family planning," "Let's not suffer from too many children, let's raise a small number of them well," "Too many children will make one a beggar," and "Bringing up a small number of children well benefits both parents and children." Slogans from the 1970s began to address the problem of Koreans' preference for male children, which often compelled a married couple to have more children so as to have at least one son: "Let's have two children regardless of their sexes," "A well brought-up daughter is as good as ten sons." Slogans from the 1980s appear to be more aggressive than previous ones: "Even two children are too many, let's have one and raise it well," "One child for happiness and love" (Kim Eun-sil 2001, 317, 319).

11 MHSA 1975a, 1976, 1980, 1981a, 1981b, 1982a, 1983, 1984, 1985, 1987c, 1989b.

12 See MHSA 1972, 1976, 1982c, 1985, 1987c.

13 Rational management of the household, characterized by savings and the efficient use and reuse of resources, could contribute to capital accumulation, especially at its earlier stage. Although Korean industrialization was financed by foreign capital, predominantly in the form of loans, domestic savings were another significant source of capital. In this context, mothers' and wives' savings from thrifty management of the household were crucial. Domestic savings represented 17 percent of the gross national product in 1970 and increased to 30 percent in 1985 (Ogle 1990, 36). While it is difficult to verify whether this increase was in part a consequence of the success of the campaign for savings and thrift, the modernizing state certainly attempted to take advantage of the positive outcome.

4. THE DECLINE OF MILITARIZED MODERNITY

1 It is noteworthy that the archetypal image associated with this event is that of young male students taking to the streets, being joined by older citizens, and fighting riot police. This masculinized image of a militant clash between young male students and the repressive state apparatus has been reinforced by the tradition of radical student activism on college campuses, particularly during the 1980s, when female students represented a significant minority. Their invisibility reflected the masculinization of female student activists (Insook Kwon 2000).

2 Immediately after the proclamation of the Yushin Constitution, college students printed underground newspapers, and their dissident activities grew into street protests. In 1973, Park Hyŏng-gyu, a Presbyterian minister, led a peaceful demonstration against the Yushin system, including the public reading of a "Christian Manifesto," which called for procedural democratization (Cumings 1997, 372). On April 3, 1974, college students in Seoul demanded "democratization of the economy and politics" in their street protest (Kang Chun-man 2002, 2:89–91, 129). A group of religious leaders, professors, journalists, politicians, and legal professionals issued joint declarations to restore procedural democracy.

3 In *Kaekchi* (Foreign Place) (1974), for instance, Hwang portrayed the lives of uprooted workers laboring at construction sites of "national land development," conveying not only their misery but also their common struggle for a better life. In *Ahopkyŏlle kuduro saranamŭn sanai* (A Man Who Survived with Nine Pairs of Shoes) (1977), Yun depicted the experience of the urban poor involved in collective rebellion to change their situation. In *Nanjangiga ssoaolin chagŭn kong* (A Small Ball Shot Upward by a Dwarf) (1978), Cho narrated the story of an informal-sector worker and his family juxtaposed with lives of the wealthy people living nearby.

4 In 1970, Chŏn, a young tailor working at the Ch'ŏng'gye Apparel Co. in Seoul, burned himself to death in a protest against the inhumane working conditions of young seamstresses in the company.

5 During the seven years of the Fifth Republic, there were at least twenty-five protests on a massive scale.

6 This practice was shaped by the history of the factory workers' lonely struggle in the 1970s. In particular, Chŏn T'ae-il, who immolated himself to protest the abject dehumanization of factory workers, wrote in his diary that he would like to have college students as his friends so that they could help him understand complicated legal documents and learn workers' rights. This record, posthumously made public, sensitized student activists exposed to Marxist-Leninist literature.

7 See Center for Security Problems 1989, 1990, 1991, 1992, 1993; National Defense University 1989, 1996; and Center for Journalism Culture 1994.

8 Women Making Peace, a grassroots middle-class women's association in Seoul,

has been leading the way by drawing public attention to still-obscure issues of peace in the Korean peninsula.

9 This movement has focused on the issues of the environmental hazards around American military bases and the crimes against Koreans committed by American soldiers. The public was particularly galvanized by the brutal murders of Korean female sex workers by American soldiers, who were not subject to the South Korean criminal justice system. American soldiers have enjoyed extraterritoriality under the Status of Forces Agreement (SOFA), and this unequal clause is still to be eliminated during the reform of SOFA in the near future.

10 In 1987 there were a record 3,749 labor disputes. While the number dropped to 1,873 in 1988, and further to 1,616 in 1989, the frequency of these disputes was still phenomenal not only for Korean history but also in the context of the world history of labor movements. These disputes enabled workers to gain real increases in wages and improvements in working conditions (Yi Hyo-jae 1997, 158).

11 One of the most conspicuous examples of this continued repression was observed in the police responses to a series of labor disputes at the Daewoo automobile company in the city of Pup'yŏng. On April 10, 2001, the police militantly suppressed a protest by laid-off autoworkers (*Hangyŏre 21*, April 26, 2001).

12 http://www.women21.or.kr/news/default.asp.

13 http://www.ccej.or.kr/english/ccej.html.

14 http://english.kfem.or.kr/aboutus/aboutus1.htm.

15 http://peoplepower21.org/pspd/org/pspd_d1.htm.

16 In 1994 the PSPD launched its annual campaign to change the popular perception of social security from a favor by the state to a duty of the state toward its citizens, and to demand the establishment of a basic social security system that would guarantee a minimum standard of living. This movement contributed to the legislation of the Minimum Standards of Living Protection Bill in 1999. In 1995, the PSPD started a campaign to reform the justice system, which had long been biased in favor of the political elite and big business. In 1996, it focused on the corruption prevention bill, which was passed in 2001. In 1997, the PSPD launched an annual campaign to exercise "small rights" of ordinary citizens and thereby make them real. In response to the Asian economic crisis, the PSPD started a campaign to organize the collective power of small-stock owners in 1998. In 1999, it organized an annual campaign to demand the release of the government budget to the public. During the parliamentary election in 2000, it joined other citizens' organizations to disseminate a list of corrupt assembly members and prevent them from being elected (http://peoplepower21.org/pspd/history/pspd_e3.htm).

17 The social relations of family and kinship also affected men's citizenship in that their relationship to the nation-state was mediated by their legal status as the household master (*hoju*). Yet the degree of mediation was far less than that for women's citizenship.

18 A parallel can be made with different types of social minorities. For instance,

people of color in the United States cannot afford to forget their race because of daily and personal experiences of racism, whereas it is easy for white people to forget their race because it rarely affects them negatively. While it is convenient for heterosexuals to claim that sexuality is a private issue and to remain apparently neutral citizens in public because their dominant sexuality rarely affects them negatively, homosexuals cannot afford to ignore their sexuality as soon as it becomes known to other people.

5. THE TRAJECTORY OF MEN'S CITIZENSHIP

1 For studies of women's military mobilization without substantial empowerment as citizens, see Hilsdon 1995 and Dolan 1993. While women who are mobilized for armed struggle can demand their rights based on their contribution and sacrifice, historical examples show that nothing comes of such claims when they are not accompanied by political leverage. The powerful tend to interpret women's military mobilization as a product of exceptional circumstances, and the restoration of order as a time for women to return to their "true" place.

2 The avoidance of a military career among qualified men implies the existence of other, more remunerative and prestigious career paths in an advanced capitalist society. It is noteworthy that the decline in the desirability of a military career coincides with its availability to women, a social group that has historically been marginal to the military. This coincidence is related to the findings of feminist scholarship on gender and professional power. That is, feminine gender negatively mediates professional power in terms of its remuneration and social prestige. The entry of women into a male-dominated profession tends to lead to their ghettoization (Riska 2001; Pringle 1998). A parallel process seems to take place in the connections between gender, military service, and citizenship.

3 There is another intriguing category of "physical abnormality" that can exempt otherwise healthy males from martial duty: the inability to produce sperm (mujŏngjajŭng). Since this physical "defect" is not externally obvious, this category of men usually performs military service anyway (Kang Sŭng-gu 1997, 14). However, the mere existence of such a category is quite revealing about the centrality of the reproductive heterosexual male body to the construction of military service as men's duty.

4 According to a survey of conscripts' perceptions conducted in 1986, 62 percent of the respondents considered the military service special cases deflating to soldiers' morale. Yet the higher the respondent's level of education, the more this percentage went down. See Hong Doo-seung 1996, 271–72.

5 In its conscription system reform bill, the Ministry of National Defense announced that by 1998, the commuting reservists would be virtually absorbed back into the general supplementary service. See *Munhwa Daily*, May 6, 1998.

6 One of the most controversial examples of the military service special cases was

the practice of granting some graduate students, categorized as "prospective special professional members," a military service term of only six months, as officers, after the completion of graduate school. The discrepancy between this form
of military service and the regular service of two years as a private is significant
enough that it stirred up controversy. Implemented between 1982 and 1990, this
case was popularly known as the system of master officers (*sŏksajangkyoje*). Their
selection was based on their academic record, recommendations from their academic chancellor and dean, an assessment of their potential contribution to their
field, and a state-administered test. Each year, about two thousand graduate students were chosen for this special case (KNA 1981, 116). Many male students attempted to go to graduate school to take advantage of this system, which rendered
admissions to graduate schools highly competitive. Throughout the 1980s, the
master officers system was tainted by the popular suspicion that it was contrived
simply to release the sons of political elites from military service. Indeed, its creation and abolition roughly coincided with the coming-of-age of the sons of the
top political elite (Sŏ Hyo-il 1995, 2:114; Kim Hwan-t'e 1993, 2:83).

7 As a consequence of rapid urbanization and industrialization, rural areas have suffered from depopulation and the feminization of labor. Exemption from military
service is intended to be an incentive for young men to pursue primary industries
in rural areas.

8 The release of such statistics on high government officials was particularly incen-
diary. For example, almost a third of ninety-six high government officials and a
quarter of 290 male legislators had themselves been exempted from regular military service. Similarly, four out of nine presidential candidates for the 1997 election had not completed military service, and only four of fifteen adult sons of
these candidates had completed regular military service (Pak Myŏng-sun 1997,
24). These rates of exemption are far above the national average of approximately
10 percent (KNA 1994, 29).

9 More recently, all of the three candidates for the 2002 mayoral election in Seoul
had been exempted from military service, and 30.4 percent of forty-six candidates
running for mayoral or provincial governor elections in 2002 had received military service exemption (*Hangyŏre Newspaper*, June 13, 2002). According to the
profiles of candidates for 2002 local elections compiled by the Central Council
for Monitoring Elections, the richer a candidate is, the more likely he is to have
gotten a military service exemption (*Hangyŏre Newspaper*, May 30, 2002).

10 I interviewed these researchers in Seoul in December 1998.

11 A foretaste of such an explosion can be observed in the national controversy over
the military service extra-points system caused by the Constitutional Court ruling
(December 23, 1999) against the legal practice of granting extra points to veterans on some public employment tests. A positive unintended consequence of this
controversy was the emergence of public debate about the conscription system,

mostly on the Internet. For the first time since the establishment of male conscription in the heavily militarized nation, young people started to discuss its
utility and relevance in contemporary Korea. Naming themselves as "a gathering of people who refuse the conscription system" (Jinggŏmo, or *jingbyŏngjerŭl
kŏbuhanŭn saramdŭrŭi moim*), this group created a Web site dedicated to discussing the elimination of the conscription system. The Seoul metropolitan police
investigated this group and other similar Web-based groups for their "criminal"
activities (*Hangyŏre 21*, March 27, 2001).

12 Membership in the metalworkers' unions almost doubled during the great workers' struggle, from 135,778 to 260,818, and that of the chemical workers' unions
grew from 154,433 to 218,269. The membership of the automobile workers' unions
showed the third largest growth, from 140,226 to 170,170. However, during this
period, the automobile workers' unions were still dominated by pro-management
leadership (Ch'oi Yŏng-gi et al. 2001, 321). Apart from these single-industry-based
unions, the Yŏnhapnoryŏn, a collection of clerical and service workers' unions,
showed the largest increase in membership during the great workers' struggle,
multiplying from 59,835 to over 320,000. See Kang In-sun 2001, 22.

13 The membership numbers for the two groups of industry-based unions in 1998
and 2000 indicate the total sum of membership in the metalworkers' unions and
in the chemical workers' unions from the two national organizations of labor
unions: the Federation of Korean Trade Unions and the Korean Confederation
of Trade Unions. Since its formation as a national body of democratic unions in
1995, the KCTU has maintained a competitive and collaborative relationship with
the FKTU, which was formerly controlled by the state and management but has
undergone significant change, becoming an autonomous and democratic organization in response to the challenge from the KCTU. See Ch'oi Yŏng-gi et al. 2001,
531–39.

14 This information is based on my conversations with Dr. Chŏng-hŭi Kim and
Dr. Seung Kyung Kim on February 28 and 29, 2004. In response to their anecdotal
discussion of college-educated male activists in the labor movement, I tried to
identify current studies on the subject; however, I was unable to locate any, even
in Korean.

15 I consulted the following sources: KCTU 1999, 2003; Hŏ Yŏng-gu 2003; An 2002;
Labor Human Rights Center 1992; *Workers Culture Correspondence*, March 1990
and July 1990; and *World of Living Together* 1989, 1990. *Workers Culture Correspondence* was the house organ of the Workers' Culture and Art Movements Alliance
(Nodongja munhwayesulyŏnhap), formed in September 1989 to overcome the dichotomy between "people's creative activities in the workplace" and "professional
artists' creative activities" and to unite them as an integral part of "the working-
class movement." See the preface of the March 1990 issue of *Workers Culture Correspondence*. *The World of Living Together* was an irregular periodical established

in August 1989 to promote political awareness among workers by publishing the current state of workers' oppression and its causes; it was published with the hope that it would be used as an elementary resource to educate union members. See the founding statement in the April 1989 issue of *The World of Living Together*.

16 This peculiar usage stems in part from the rise of the "citizens' movement" led largely by middle-class professionals in the 1990s (see chapter 4) and in part from ideological hostility to the term *citizenship* as a bourgeois sham among a radical segment of the labor movement.

17 An exception to this tendency was an assessment of the great workers' struggle by An Sŭng-ch'ŏn, a former worker and vice president of the Socialist Party: "Workers acquired citizenship through the labor union movement" (An 2002, 103).

18 For writings of individual workers describing their experiences in the workplace and their personal life histories, see Yi T'ae-ho 1986a, 1986b; Yi Tal-hyŏk et al. 1985; and Tolbege Editorial Division 1983.

19 Translation mine; the complete script of this play was printed in *Nodongjamunhwa t'ongsin* 2 (July 1990): 146–56.

20 To give a few examples of such battles, as early as December 1988, announcing the Special Measures on Civil Life and Security, Roh Tae Woo's government dispatched a police force of 3,400 to the Angang plant owned by the Poongsan Metal Co. to break the workers' strike. The police rounded up thirty-seven workers and arrested four of them (Ch'oi Yŏng-gi et al. 2001, 343). The authorities also put down a 128-day strike waged by workers of the Hyundai Heavy Industry Co. between December 1988 and April 1989 (246), using a massive military-style operation involving the riot police. In 1988 and 1989, Roh's government arrested 1,093 workers, more than the total number of workers arrested during the Fifth Republic, which had maintained extremely repressive labor control. Most of the 1,093 workers were arrested on charges other than breaking labor laws, because the government attempted to segregate labor activists from labor unions as a tactic to curb the growth of autonomous labor unions (202). The release of the arrested union workers became a major demand of the workers participating in labor disputes. A dramatic example of a violent clash between the state's repressive apparatus and workers over this type of political issue can be observed in the Goliath (referring to a huge crane) struggle launched, again, by workers of the Hyundai Heavy Industry Co. in early 1990. Responding to the severe sentencing imposed on five union leaders who had led the 128-day strike, unionized workers launched a protest strike which resulted in the arrest of six more unionists. In comparison, all the striking union members of the Korea Broadcasting Standard, white-collar workers employed by a public corporation, were released. This differential treatment struck a sensitive chord among manual workers at Hyundai Heavy Industry because manual workers had long been despised, and they had been fighting for

humane treatment by management and destigmatization of their collective identity in society. Interpreting the series of events as a deliberate effort to repress the
union and unionized workers in general, the Hyundai union started yet another
strike. On the fourth day of the strike, alarmed by its ramifications for a nationwide strike planned by the National Council of Labor Unions (Chŏnnohyŏp), the
authorities deployed 18,000 land, sea, and air troops to break the strike. After this
massive military operation, seventy-some unionists climbed up the eighty-two-
meter-high Goliath crane to continue their struggle, but this struggle was also
put to an end with fifteen more arrests (Ch'oi Yŏng-gi et al. 2001, 377–79). The
political nature of the workers' demands, including the release of their arrested
leaders and coworkers, the repeal of their harsh sentences, and the recognition
of democratic labor unions, highlights the workers' determination to alter their
relationship to the state.

21 See the platform of the Workers' Culture and Art Movement Alliance printed in
the founding issue of the *Workers Culture Correspondence* (spring 1990): 191–200.

22 As recently as April 2003, under Roh Moo Hyon's "government of participation,"
most strikes imply illegal actions (Hŏ Yŏng-gu 2003, 73). For instance, public employees cannot strike for wage increases beyond the government's guidelines, and
private employees are responsible for damages and indirect loss of profit caused
by a strike. Although the arrest and expulsion of unionized workers are pervasive, workers' collective demands for their release and reinstitution are considered
illegal (89, 90).

23 In December 1998, the total number of state employees was 888,217 (Presidential
Commission on Women's Affairs 1999, 318).

6. THE TRAJECTORY OF WOMEN'S CITIZENSHIP

1 As of 1999, its membership was 2,475. In 2003 it included eight women workers'
associations.

2 The KWWAC continued the leadership-training education, emphasizing the goal
of democratization. Its 2003 educational manual for women union leaders started
with a section on self-discovery and development, emphasizing democratic quali-
ties and fighting against authoritarian behavior and psychology in the self
(KWWAC 2003a).

3 Realizing the limits of working within labor unions dominated by men, in 1999
women workers established the National Women's Labor Union (NWLU), encom-
passing occupational groups of broadcasters, librarians, nutritionists, and hotel
maids, as well as school custodians (KWWAC 2003a, 27). The absence of factory
workers in manufacturing in the NWLU seems to reflect the shift in the center of
the women's union movement from manufacturing industries to service industries.

4   However, this highest recent rate is still far lower than the 19.3 percent figure in 1975, when the women workers' union movement was most vibrant. Just before the great workers' struggle, the rate dropped to 9.5 percent (KWDI 1999, 260).

5   This assessment is based on my survey of the quarterly from vol. 1 to vol. 17 (fall 1994).

6   In 1989 she won her case after a six-year legal battle. However, her case did not end with this victory. In 1987 the public corporation established different retirement ages for "general positions" (ilbanjik) and "telephone operators" (kyohwanwŏn). Subject to the retirement age of fifty-three years applied to telephone operators, Ms. Kim was forced to retire from her position in 1992. She resumed her legal battle in 1993 but was defeated. Later she appealed to the Central Labor Council and won. In response, the public corporation filed a countersuit with the High Court and was defeated, but then appealed to the Supreme Court, which issued a reversal of the original ruling. In 1997 the Korean Women's Associations Council filed litigation with the Supreme Court, and the case was pending in the court as of 1999 (Pak Suk-ja 2000, 240).

7   Its enactment appeared as a potential women's policy issue in 1985, when the Ministry of Labor announced its plan to remedy employment discrimination against women in hiring, promotion, and retirement. This attention was a response to persistent demands for equal employment voiced by women's associations since the mid-1970s. Soon the Korean Women's Development Institute began to study the equal-employment laws of other countries in preparation for an equal-employment bill. However, Chun Doo Hwan's regime did not allow the result of this study to be made public, supposedly because it was "too early" for Korean society to enforce such a law. In contrast to this dismissal, in December 1986 the ruling Democratic Justice Party (DJP) picked up the issue of equal employment and monopolized the drafting of the bill. The bill was passed by the National Assembly in 1987 and enforced beginning in 1988. See Dong-A Daily (Seoul), January 11, 1989.

8   Women's associations indicated the following problems: (1) it failed to define sex discrimination clearly; (2) it excluded the principle of equal pay for work of equal or comparable value; and (3) it lacked any serious punishment to ensure employers' compliance (Chŏng Kang-ja 1998, 51, 52).

9   The automation of office work in the name of "management rationalization" to compete in the global market aggravated women's equal employment in traditionally feminized clerical positions. In the early 1990s, PFS members, in collaboration with other social movement organizations, fought to prevent passage of the Dispatch Law (p'agyŏnbŏp), which would enable employers to replace permanent workers with temporary or part-time workers (Minuhoe 1997, 31).

10 Founded in 1987 by some two hundred women, the PFS was composed of women political activists, wives of male political activists, and clerical workers involved in

the union movement in the 1980s. By 1997, its membership had grown to around four thousand members (Minuhoe 1997, 13). Initially intending to reach out to a broad spectrum of women, including factory workers, clerical workers, housewives, and younger-generation women, the PFS had to modify this ambitious goal because it could not attract factory workers, who did not have time to pursue voluntary association activities and were afraid of the negative consequences of involvement in the social movement because of the violent punishment of labor activism by the state and employers. In January 1989, after a long internal debate on its organizational identity, the PFS decided to concentrate on white-collar workers—including clerical workers, professionals, and sales workers—and housewives as its membership base (10, 11). Pursuing the ultimate goal of building a democratic society, the PFS worked to create and maintain democratic processes in its members' participation in various small-group activities. Conscious of a popular view that only privileged women participated in the women's movement, PFS members attempted to work with the masses of women in their local communities and to deal with issues relevant to their daily lives (Minuhoe 1997, 25, 28).

11 The discussion of the activities of the equal employment promotion headquarters here is also based on my interview with Ms. Chŏng Kang-ja, corepresentative of Minhuhoe, on October 4, 2004.

12 I have discussed this process in detail in S. Moon 2002a.

13 The difference between public and private corporations results from the fact that the extra-points system required only public corporations to observe it. The difference between larger and smaller private firms stems from the fact that larger firms could afford to offer more benefits to their employees in general and could therefore also afford to offer more benefits tied to military service.

14 The force of economic globalization has yet to undermine conventional practices among many private and public corporations that recognize military service as a form of employment experience to be reflected in pay, promotion, or both. While the specific details have varied from one employer to another and even within a firm over time, there are two common elements shared by private and public corporations. According to a 1994 study of eighty-one private and public corporations of large size (300 employees and more) and of medium or small size (fewer than 300 employees), 90 percent of the large companies offered former conscripts higher pay than did their counterparts. This percentage was lower (64 percent) in medium or small companies. The same study also showed that 54 percent of the large corporations and 46 percent of the medium and small corporations considered military service as work experience, to be taken into consideration in promotion (KIDA 1995a, 35, 36). This practice was less prevalent among the public corporations (35 percent) than among private ones. A 1998 study of personnel management practices among companies of five major economic conglomerates

showed that all of them rewarded military service in the form of higher pay. Two of these five companies incorporated military service into the evaluation of employees for promotion (Kim T'ae-hong 1998, 18).

15 Elsewhere I have discussed the shifting attitude of the state toward the women's policy to promote gender equality in the context of globalization and the political transition to procedural democracy. See S. Moon 2000.

16 The KWAU maintained a slightly more cautious approach to this issue, for strategic reasons. First, understanding the extra-points system merely as the tip of the deeper issue of conscription, it did not want to alienate the masses of lower-class men who perform regular military service disproportionately to their upper-class counterparts. Second, issues regarding conscription were tightly interwoven with the dominant ideologies of national security and anticommunism. The KWAU seems to have learned caution about dealing with sensitive military issues from its own past experience. In fact, the KWAU has long been aware of the centrality to the Korean women's movement of national division and the military confrontation between South and North. It started a peace unification movement and focused on the reduction of defense spending as early as 1990. However, this movement failed to draw popular attention (Yi Hyo-jae 1996, chaps. 6–7; Yi Mi-kyŏng 1998, 27–29).

17 This information is based on my phone inquiry with the office of the KWAC in October 1998.

18 See P'yŏngdŭng 1998; Hangyŏre Newspaper, September 9, 1998; Seoul Newspaper, May 13, 1998; Kang Ki-wŏn 1998; Yi Uk-han 1998.

19 This information is based on a petition prepared by attorneys Kang Ki-wŏn, Yi Sŏk-yŏn, and Ch'oi Ŭn-sun, who were advocates for the six plaintiffs.

20 In 1992, Orient labor union in Sŏngnam established the first child-care center run by a factory labor union (KWWAC 1997, 107).

21 For example, in 1989 the SWWA opened a "healthy children's home," a nonprofit child-care center in the Kuro region in Seoul, to take care of children between the ages of two and five, using volunteer college students (KWWAC 1997, 96).

CONCLUSION

1 In 1890 the Meiji state passed a law banning women's participation in political activities (Sievers 1983, 53).

2 In multiethnic and multiracial societies, race and ethnicity will generate hierarchy in access to, and practices of, citizenship. As recent studies of sexuality in Western democratic societies suggest, sexuality has also been a social structure of inequality that affects the access to, and practices of, citizenship. See Bell and Binnie 2000.

3 The state's ongoing involvement in gender politics does not imply its fixed na-

ture as a patriarchal institution. V. Spike Peterson (1996) argues that the nation-state is "masculinist" in how it constitutes the identities of workers and citizens. "The nation-state tends to construct workers as wage-earning and/or property-owning family providers and citizens as rational and autonomous individuals, engaging in the public/political sphere and protecting their women and their nation" (9).

REFERENCES

Abelmann, Nancy. 1996. *Echoes of the Past, Epics of Dissent: A South Korean Social Movement*. Berkeley: University of California Press.

Afshar, Haleh. 1985. *Women, Work, and Ideology in the Third World*. New York: Tavistock.

Althusser, Louis. 1971. *Lenin and Philosophy, and Other Essays*. New York: Monthly Review Press.

Alvarez, Sonia. 1990. *Engendering Democracy in Brazil: Women's Movement in Transition Politics*. Princeton: Princeton University Press.

Amin, Samir. 1989. *Eurocentrism*. New York: Monthly Review Press.

Amsden, Alice. 1989. *Asia's Next Giant: South Korea and Late Industrialization*. New York: Oxford University Press.

An Sŭng-ch'ŏn. 2002. *Han'guk nodongjaundong, t'ujaengŭi kirok: Chŏn T'ae-ilesŏ minjunoch'ong'kkaji* [Korean workers' movement, record of struggle: From Chŏn T'ae-il to the Korean Confederation of Trade Unions]. Seoul: Pakchongch'ŏl.

Anderson, Benedict. 1991. *Imagined Communities: Reflections on the Origin and Spread of Nationalism*. Rev. ed. New York: Verso.

Bae, Kyuhan. 1987. *Industrialization and Korean Blue-Collar Workers*. Seoul: Seoul National University Press.

Barber, Benjamin R. 2001. *Jihad vs. McWorld*. New York: Ballantine Books.

Bell, David, and Jon Binnie. 2000. *The Sexual Citizen: Queer Politics and Beyond*. Cambridge, U.K.: Polity Press.

Bello, Walden, and Stephanie Rosenfeld. 1990. *Dragons in Distress: Asia's Miracle Economies in Crisis*. Harmondsworth: Penguin.

Bendix, Reinhard. 1977. *Nation Building and Citizenship: Studies of Our Changing Social Order*. Berkeley: University of California Press.

Beneria, Lourdes, and Martha Roldan. 1987. *The Crossroads of Class and Gender: Industrial Homework, Subcontracting, and Household Dynamics in Mexico City*. Chicago: University of Chicago Press.

Berger, Peter, and Hsin-huang Hsiao. 1988. *In Search of an East Asian Development Model*. New Brunswick: Transaction Books.

Brinton, Mary. 1993. *Women and the Economic Miracle: Gender and Work in Postwar Japan*. Berkeley: University of California Press.

———. 2001. *Women's Working Lives in East Asia*. Stanford: Stanford University Press.

Brubaker, Rogers. 1992. *Citizenship and Nationhood in France and Germany*. Cambridge: Harvard University Press.

Bureau of Labor. 1971. *Nodongbaeksŏ* [White paper on labor]. Seoul: Bureau of Labor, Republic of Korea.

———. 1972. *Kŭlloyŏsŏngŭi hyŏnhwang* [The current state of working women]. Seoul: Bureau of Labor, Republic of Korea.

Burstyn, Varda. 1985. Masculine Dominance and the State. In *Women, Class, Family and the State*, ed. Varda Burstyn and Dorothy Smith. Toronto, Ontario: Garamond Press.

Catholic Human Rights Council. 2001. *Sabŏbsarin: 1975nyŏn 4wŏrŭi haksal* [Legal murder: the killing of April 1975]. Seoul: Hangminsa.

Center for Journalism Culture. 1994. *94nyŏn pŏmkungmin anboŭisik chosa* [1994 national survey of security perception]. Seoul: Sŏgang University.

Center for Security Problems. 1989. *Pŏmgungmin anboŭisikchosa* [A national survey of security perception]. Seoul.

———. 1990. *Pŏmgungmin anboŭisikchosa* [A national survey of security perception]. Seoul.

———. 1991. *Pŏmgungmin anboŭisikchosa* [A national survey of security perception]. Seoul.

———. 1992. *Pŏmgungmin anboŭisikchosa* [A national survey of security perception]. Seoul.

———. 1993. *Pŏmgungmin anboŭisikchosa mit chŏngch'aekdaean yŏn'gu* [A study of a national survey of security perception and policy measures]. Seoul.

Ch'a Chae-ik. 1989. *Chogugŭl wihayŏ* [For the ancestor land]. Seoul: Koryŏwŏn.

Chakravarty, Sukhamoy. 1988. Development Strategies in the Asian Countries. In *Development Policies and the Crisis of the 1980s*, ed. Louis Emmerij. Paris: Development Center of the OECD.

Chang Chi-yŏn. 1990. Han'guksahoe chigŏbŭi sŏngbyŏl punjŏlhwawa kyŏngjejŏk pulp'yŏngdŭng: Sŏngbyŏl imgŭm kyŏkch'a punsŏgŭl chungsimŭro [Occupational segregation by gender and economic inequalities in South Korea: An analysis of wage differences by gender]. In *Han'guksahoeŭi yŏsŏngkwa kajok* [Women and the family in Korean society], ed. Han'guksahoesayŏn'guhoe (Korean Society Studies Association). Seoul: Munhakkwajisŏngsa.

Chang Ha-jin. 1991. Han'guksahoegujowa yŏsŏngmunje [The structure of Korean society and women's issues]. In *Yŏsŏnghakkang'ŭi* [Women's studies lectures], ed. Han'gungyŏsŏngyŏn'guhoe (Korean Women's Studies Association). Seoul: Tongnyŏk.

Chang Min-sŏ, and Yi Yeha. 1998. *Kundae chedaero algogagi* [Going to the military after learning about it]. Seoul: Chŏngbonara.

Chatterjee, Partha. 1993. *The Nation and Its Fragments: Colonial and Postcolonial Histories*. Princeton, N.J.: Princeton University Press.

Chin Chae-mun. 1999. Kungminŭi chŏngbu koyongbohŏm ilnyŏnŭi py'ŏnggawa kwaje [The people's government's employment insurance policy: Its evaluation and related issues after its first year]. *Wŏlganbokchidonghyang* [Monthly welfare trend] 6 (March): 15–18.

Cho Hŭi-yŏn. 1995. Minjungundongkwa "siminsahoe," "siminundong" [The people's movement, "civil society," and the "citizens' movement"]. In *Siminsahoewa siminundong* [Civil society and the citizens' movement], ed. Yu P'al-mu and Kim Ho-gi. Seoul: Han'ul.

Cho, Hwa Soon. 1988. *Let the Weak Be Strong: A Woman's Struggle for Justice*. Bloomington, Ind.: Meyerstone Books.

Cho Pong-jin, and Hong Sŏng-t'ae, eds. 1995. *Hoesagamyŏn chungnŭnda: Kyŏngjejuŭi damnonŭi pip'anŭlwihan pildstŏdi* [If you work in a company, you will be dead: A field study to criticize the discourse of economism]. Seoul: Hyŏnsilmunwhayŏn'gu.

Cho Pyŏng-t'ae. 1975. Han'guk yŏjanomukwallie kwanhan yŏn'gu [A study of the management of women workers in South Korea]. M.A. thesis, Dong-A University.

Cho Se-hŭi. 1978. *Nanjangiga ssoaolin chagŭn'gong* [A small ball shot upward by a dwarf]. Seoul: Munhakkwajisŏngsa.

Cho Sŏng-lyul. 1996. Chaehaksaeng ibyŏng (sojip) yŏn'gijedoŭi pyŏnch'ŏn kwajŏng [A process of change in the students' enlistment postponement system]. *Pyŏngmu* [Military duty] 32 (winter): 84–87.

Cho Sŏng-suk. 1997. Kundaemunhwawa namsŏng [Military culture and men]. In *Namsŏngkwa han'guksahoe* [Men and Korean society], ed. Yŏsŏnghan'guksahoeyŏn'guhoe [Korean Women's Society Studies Association]. Seoul: Sahoemunhwayŏn'guso.

Cho Tae-yŏp. 2000. *Han'gugŭi siminundong: Chŏhangkwa ch'amyŏŭi tonghak* [Social movements in Korea: The politics of protest and participation]. Seoul: Na'nam.

Cho Uhn. 1983. Sanŏphwawa singabujangje [Industrialization and neo-patriarchy]. In *Han'guksahoe ŏdiro kagoinna* [Where is Korean society headed?], ed. Korean Sociological Association. Seoul: Hyŏndaesahoeyŏn'guso (Contemporary Society Studies Center).

Cho Yŏng-min. 2001. Chŏnhyangjedowa kamogŭi yaman [The conversion system and savagery of the prison]. In *20segi han'gugŭi yaman* [Savagery in twentieth-century Korea], ed. Yi Pyŏng-ch'ŏn and Yi Kwang-il. Seoul: Ilbit.

Choi, Chungmoo. 1995. The Minjung Culture Movement and the Construction of Popular Culture in Korea. In *South Korea's Minjung Movement: The Culture and Politics of Dissidence*, ed. Kenneth M. Wells. Hǫnolulu: University of Hawaii Press.

Choi, Jae-Hyeon. 1986. Strategic Groups of Nationalism in Nineteenth-Century Korea. *Journal of Contemporary Asia* 16 (2): 223–36.

Ch'oi Jang-jip, and Ko Sŏng-guk. 1989. Hyŏndan'gye han'guksahoeŭi chibaegujowa minjokminju undong [The current stage of the structure of ruling and the nationalist democracy movement in South Korea]. In *1980nyŏndae han'guksahoewa chibaegujo* [The structure of ruling in 1980s Korean society], ed. Haksuldanch'ehyŏbŭihoe. Seoul: P'ulbit.

Ch'oi Kwang-p'yo. 1997. Nambukhan pyŏngmuinsajedowa t'ongilhan'gukkun [Military service personnel systems in South and North Korea and the unified Korean military]. *Han'gukkunsa* [South Korean military affairs] 5 (7): 91–110.

Ch'oi Kyun. 1998. Sahoebokji chŏngch'aek [Social welfare policy]. In *Kim Young Sam chŏngbuŭi kukchŏng p'yŏnggamit ch'agijŏngbuŭi chŏngch'aekkwaje* [The evaluation of Kim Young Sam's government policy and the next government's policy issues], ed. Narajŏngch'aek'yŏn'guhoe (National Policy Studies Association). Seoul: Hyŏndaejŏngbo'munhwasa.

Ch'oi Pyŏng-du. 1991. Pyŏngyŏkpongmuga kukgasanŏppaljŏne mich'inŭn yŏnghyang [The effect of military service on national industrial development]. *Pyŏngmu* 18:46–48.

Ch'oi Yŏng-gi, et al. 2001. *1987nyŏn ihuŭi han'gugŭi nodongundong* [The labor movement in Korea after 1987]. Seoul: Han'guknodongyŏn'guwŏn (Korean Labor Studies Center).

Chŏn T'ae-il. 1988. *Naŭi chukŭmŭl hŏttoei malla* [Don't waste my death: A collection of Chŏn's writings]. Seoul: Tolbege.

Chŏng Hwan-sik. 1995. Pyŏngnyŏkdongwŏn hullyŏnsojipjedo pyŏnch'ŏnmit ch'ujinbanghyang [The direction of change in the military manpower mobilization enlistment system]. *Pyŏngmu* 31 (fall): 26–29.

Chŏng Hye-sŏn, Kim Kyŏng-hŭi, Ch'a In-sun, and Nam Yun-ju. 1989. Han'guk yŏsŏng nodongjaŭi ch'abyŏljŏk chŏimgŭm silt'aewa kŭkbokpang'an [Korean women workers' discriminatory low pay and its solution]. In *Yŏsŏng 3* [Women 3], ed. Yŏsŏngyŏn'guhoe (Women's Studies Association). Seoul: Ch'angjakkwabip'yŏngsa.

Chŏng Kang-ja. 1998. Samujik yŏsŏngnodongja undong [Clerical women workers' movement]. In *Yŏlin hŭimang: Han'guk yŏsŏngdanch'eyŏnhap simnyŏnsa* [Open hope: A ten-year history of the Korean Women's Associations United], ed. Han'guk yŏsŏngdanch'eyŏnhap. Seoul: Dongdŏk Women's University, Korean Women's Studies Center.

Chŏng Kyŏng-hyŏn. 1990a. Urinaraŭi pyŏngyŏkjedo ŏttŏke paljŏndoiŏ wanna? Koryŏ hugi p'yŏn [How did our nation's military service system come to develop? The late Koryŏ period]. *Pyŏngmu* 16 (November): 11–15.

———. 1990b. Urinaraŭi pyŏngyŏkjedo ŏttŏke paljŏndoiŏ wanna? Koryŏ jŏngi p'yŏn [How did our nation's military service system come to develop? The early Koryŏ period]. *Pyŏngmu* 15 (September): 42–47.

———. 1990c. Urinaraŭi pyŏngyŏkjedo ŏttŏke paljŏndoiŏ wanna? Kodae p'yŏn [How did our nation's military service system come to develop? The ancient period]. *Pyŏngmu* 14 (May): 14–19.

──────. 1991a. Chosŏnsidaeŭi pyŏngyŏkjedo: Chosŏnhugi p'yŏn [The military service system in the Chosŏn dynasty: The late Chosŏn period]. *Pyŏngmu* 19:13–18.

──────. 1991b. Chosŏnsidaeŭi pyŏngyŏkjedo: Chosŏnjŏngi p'yŏn [The military service system in the Chosŏn dynasty: The early Chosŏn period]. *Pyŏngmu* 18 (April): 8–13.

──────. 1992. Kaehanghuŭi kunsawa pyŏngyŏkjedo [The military and the military service system after the opening]. *Pyŏngmu* 21 (January): 27–31.

Chŏng Su-bok. 1994. *Ŭimisegyewa sahoeundong* [The world of meanings and social movements]. Seoul: Minyŏngsa.

Chŏng-Pak Mi-kyŏng. 2003. Yŏgun, chuingonginga, chubyŏnininga [Women soldiers, are they protagonists or extras?]. *Feminist Journal If* (spring): 94–99.

Chow, Esther Ngan-ling, ed. 2002. *Transforming Gender and Development in East Asia*. New York: Routledge.

Chung Hyun-baek. 1985. Yŏsŏng nodongjaŭi ŭisikkwa nodong sekye: Nodongja sugi punsŏgŭl chungsimŭro [Women workers' consciousness and their world of labor: Focusing on their essays]. *Yŏsŏng* [Women] 1:116–62.

Citizens' Coalition for Economic Justice (CCEJ) (Kyŏngsilyŏn). http://www.ccej.or.kr.

Connell, Robert. 1995. *Masculinities*. Berkeley: University of California Press.

Cumings, Bruce. 1981. *The Origins of the Korean War: Liberation and the Emergence of Separate Regimes, 1945–1947*. Princeton: Princeton University Press.

──────. 1984. The Legacy of Japanese Colonialism in Korea. In *The Japanese Colonial Empire, 1895–1945*, ed. Ramon H. Myers and Mark R. Peattie. Princeton: Princeton University Press.

──────. 1990. *The Roaring of the Cataract, 1947–1950*. Vol. 2 of *The Origins of the Korean War*. Princeton: Princeton University Press.

──────. 1997. *Korea's Place in the Sun: A Modern History*. New York: W. W. Norton.

Daily Economy Newspaper Co. 1977. *The Road to National Survival: Korean President Park Chung Hee's Leadership Philosophy and Action Programs*. Seoul.

Deyo, Frederic. 1987. *The Political Economy of the New Asian Industrialism*. Ithaca, N.Y.: Cornell University Press.

Diamond, Larry, and Byung-Kook Kim. 2000. *Consolidating Democracy in South Korea*. Boulder, Colo.: Lynn Rienner.

Dietz, Mary. 1996. *Turning Operations: Feminism, Arendt, Politics*. London: Routledge.

Dolan, Maureen. 1993. *Gender, Militarism and the State in Nicaragua: The Emergence of Feminism in a Political Culture of Violence*. Ph.D. diss., University of Wisconsin, Madison.

Dore, Ronald P. 1987. *Taking Japan Seriously: A Confucian Perspective on Leading Economic Issues*. Stanford: Stanford University Press.

Duncan, John. 2002. The Problematic Modernity of Confucianism: The Question of "Civil Society" in Chosŏn Dynasty Korea. In *Korean Society: Civil Society, Democracy, and the State*, ed. Charles K. Armstrong. New York: Routledge.

Eckert, Carter. 2000. Korea's Transition to Modernity: A Will to Greatness. In *His-*

torical Perspectives on Contemporary East Asia, ed. Merle Goldman and Andrew Gordon. Cambridge: Harvard University Press.

Eckert, Carter, et al. 1990. *Korea Old and New: A History.* Cambridge: Harvard University Press.

Economic Planning Board. 1960. *Census Report of Population and Housing.* Seoul.

————. 1970. *Census Report of Population and Housing.* Seoul.

————. 1980. *Census Report of Population and Housing.* Seoul.

————. 1991. *Annals of the Economically Active Population.* Seoul.

Edgerton, Robert. 1997. *Warriors of the Rising Sun: A History of the Japanese Military.* New York: Norton.

Editorial Board. 1994. Yulgolsaŏbiran muŏsinga? [What is yulgolsaŏp?]. *Kunsajŏnŏl* [Military journal] 18 (August): 102–7.

Elias, Norbert. 1939/1997. *The Civilizing Process: The History of Manners and State Formation and Civilization.* Trans. Edmund Jephcott. Oxford: Blackwell.

Elson, Dianne, and Ruth Pearson. 1981. *The Latest Phase of the Internationalization of Capital and Its Implications for Women in the Third World.* Brighton: Institute of Development Studies at the University of Sussex.

Enloe, Cynthia. 1980. *Ethnic Soldiers: State Security in Divided Societies.* London: Penguin.

————. 2000. *Maneuvers: The International Politics of Militarizing Women's Lives.* Berkeley: University of California Press.

Escobar, Arturo. 1995. *Encountering Development: The Making and Unmaking of the Third World.* Princeton: Princeton University Press.

Feinman, Ilene Rose. 2000. *Citizenship Rites: Feminist Soldiers and Feminist Antimilitarists.* New York: New York University Press.

Flax, Jane. 1990. *Thinking Fragments: Psychoanalysis, Feminism, and Postmodernism in the Contemporary West.* Berkeley: University of California Press.

Foley, James A. 2003. *Korea's Divided Families: Fifty Years of Separation.* New York: Routlege Curzon.

Foreit, K. G., K. S. Koh, and M. H. Suh. 1980. Impact of the National Family Planning Program on Fertility in Rural Korea: A Multivariate Areal Analysis. *Studies in Family Planning* 11 (March): 79–90.

Foucault, Michel. 1979. *Discipline and Punish: The Birth of the Prison.* New York: Pantheon Books.

————. 1984. What Is Enlightenment? In *The Foucault Reader,* ed. Paul Rabinow. New York: Pantheon Books.

Frank, Andre Gunder. 1998. *ReOrient: Global Economy in the Asian Age.* Berkeley: University of California Press.

Giddens, Anthony. 1987. *The Nation-State and Violence.* Berkeley and Los Angeles: University of California Press.

Gills, Barry K. 1996. *Korea versus Korea: A Case of Contested Legitimacy.* New York: Routledge.

Gramsci, Antonio. 1971. *Selections from the Prison Notebooks*. Ed. and trans. Quintin Hoare and Geoffrey Nowell-Smith. New York: International Publishers.

Haggard, Stephen. 1990. *Pathways from the Periphery: The Politics of Growth in the Newly Industrializing Countries*. Ithaca: Cornell University Press.

Ham In-hŭi, et al. 2001. *Chungsanch'ŭngŭi chŏngch'esŏngkwa sobimunhwa* [Middle-class identity and consumer culture]. Asan Foundation Research Monograph Series, no. 80. Seoul: Chimmundang.

Hamm, Taik-young. 1999. *Arming the Two Koreas: State, Capital, and Military Power*. New York: Routledge.

Han Sang-jin. 1998. Kwangju minjuhwaundongesŏ pon kungminjukwŏnkwa sŭngint'ujaeng [A struggle for people's sovereignty and approval from the standpoint of the Kwangju democracy movement]. In *Segyehwasidaeŭi inkwŏnkwa sahoeundong: 5.18 Kwangjuminjuhwaundongŭi chaejomyŏng* [Human rights and social movements in the age of globalization: Rethinking the May 18 democracy movement in Kwangju], ed. Korean Sociological Association. Seoul: Na'nam.

Han Sang-t'ae. 1995. Hyŏnyŏkbyŏng ibyŏngjedoŭi pyŏnch'ŏn [The change in the institution of conscripts' enlistment]. *Pyŏngmu* 31 (fall): 20–22.

Han Sŭng-hŏn. 1997. *Puraenghan chogugŭi imsangnotŭ: Chŏngch'ijaep'anŭi hyŏnjang* [The unfortunate nation's clinical notes: Scenes from political trials]. Seoul: Iryosinmunsa.

Han, Sungjoo. 1978. South Korea's Participation in the Vietnam Conflict: An Analysis of the U.S.-Korean Alliance. *Orbis* 21:893–912.

Han'guk'kyoyungmunjeyŏn'guhoe [Korean Educational Issues Research Association]. 1989. Che 6 konghwagugŭi kyoyuge taehan chibaejŏngch'aek [The Sixth Republic's ruling policy on education]. In *1980nyŏndae han'guksahoewa chibaegujo* [The structure of ruling in Korean society in the 1980s]. Seoul: P'ulbit.

Hart-Landsberg, Martin. 1993. *The Rush to Development: Economic Change and Political Struggle in South Korea*. New York: Monthly Review Press.

———. 1998. *Korea: Division, Reunification, and U. S. Foreign Policy*. New York: Monthly Review Press.

Hegel, G. W. F. 1807/1967. *The Phenomenology of Mind*. Trans. J. B. Baillie. New York: Harper and Row.

Herbert, Melissa. 1998. *Camouflage Isn't Only for Combat: Gender, Sexuality, and Women in the Military*. New York: New York University Press.

Hilsdon, Anne-Marie. 1995. *Madonnas and Martyrs: Militarism and Violence in the Philippines*. St. Leonards, Australia: Allen and Unwin.

Hŏ Sang-gu. 1990. Pyŏngyŏkt'ŭngnyebŏp sihaengnyŏng ŏttŏke kaejŏngdoeŏnna? [How did the enforcement ordinance of the military service special cases law change?] *Pyŏngmu* 15:60–63.

Hŏ Yŏng-gu. 2003. *Kŭrae, wurin nodongjayo* [Yes, we are workers]. Seoul: Siminbangsong.

Hobsbawm, Eric, and Terence Ranger, eds. 1983. *The Invention of Tradition*. Cambridge: Cambridge University Press.

Hong Doo-Seung. 1996. *Han'gukkundaeŭi sahoehak* [Sociology of the Korean military]. Expanded ed. Seoul: Na'nam.

————. 1999. Profile of the Korean Middle Class. In *East Asian Middle Classes in Comparative Perspective*, ed. H. Michael Hsiao. Taipei: Institute of Ethnology, Academia Sinica.

Hong Tŏng-yul. 1999. Kim Dae Jung chŏngbuŭi kaehyŏk ilnyŏnŭl p'yŏnggahanda [We evaluate the first-year restructuring of Kim Dae Jung's government]. *Tonghyangkwajŏnmang* [Trend and prospect] 40 (January): 131–48.

Hong Yŏng-ju. 1984. Tagukjŏk kiŏpŭi yŏsŏngnodonge kwanhan ilgoch'al: Chŏnjaŏpkye saryerŭl chungsimŭro [A study of women workers in the multinational corporations: A focus on the electronics industry]. M.A. thesis, Ehwa Women's University, Seoul.

Hong Yong-p'yo. 1997. Kukkaanbowa chŏnggwŏnanbo: Yisŭngman daet'ongnyŏngŭi anbochŏngch'aekŭl chungsimŭro, 1953–1960 [State security and regime security: A focus on the President Rhee Syngman's security policy, 1953–1960]. *Kukchejŏngch'i'nonch'ong* [International relations studies] 36 (3): 237–62.

Horton, Susan, ed. 1996. *Women and Industrialization in Asia*. New York: Routledge.

Hsiung, Ping-Chun. 1996. *Living Rooms as Factories: Class, Gender, and the Satellite Factory System in Taiwan*. Philadelphia: Temple University Press.

Hwang Sŏk-yŏng. 1974. *Kaekchi* [A foreign place]. Seoul: Ch'angjakkwabip'yŏngsa.

Ilnari, Virgilio. 1994. Penelope's Web: Female Military Service in Italy; Debates and Draft Proposals, 1945–92. In *Women Soldiers: Images and Realities*, ed. Elisabetta Addis, Valeria E. Russo, and Lorenza Sebesta. New York: St. Martin's Press.

Isacsson, Eva, ed. 1988. *Women and the Military System*. Proceedings of a symposium arranged by the International Peace Bureau and Peace Union of Finland. London: Harvester Wheatsheaf.

Janelli, Roger. 1993. *Making Capitalism: The Social and Cultural Construction of a South Korean Conglomerate*. Stanford: Stanford University Press.

Janoski, Thomas. 1998. *Citizenship and Civil Society: A Framework of Rights and Obligations in Liberal, Traditional, and Social Democratic Regimes*. New York: Cambridge University Press.

Janowitz, Morris. 1964. *The Military in the Political Development of New Nations: An Essay in Comparative Analysis*. Chicago: University of Chicago Press.

Jaquette, Jane. 1994. *The Women's Movement in Latin America: Participation and Democracy*. Boulder: Westview Press.

Jayawardena, Kumari. 1986. *Feminism and Nationalism in the Third World*. Totowa, N.J.: Zed Books.

Johnson, John. 1962. *The Role of the Military in Underdeveloped Countries*. Princeton, N.J.: Princeton University Press.

————. 1964. *The Military and Society in Latin America*. Stanford: Stanford University Press.

Kang Chun-man. 1998. *Kamelleonkwa haiena: Han'guk ŏllon 115 nyŏnsa, 1883–1998* [Chameleon and hyena: A history of 115 years of Korean mass media]. Seoul: Inmulkwasasangsa.

————. 2002. *Han'guk hyŏndaesa sanch'aek: 1970nyŏndaep'yŏn* [Strolling through contemporary Korean history: The 1970s]. 3 vols. Seoul: Inmulkwasasangsa.

Kang In-sun. 2001. *Hangukyŏsŏngnodongja undongsa 2* [A history of the Korean women workers' movement]. Vol. 2. Seoul: Han'ul.

Kang I-su, and Pak Ki-nam. 1991. Yŏsŏngkwa nodong [Women and labor]. In *Yŏsŏnghak kang'ŭi: Han'guk yŏsŏng hyŏnsilŭi ihae* [Women's studies lectures: Understanding Korean women's reality], ed. Han'gukyŏsŏngyŏn'guhoe (Korean Women's Studies Association). Seoul: Tongnyŏk.

Kang Ki-wŏn. 1998. Kun'gyŏngyŏk samjung hyet'aek muŏsi munjeinga? [What is the problem with the triple benefits of military service?]. An emergency discussion in Seoul organized by the Korean Women's Associations Council, the Korean Women's Associations United, the Citizens' Coalition for Economic Justice, and the People's Solidarity for Participatory Democracy, September 16, 1998.

Kang Kyŏng-hwan. 1996. Pyŏngyŏkpŏmnyŏngŭi chejŏngkwa chuyo gaejŏngnaeyong [The establishment of conscription law and its revisions]. *Pyŏngmu* 32 (winter): 68–70.

Kang Man-gil. 1985. Tongdosŏgironŭi chaeŭmmi [Rethinking the theory of Eastern morality and Western technology]. In *Han'guk minjokundongsaron* [A history of the Korean people's movement], by Kang Man-gil. Seoul: Han'gilsa.

Kang Sŭng-gu. 1997. Kundaeangagi p'inanŭn 'ch'ejungkwaŭi chŏnjaeng' [Not going to the military: A bloody war against body weight]. *Nyusŭp'ŭlŏsŭ* [News plus], 14 August, 14.

Karner, Tracy Xavia. 1998. Engendering Violent Men: Oral Histories of Military Masculinity. In *Masculinities and Violence*, ed. Lee H. Bowker. Thousand Oaks, Calif.: Sage Publications.

Kasza, Gregory. 1995. *Conscription Society: Administered Mass Organizations*. New Haven: Yale University Press.

KCTU. *See* Korean Confederation of Trade Unions.

Kearney, Robert. 1991. *The Warrior Worker: The Challenge of the Korean Way of Working*. New York: Henry Holt.

Ki Yong-ju. 1995. Pyŏngmuhaengjŏng swoesin ŏdikkaji wannŭnga? [How far has the military service administration reform come?]. *Pyŏngmu* 31 (fall): 30–33.

KIDA. *See* Korean Institute for Defense Analysis.

Kil, Sung-hum, and Chung-In Moon. 2001. *Understanding Korean Politics: An Introduction*. Albany: State University of New York Press.

Kim Chae-il. 1996. Hyangt'oyebigun ŏpmu pyŏnch'ŏn [The change in the homeland reserve force's task]. *Pyŏngmu* 32 (winter): 80–83.

Kim Cha-ju. 1994. Chŏngbuŭi taebukkang'onch'aek ınyŏnŭl kŏttoratta [The government's hard-line and soft-line northern policy wandered for a year]. *Sindonga* [New East Asia] (May): 208–23.

Kim Chang-ho. 1986. Urinara yŏsŏng nodongnyŏgŭi sugŭpkujo pyŏnhwawa kihon yŏsŏngŭi nodongch'amga [The change in the supply of female labor and married women's participation in the labor market]. *Aseayŏsŏngyŏn'gu* [Asia women's studies] 26:133–59.

Kim Chin-dae. 1996. Tokcha poch'ungyŏk chedoŭi pyŏnch'ŏn [The change in the assignment of only sons to the supplementary service]. *Pyŏngmu* 32 (winter): 74–76.

Kim Chin-gyun. 1996. 1990nyŏndae han'guk kunsusanŏbŭi tonghyangkwa "kyŏngjeŭi kunsahwa munje" [A trend in Korean military industry in the 1990s and "the problem of militarization of the economy"]. In *Kunsinkwa hyŏndaesahoe* [Mars and contemporary society], ed. Kim Chin-gyun and Hong Sŏng-t'ae. Seoul: Munhwa'kwahaksa.

Kim Chin-kyun, and Hong Sŭnghŭi. 1991. Han'guksahoeŭi kyoyukkwa chibaeideologi [Education and ruling ideologies in Korean society]. In *Han'guksahoe'wa chibae ideologi* [Korean society and ruling ideologies], ed. Han'guksanŏpsahoe yŏn'guhoe (Korean Industrial Society Studies Association). Seoul: Nokdu.

Kim Chong-il. 1995. Nugurŭl wihan kyŏngyŏnghyŏksininga? [For whom is management innovation?]. In *Hoesagamyŏn chungnŭnda* [If you work in a company, you will be dead], ed. Cho Pong-jin and Hong Sŏng-ta'e. Seoul: Hyŏnsilmunhwayŏn'gu.

Kim Chong-sŏng. 1997. Chedae'kunin kwallyŏn ippŏp silt'aewa panghyang" [Legislation of veterans-related acts: Its actual conditions and directions]. *Han'gukkunsa* [Korean military affairs] 5 (July): 164–72.

Kim, Choong Soon. 1992. *The Culture of Korean Industry: An Ethnography of Poongsan Corporation*. Tucson: University of Arizona Press.

Kim Ch'ung-sik. 1992. *Chŏngch'igongjaksaryŏngbu namsanŭi pujangdŭl* [Chiefs of the south mountain, political machination headquarters]. Seoul: Dong-a'ilbosa.

Kim Chu-suk. 1990. Nong'ŏpsaengsan kujoŭi pyŏnhwawa kajok. [The change in the structure of agricultural production and the family]. In *Han'gukkajongnon* [Studies of Korean families], ed. Yŏsŏnghan'guksahoeyŏn'guhoe (Women's Korean Society Studies Association), Seoul.

Kim, Elaine H. 1997. Men's Talk: A Korean American View of South Korean Constructions of Women, Gender, and Masculinity. In *Dangerous Women: Gender and Korean Nationalism*, ed. Elaine H. Kim and Chungmoo Choi. New York: Routledge.

Kim, Eun Mee. 1997. *Big Business, Strong State: Collusion and Conflict in South Korean Development, 1960–1990*. Albany: State University of New York Press.

Kim Eun-sil. 2001. *Yŏsŏngŭi mom, momŭi munhwajŏngch'ihak* [Woman's body, the cultural politics of the body]. Seoul: Ttohanaŭi munhwa.

Kim Ho-jin. 1999. Kim Dae Jung chŏngbuŭi kukkagaehyŏk: T'ŭksŏngkwa kanŭng-sŏng [The Kim Dae Jung government's state restructuring: Its characteristics and possibilities]. *Chŏngbuhakyŏn'gu* [Government studies] 5 (2): 157–76.

Kim Hwan-t'ae. 1993. *Yukdup'um soryŏngŭi kundaeiyagi, sang; ha* [A sixth dup'um major's military story]. 2 vols. Seoul: Chaenggi.

Kim Hyo-jae. 1993. Kun sangch'ŭngbuŭi choegŭn tonghyang [A recent trend in the top echelon of the military]. *Wŏlganjosŏn* 157 (April): 228–41.

Kim Hyŏn-a. 2001. Han'gukkunŭi betŭnam ch'amjŏnkwa minganin haksal [Korea's military participation in the Vietnam War and the massacre of civilians]. In *20segi han'kugŭi yaman* [Savagery in twentieth-century Korea], ed. Yi Pyŏng-hŏn and Yi Kwang-il. Seoul: Ilbit.

Kim In-ok. 1990. T'ujaengsogesŏ t'aeŏnan munhwa, t'ujaengŭro kŏnsŏldoel munhwa: Ulsan Ulju nodongja p'ungmulp'ae yŏnhapgongyŏnŭl tanyŏwasŏ [Culture born in the midst of struggle, culture to be built by struggle: Visiting the allied perfor-mance of Ulsan and Ulju workers' *p'ungmul* groups]. *Nodongja munhwa t'ongsin* [Workers Culture Correspondence] 1 (March): 138–43.

Kim Ki-jung. 2000. Chŏnch'ejuŭijŏk pŏpchilsŏŭi t'odae, chumindŭngnokche [A foundation of the totalitarian legal order, the resident registration system]. In *Urianŭi p'asijŭm* [Fascism inside us], ed. Im Chi-hyŏn et al. Seoul: Samin.

Kim Kyu-ch'ang. 1985. Yŏsŏng nodongjaŭi ch'uiŏpsilt'ae mit koyonggwalli kaesŏn pangan [A proposal for the improvement of women workers' employment and their management]. *Aseayŏsŏngyŏn'gu* 14:359–76.

Kim Mi-suk. 1990. Chungsodosi pinmingajogŭi sahoegyŏngjejŏk sŏnggyŏk [Socio-economic characteristics of poor families in medium and small cities]. In *Han'guk kajongnon* [A study of Korean families].

Kim Nam-guk. 1995. *Kungminŭi kundae, kŭdŭrŭi kundae* [People's army, their army]. Seoul: P'ulbit.

Kim Ok-yŏl, and Kim T'ae-hŭi. 1973. Kullo yŏsŏngŭi silt'ae punsŏke kwanhan yŏn'gu [An analysis of the working conditions of women workers]. *Aseayŏsŏngyŏn'gu* 12:1–44.

Kim Sam-sŏk. 2001. *Pangapta, kundaeya* [Glad to meet you, the military]. Seoul: Salimtŏ.

Kim, Se Jin. 1971. *The Politics of Military Revolution in Korea.* Chapel Hill: University of North Carolina Press.

Kim, Seung-Kyung. 1997. *Class Struggle or Family Struggle: The Lives of Women Fac-tory Workers in South Korea.* Cambridge: Cambridge University Press.

Kim Sŏng-guk. 1998. Kukka'e taehanghanŭn siminsahoe [Civil society resisting the state]. In *Segyehwasidaeŭi inkwŏnkwa sahoeundong: 5.18 Kwangju minjuhwaun-dongŭi chaejomyŏng* [Human rights and social movements in the period of global-ization: Recasting the May 18 Kwangju democracy movement], ed. Korean Socio-logical Association. Seoul: Na'nam.

————. 2002. Han'guk siminsahoeŭi sŏngsukkwa siminsahoeundongŭi kwaje [The maturing of Korean civil society and issues for citizens' social movements]. In *Ch'amyŏ'minjujuŭi silhyŏnŭl wihan siminsahoewa siminundong* [Civil society and citizens' movements for the realization of participatory democracy], ed. Civil Society Forum and Chung'ang Daily Civil Society Research Center. Seoul: Arŭke.

Kim Sun-kwŏn. 1991. *Chŏlmŭmŭl pach'inŭn saramdŭl* [Those who dedicate their youth]. Seoul: K'umran.

Kim T'ae-hong. 1998. Kunbongmukyŏngnyŏk injŏngjŏngch'aekŭi hyokwawa kaep'-yŏnbang'an [The effect of the policy to recognize military service as work experience and its reform direction]. Emergency discussion meeting organized by the Korean Women's Associations United, the Korean Women's Associations Council, the Economic Justice Practice United, and the Participation United, and sponsored by the Special Council for Women, September 16, Seoul.

Kim, Taek Il, and Syng Wook Kim. 1966. Mass Use of Intra-uterine Contraceptive Devices in Korea. In *Family Planning and Population Programs: A Review of World Development*. Proceedings of the International Conference on Family Planning Programs, Geneva, 1965. Chicago: University of Chicago Press.

Kim Tŏk-han. 1996. Sinsedaenŭn ŏtŏke kuninŭro mandŭrŏjina [How is the new generation transformed into soldiers?]. *Wŏlganjosŏn* [Monthly chosŏn] 196 (July): 402–15.

Kim, Yong Cheol, and Chung-In Moon. 2000. Globalization and Workers in South Korea. In *Korea's Globalization*, ed. Samuel S. Kim. Cambridge: Cambridge University Press.

Kim Yŏn-myŏng. 1999. Yŏn'gŭm, ŭiryobohŏmŭi pyŏnhwa: Paejeŭi chŏngch'iŭi chongŏn [Pension and health insurance change: The end of the politics of exclusion]. *Wŏlganbogjidonghyang* [Monthly welfare trend] 6 (March): 11–14.

Kim Yŏng-mo. 1997. *Han'guk chungsanch'ŭng yŏn'gu* [A study of the Korean middle class]. Seoul: Chung'ang University Press.

Kim Yong-su, and Lee Yong-ok. 1976. Yŏsŏng nodonjaŭi koyong sangt'ae [Women workers' employment situation]. *Yŏsŏngmunjeyŏn'gu* [Women's issues studies] 5–6 (September): 85–95.

Kiŏpkyŏngyŏng [Enterprise management]. 1967. Urinara yŏsŏng'illyŏkjawŏnkwa kŭ tongt'ae [Our nation's female human resource and its mobility]. *Kiŏpkyŏngyŏng* 68:65–68.

Klein, Uta. 1999. "Our Best Boys": The Gendered Nature of Civil-Military Relations in Israel. *Men and Masculinities* 2 (1): 47–65.

KNA. *See* Korean National Assembly.

Koo, Hagen. 1990. From Farm to Factory: Proletarianization in Korea. *American Sociological Review* 55 (October): 660–81.

————. 1999. The Middle Class in the East Asian Newly Industrialized Societies: Issues, Preliminary Findings and Further Questions. In *East Asian Middle Classes in Comparative Perspective*, ed. Hsin-Huang Michael Hsiao. Taipei: Institute of Ethnology, Academia Sinica.

————. 2001. *Korean Workers: The Culture and Politics of Class Formation*. Ithaca, N.Y.: Cornell University Press.

Korean Confederation of Trade Unions (KCTU). 1999. *Nodongkwa segye, che 1kwŏn* [Labor and the world]. Vol 1. Seoul: KCTU.

————. 2003. *Nodongkwa segye, che 2kwŏn* [Labor and the world]. Vol. 2. Seoul: KCTU.

Korean Federation for Environmental Movement (KFEM) (Hwankyŏngyŏnhap). http://english.kfem.or.kr/aboutus/founding.htm.

Korean Institute for Defense Analysis (KIDA). 1995a. *Hyŏnyŏk ŭimubongmuja puriik bosangbang'an yŏn'gu: Chedaehu sahoesaenghwal chiwŏnŭl chungsimŭro* [A study of the methods to compensate regular military service performers for their disadvantage: A focus on their employment after the completion of military service].

————. 1995b. *Pyŏngyŏgjedo kaesŏnbanghyang yŏn'gu: Kugbangŭimuŭi kaenyŏm chaejŏngnip mit chingjipingyŏ illyŏgŭi hyoyulhwarŭl chungsimŭro* [A study of the conscription system reform directions: Focusing on the reestablishment of the concept of national defense duty and the effective use of surplus manpower for conscription].

Korean National Assembly (KNA). 1981. Chegaejŏng pŏmyulhaesŏl: Pyŏngyŏkpŏpchung kaejŏngbŏmyul [The commentary on enacted or reformed bills: The military service law reform]. *Kukhoebo* [National Assembly paper], vol. 180 (August), 107th National Assembly special session, May 4–19.

————. 1991. Che 13dae kugbangwiwŏnhoe hoeŭirok [The record of the 13th National Defense Committee meeting]. The 152nd National Assembly, 4th session, February 4.

————. 1993. 1993nyŏndo kugjŏnggamsa: Che 14dae kugbangwiwŏnhoe hoeŭirok [1993 parliamentary inspection of the administration: The record of the 14th National Defense Committee meeting], October 8.

————. 1994. 1994nyŏndo kugjŏnggamsa: Che 14dae kugbangwiwŏnhoe hoeŭirok [1994 parliamentary inspection of the administration: The record of the 14th National Defense Committee meeting], October 14.

————. 1998. The Abstract of the 14th Regular Meeting of the Supreme Council for the National Reconstruction. The Record of Legislation and Revision, June–July 1961. DOCID 002558-AA03XX-B101 0001. Seoul.

Korean Public Corporation for Vocational Training. 1985a. *Annual Statistics on National Skill Licenses*. Seoul.

————. 1985b. *Annual Statistics of the State's Technical Certification*.

Korean Rural Community Research Center. 1989. 1980nyŏndae nong'ŏpchŏngch'aegŭi tonghyangkwa sŏnggyŏk [The trend and nature of the agrarian policy in the 1980s]. In *1980nyŏndae han'guk sahoewa chibaegujo* [The ruling structure of Korean society in the 1980s].

Korean Women's Associations United (KWAU). 1998. *Yŏlin hŭimang: Han'guk yŏsŏng-danch'eyŏnhap simnyŏnsa* [Open hope: A ten-year history of the Korean Women's Associations United]. Seoul: Dongdŏk Women's University, Korea Women's Studies Center.

———. http://www.women21.or.kr.

Korean Women's Development Institute (KWDI). 1983. *Yŏsŏng illŏk paljŏnŭi chedojŏk, sahoejŏk chŏhaeyoin chosa* [A study of institutional and social factors preventing women workers' development]. Seoul.

———. 1984. *Saengsanjik nodongyŏsŏngŭi kŭlojogŏne kwanhan yŏn'gu* [A study of the working conditions of women factory workers].

———. 1985a. *Yŏsŏngbaeksŏ* [White paper on women].

———. 1985b. *Yŏsŏng koyongch'ojin pŏbje'e kwahan yŏn'gu* [A study of legislation to promote women's employment].

———. 1990a. *Han'guk kajokchŏngch'aege kwanhan yŏn'gu* [A study of family policy in Korea], research report 200-6.

———. 1990b. *Uri nongch'onkwa yŏsŏng* [Our rural communities and women], educational material 300-16.

———. 1991. *Yŏsŏngbaeksŏ* [White paper on women].

———. 1995. *Statistical Yearbook on Women.*

———. 1997. *Statistical Yearbook on Women.*

———. 1999. *Statistical Yearbook on Women.*

———. 2001. *Statistical Yearbook on Women.*

Korean Women Voters' League. 1980. *Yŏsŏng nodongja silt'ae chosa pogosŏ: Kuro, Kumi kongdaŭl chungsimŭro* [A report of the working conditions of women workers: Kuro and Kumi industrial estates]. Seoul.

Korean Women Workers Associations Council. 1997. *Yŏsŏngnodongjahoe simnyŏnsa: Dŭlkoch'iyŏ! bulkoch'iyŏ kŭdae irŭmŭn yŏsŏngnodongja* [A ten-year history of the Women Workers Associations Council: Wild flowers! Fire flowers, your name is women workers].

———. 1998. Saengsanjik yŏsŏngnodongjaundong [Women production workers' movement]. In *Yŏlin hŭimang: Han'guk yŏsŏngdanch'eyŏnhap simnyŏnsa* [Open hope: A ten-year history of the Korean Women's Associations United], ed. Han'gukyŏsŏngdanch'eyŏnhap. Seoul: Dongdŏk Women's University, Korea Women's Studies Center.

———. 1999. *1999nyŏn p'yŏngdŭngŭijŏnhwa sangdamsaryejip* [The 1999 collection of equality hot line counseling cases].

———. 2003a. *Yŏsŏng nodongundongga yangsŏngkyoyuk* [Education for cultivating women labor activists]. Seoul.

———. 2003b. *2002nyŏn p'yŏngdŭngŭijŏnhwa sangdamsaryejip* [The 2002 collection of equality hot line counseling cases].

Kwack, Sung Young. 1986. The Economic Development of the Republic of Korea, 1965–1981. In *Models of Development: A Comparative Study of Economic Growth in South Korea and Taiwan*, ed. Lawrence J. Lau. San Francisco: Institute for Contemporary Studies.

KWAU. *See* Korean Women's Associations United.

KWDI. *See* Korean Women's Development Institute.

Kwŏn Hyŏk-pŏm. 2000. Naemomsogŭi pankongjuŭi hoerowa kwŏllyŏk [Anticommunist circuit and power in my body]. In *Urianŭi p'asijŭm* [Fascism inside us], ed. Chi-hyŏn Im et al. Seoul: Samin.

Kwon, Insook. 2000. Militarism in My Heart: Militarization of Women's Consciousness and Culture in South Korea. Ph.D. diss., Clark University.

Kwŏn Sŏn-jin. 1997. *P'arasyutŭ: Kundaeiyagi, yŏjaiyagi, sesangiyagi* [Parachute: Stories of the military, women, and the world]. Seoul: Changmunsan.

KWWAC. *See* Korean Women Workers Associations Council.

Labor Human Rights Center. 1992. *1991 Nodonginkwŏn pogosŏ* [1991 labor human rights report], vol. 2. Seoul: Yŏksabip'yŏngsa.

Leblanc, Robin. 1998. *Bicycle Citizens: The Political World of the Japanese Housewife*. Berkeley and Los Angeles: University of California Press.

Lee, Ching Kwan. 1998. *Gender and the South China Miracle: Two Worlds of Factory Women*. Berkeley: University of California Press.

Lee, Chulwoo. 1999. Modernity, Legality, and Power in Korea under Japanese Rule. In *Colonial Modernity in Korea*, ed. Gi-Wook Shin and Michael Robinson. Cambridge: Harvard University Press.

Lee, June J. H. 2001. Discourses of Illness, Meanings of Modernity: A Gendered Construction of *Sŏnginbyŏng*. In *Under Construction: The Gendering of Modernity, Class, and Consumption in the Republic of Korea*, ed. Laurel Kendall. Honolulu: University of Hawaii Press.

Lee, Ki-baik. 1984. *A New History of Korea*. Trans. Edward Wagner, with Edward Schultz. Cambridge: Harvard University Press.

Lie, John. 1998. *Han Unbound: The Political Economy of Korea*. Stanford: Stanford University Press.

Lister, Ruth. 1990. Women, Economic Dependency and Citizenship. *Journal of Social Policy* 19 (4): 445–67.

———. 1997. *Citizenship: Feminist Perspectives*. New York: New York University Press.

Liu, Lydia H. 1993. Translingual Practice: The Discourse of Individualism between China and the West. *Positions* 1 (1): 160–93.

Lown, Judy. 1990. *Women and Industrialization: Gender at Work in Nineteenth-Century England*. Minneapolis: University of Minnesota Press.

Lucassen, Jan, and Erik Jan Zürcher. 1999. Conscription and Resistance: The Historical Context. Introduction to *Arming the State: Military Conscription in the Middle East and Central Asia, 1775–1925*, ed. Erik J. Zürcher. New York: I. B. Tauris.

Lyotard, Jean-François. 1984. *The Postmodern Condition: A Report on Knowledge*. Minneapolis: University of Minnesota Press.

Mann, Michael. 1984/1992. Capitalism and Militarism. In *States, War and Capitalism: Studies in Political Sociology*. Oxford: Blackwell.

Marchand, Marianne J., and Jane Parpart, eds. 1995. *Feminism/Postmodernism/Development*. New York: Routledge.

Marshall, T. H. 1950. *Citizenship and Social Class*. Cambridge: Cambridge University Press.

MHSA. *See* Ministry of Health and Social Affairs.

Ministry of Health and Social Affairs (MHSA). 1972. *Kajŏngŭirye haesŏl* [Family ritual commentaries].

————. 1975a. *Punyŏgyosil* [Women's class].

————. 1975b. *Segye yŏsŏngŭi haewa han'gukyŏsŏng* [The world women's year and Korean women].

————. 1976. *Kajŏngŭirye haesŏl* [Family ritual commentaries].

————. 1980. *Saemaŭlbunyŏhoe kyojae* [Textbook for the new village women's association].

————. 1981a. *Saemaŭlbunyŏhoe chidosuch'ŏp* [Pocketbook for guiding the new village women's association].

————. 1981b. *Yŏsŏngkwa saemaŭlundong* [Women and the new village movement].

————. 1982a. *UN yŏsŏng 10nyŏn hubangi saŏp hyŏnhwang* [The current state of the second half of the UN Women's Decade project].

————. 1982b. *Punyŏbokjisisŏrŭi hyŏnhwang* [The current state of women's welfare facilities].

————. 1982c. *Kŏnjŏnhan kajŏngŭirye* [Wholesome family rituals].

————. 1983. *Haengbokhan kajŏngsaenghwal* [Happy family life].

————. 1984. *Haengbokhan kajŏngsaenghwal* [Happy family life].

————. 1985. *Kŏnjŏnhan kajŏngŭirye* [Wholesome family rituals].

————. 1987a. *Punyŏhaengjŏng 40nyŏnsa* [Forty-year history of the administration of women].

————. 1987b. *Che 6ch'a kyŏngjesahoebaljŏn 5gaenyŏn kyehoek: Pogŏnsahoebumun kyehoek, 1987-1991* [The sixth five-year economic and social development plan: Health and social sectors, 1987-1991].

————. 1987c. *Chihyeroun kajoksaenghwal* [Wise family life].

————. 1989a. *Punyŏbogjisaŏp chich'im* [Guidelines for women's welfare projects].

————. 1989b. *Kajokpogŏnsaŏp ch'amgojaryo* [Reference resource for the family health project].

————. 1992. *Sido yŏsŏnghoekwan choryejip* [The collection of municipal and provincial ordinances of women's centers]. Seoul.

Ministry of Labor (ML). 1983. *Yŏsŏngkwa chigŏp* [Women and occupation].

————. 1984. *Yŏsŏngkwa koyong* [Women and employment].

————. 1989. *Nodongpaeksŏ* [White paper on labor].

————. 1992a. *Nodongpaeksŏ* [White paper on labor].

———. 1992b. *Nodongt'onggyeyŏn'gam* [Labor statistics yearbook].

———. 1997. *Nodongpaeksŏ* [White paper on labor].

———. 1999. *Nodongt'onggyeyŏn'gam* [Labor statistics yearbook]. Seoul.

Ministry of National Defense (MND). 1988. *Kukbangpaeksŏ* [White paper on national defense].

———. 1989. *Kukbangpaeksŏ* [White paper on national defense].

———. 1990. *Kukbangpaeksŏ* [White paper on national defense].

———. 1991. *Kukbangpaeksŏ* [White paper on national defense].

———. 1997. *Kukbangpaeksŏ* [White paper on national defense].

———. 1998. *Kukbangpaeksŏ* [White paper on national defense]. Seoul.

Minuhoe (PFS: People's Friends Society). 1996. *96nyŏn koyongp'yŏngdŭngch'ujinbonbu hwaldong mit kiŏpp'yŏngga pokosŏ* [1996 report on activities of the equal employment promotion headquarters and assessment of corporations]. Seoul: Han'gukyŏsŏngminuhoe.

———. 1997. *Han'gukyŏsŏngminuhoe 10nyŏnsa* [A ten-year history of the Korean women people's friends association]. Seoul: Han'gukyŏsŏngminuhoe.

———. 2000. *Sŏnghŭirong: Tangsinŭi chikchangŭn anjŏnhamnigga?* [Sexual harassment: Is your workplace safe?]. Seoul: 21 segibuks.

ML. *See* Ministry of Labor.

MND. *See* Ministry of National Defense.

Mohanty, Chandra T. 1987. Under Western Eyes: Feminist Scholarship and Colonial Discourses. *boundary 2* (13):333–58.

Moon, Chung-In. 1989. Technological Dependence, Supplier Control and Strategies for Recepient Autonomy. In *The Dilemma of Third World Defense Industries: Supplier Control or Recipient Autonomy?* ed. Kwang-Il Baek, Ronald D. McLaurin, and Chung-In Moon. Pacific and World Studies Series, no. 3. Boulder: Westview Press.

———. 1998. South Korea: Recasting Security Paradigms. In *Asian Security Practice: Material and Ideational Influences*, ed. Muthiah Alagappa. Stanford: Stanford University Press.

Moon, Seungsook. 1997. Begetting the Nation: The Androcentric Discourse of National History and Tradition in South Korea. In *Dangerous Women: Gender and Korean Nationalism*, ed. Elaine H. Kim and Chungmoo Choi. New York: Routledge.

———. 1998. Gender, Militarization, and Universal Male Conscription in South Korea. In *The Women and War Reader*, ed. Lois Lorentzen and Jennifer Turpin. New York: New York University Press.

———. 2000. Overcome by Globalization: The Rise of a Women's Policy in South Korea. In *Korea's Globalization*, ed. Samuel S. Kim. Cambridge: Cambridge University Press.

———. 2001. The Production and Subversion of Hegemonic Masculinity: Reconfiguring Gender Hierarchy in Contemporary South Korea. In *Under Construction:*

The Gendering of Modernity, Class, and Consumption in the Republic of Korea, ed. Laurel Kendall. Honolulu: University of Hawaii Press.

———. 2002a. Imagining a Nation through Differences: Reading the Controversy Concerning the Military Service Extra Points System in South Korea. *Review of Korean Studies* 5 (2): 73–109.

———. 2002b. Beyond Equality versus Difference: Professional Women Soldiers in the South Korean Army. *Social Politics: International Studies in Gender, State, and Society* 9 (2): 212–47.

———. 2002c. Carving Out Space: Civil Society and the Women's Movement in South Korea. *Journal of Asian Studies* 61 (2): 473–500.

———. 2003. Redrafting Democratization through Women's Representation and Participation in the Republic of Korea. In *Korea's Democratization*, ed. Samuel S. Kim. Cambridge: Cambridge University Press.

Morishima, Michio. 1982. *Why Has Japan "Succeeded"?: Western Technology and the Japanese Ethos*. New York: Cambridge University Press.

Mun Suk-jae, et al. 2000. *Han'guk chungsanch'ŭngŭi saenghwalmunhwa* [Living culture of the Korean middle class]. Asan Foundation Research Monograph Series, no. 68. Seoul: Chimmundang.

Nair, Elizabeth. 1994. Nation-Building through Conscript Service in Singapore. In *The Military in the Service of Society and Democracy: The Challenge of the Dual-Role Military*, ed. Daniella Ashkenazy. Contribution to Military Studies series, no. 153. Westport, Conn.: Greenwood Press.

Nam, Jeong-Lim. 1996. Labor Control of the State and Women's Resistance in the Export Sector of South Korea. *Social Problems* 43 (3): 327–38.

Narayan, Uma. 1997. *Dislocating Cultures: Identities, Traditions, and Third-World Feminism*. New York: Routledge.

National Defense University. 1989. *Kungmin anboŭisik chosa* [A national survey of security perception].

———. 1996. *Pŏmkungmin anboŭisik chosabunsŏk* [An analysis of a national survey of security perception]. Seoul.

Nelson, Laura C. 2000. *Measured Excess: Status, Gender, and Consumer Nationalism in South Korea*. New York: Columbia University Press.

Nolan, Janne E. 1986. *Military Industry in Taiwan and South Korea*. New York: St. Martin's Press.

Office of Military Manpower (OMM). 1986. *Pyŏngmuhaengjŏngsa, ha* [A history of military service administration]. Vol. 2. Seoul.

Ogasawara, Yuko. 1998. *Office Ladies and Salaried Men: Power, Gender, and Work in Japanese Companies*. Berkeley: University of California Press.

Ogle, George. 1990. *South Korea: Dissent within the Economic Miracle*. Atlantic Highlands, N.J.: Zed Books.

O-jang Mi-kyŏng. 2003. *Yŏsŏngnodongundongkwa simingwŏnŭi chŏngch'i* [The women's labor movement and the politics of citizenship]. Seoul: Arŭke.

Olsen, Edward. 1986. The Societal Role of the ROK Armed Forces. In *The Armed Forces in Contemporary Asian Societies*, ed. Edward Olsen and Stephen Jurika. Boulder, Colo.: Westview Press.

Ŏm Kyu-suk. 1999. Yŏsŏngdŭri sarajigo itta [Women are disappearing]. In *Yŏsŏngŭi ilch'atki sesangbakkugi* [Women's search for work and changing the world]. Seoul: Ttohanaŭi munhwa (Alternative Culture).

OMM. *See* Office of Military Manpower.

Paek, Chong-chŏn. 1985. Military Education System and National Development: The Case of the Republic of Korea (ROK) Army. *Korea Observer* 14 (winter): 400–431.

Pak Chae-ch'ang. 2002. Kukkayuhyŏngkwa NGOŭi chŏngch'aekch'amyŏ: P'yŏnggaronjŏk chŏbgŭn [Typology of the state and the NGOs' participation in policy making: An evaluative approach]. In *Ch'amyŏminjujuŭi silhyŏnŭl wihan simin sahoewa siminundong* [Civil society and citizens' movements for participatory democracy], ed. Siminsahoeporŏm (Civil Society Forum). Seoul: Arŭke.

Pak Dong-su. 1990. Chŏnp'yŏng ihu, ch'oidaeŭi minjunojo kyŏljipch'e, chŏnnohyŏp [After the national labor union, the largest alliance of democratic labor unions, the national council of labor unions]. *Hamggesanŭn sesang* [The world of living together] 2 (January): 69–78.

Pak Ki-yŏl. 1989. *Chŏlmŭn sakwanhubosaengŭi sŭlp'ŭn yŏn'ga* [A young cadet's sad elegy]. Seoul: Miraemunhwasa.

Pak Kyŏng-nam. 1990. T'anabŭl titko irŏsŏnŭn kangch'ŏldongjidŭl: Mach'angnoryŏnŭl tanyŏwasŏ [Steely comrades standing up to overcome oppression: Visiting the Masan-Changwon labor union federation]. *Nodongja munhwa t'ongsin* [Workers culture correspondence] 1 (March): 148–54.

Pak Myŏng-sun. 1997. Haggyoesŏŭi namsŏngsahoehwa [Men's socialization in schooling]. In *Namsŏngkwa han'guksahoe* [Men and Korean society], ed. Yŏsŏnghan'guksahoeyŏn'guhoe (Women's Korean Society Studies Association). Seoul: Sahoemunhwayŏn'guso.

Pak No-ja. 2003. *Narŭl paebanhan yŏksa* [A history that betrayed me]. Seoul: Inmulkwasasangsa.

Pak Sang-wŏn. 1995. Chingbyŏnggŏmsa jedoŭi pyŏnch'ŏn [The change in the conscription test system]. *Pyŏngmu* 31 (fall): 16–19.

Pak Suk-ja. 1997. Tŭrama sogŭi namsŏngmunhwa [Masculine culture in television sitcoms]. In *Namsŏngkwa han'guksahoe* [Men and Korean society], ed. Yŏsŏnghan'guksahoeyŏn'guhoe (Women's Korean Society Studies Association). Seoul: Sahoemunhwayŏn'guso.

———. 2000. Yŏsŏngkwa kyŏngjehwaldong [Women and economic activities]. In *Saerossŭnŭn yŏsŏngkwa han'guksahoe* [Rewriting women and Korean society], ed. Yŏsŏnghan'guksahoeyŏn'guhoe (Women's Korean Society Studies Association). Seoul: Sahoemunhwayŏn'guso.

Palais, James. 1996. *Confucian Statecraft and Korean Institutions: Yu Hyongwon and the Late Chŏson Dynasty*. Seattle: University of Washington Press.

Peattie, Mark R. 1984a. Introduction to *The Japanese Colonial Empire, 1895–1945.* Princeton, N.J.: Princeton University Press.

———. 1984b. Japanese Attitudes toward Colonialism, 1895–1945. In *The Japanese Colonial Empire, 1895–1945.* Princeton, N.J.: Princeton University Press.

People's Solidarity for Participatory Democracy (PSPD) (Ch'amyŏyŏndae). http:// peoplepower21.org.

Peterson, V. Spike. 1996. The Politics of Identification in the Context of Globalization. *Women's Studies International Forum* 19 (1–2): 5–15.

Planned Parenthood Federation of Korea (PPFK). 1975. *Kahyŏp 10nyŏnsa* [A ten-year history of the PPFK].

———. 1983. *Kahyŏp 20nyŏnsa* [A twenty-year history of the PPFK]. Seoul: PPFK.

Porter, Bruce D. 1994. *War and the Rise of the State: The Military Foundations of Modern Politics.* New York: Free Press.

PPFK. *See* Planned Parenthood Federation of Korea.

Presidential Commission on Women's Affairs. 1999. *Yŏsŏngpaeksŏ* [White paper on women]. Seoul.

Pringle, Rosemary. 2001. *Sex and Medicine: Gender, Power and Authority in the Medical Profession.* Cambridge: Cambridge University Press.

Pyle, Jean. 1990. *The State and Women in the Economy: Lessons from Sex Discrimination in the Republic of Ireland.* Albany, N.Y.: SUNY Press.

Pyŏn Hwa-sun. 1989. Han'guk kajokchŏngch'aege kwanhan chonghapjŏk chŏpkŭn [A comprehensive approach to Korean family policy]. *Yŏsŏngyŏn'gu* 22:140–59.

———. 1991. Kukka chŏngch'aekkwa yŏsŏng: Ch'ulsan chŏngch'aekkwa sŏngbi pulkyunhyŏng hyŏnsangŭl chungsimŭro [The state's policy and women: Birth control policy and sex ratio imbalance]. *Yŏsŏngyŏn'gu* [Women's studies] 29:109–33.

Pyŏngmu. 1995. Pyŏngmuch'ŏng ch'angsŏl 25nyŏn paljach'ui [A twenty-five-year history of the office of military manpower]. *Pyŏngmu* 31 (fall): 16–33.

———. 1998a. Pyŏngyŏkŭimu, kungmindŭrŭn irŏkke saenggakhago itda (I) [Military service, the Korean people think this way]. *Pyŏngmu* 38:23–29.

———. 1998b. Pyŏngyŏkŭimu, kungmindŭrŭn irŏkke saenggakhago itda (II) [Military service, the Korean people think this way]. *Pyŏngmu* 39:30–35.

P'yŏngdŭng. 1998. T'ŭkchip: IMF sidaeŭi yŏsŏngnodongja [Special report: Women workers in the IMF era]. *P'yŏngdŭng* 9 (January–February): 20–29.

Research Center for Population and Health. 1986. *Yebigun kajokkyehoek silt'ae chosa bogo* [A report on the family planning practices among reserve army soldiers]. Seoul.

Rhee, Chong-ch'an. 1994. *The State and Industry in South Korea: The Limits of the Authoritarian State.* New York: Routledge.

Riska, Elianne. 2001. Towards Gender Balance: But Will Women Physicians Have an Impact on Medicine? *Social Science and Medicine* 52: 179–87.

Rofel, Lisa. 1999. *Other Modernities: Gendered Yearnings in China after Socialism.* Berkeley: University of California Press.

Rostow, Walt Whitman. 1960. *The Stages of Economic Growth: A Non-Communist Manifesto.* Cambridge: Cambridge University Press.

Ryu Yŏn-kwŏn. 1989. Pyŏngyŏkp'ungt'o, ŏttŏke pyŏnch'ŏndoeŏ wanna? [Social perception of military service, how has it changed?]. *Pyŏngmu* 12:18–22.

Said, Edward. 1978. *Orientalism.* New York: Pantheon Books.

Sassen, Saskia. 1998. *Globalization and Its Discontents: Essays on the New Mobility of People and Money.* New York: New Press.

Sebesta, Lorenza. 1994. Women and the Legitimation of the Use of Force: The Case of Female Military Service. In *Women Soldiers: Images and Realities,* ed. Elisabetta Addis et al. New York: St. Martin's Press.

Shim Yŏng-hŭi. 1988. Nodongsijang kujoŭi pyŏnhwawa yŏsŏngnodongŭi silt'ae: Chunghwahak kongŏpbumunŭl chungsimŭro [The transformation of the labor market structure and the reality of women's labor: A focus on heavy and chemical industries]. *Han'gukyŏsŏnghak* [Korean women's studies] 4:101–54.

Shin, Doh C. 1999. *Mass Politics and Culture in Democratizing Korea.* New York: Cambridge University Press.

Shin, Gi-Wook, and Do-Hyun Han. 1999. Colonial Corporatism: The Rural Revitalization Campaign, 1932–1940. In *Colonial Modernity in Korea,* ed. Gi-Wook Shin and Michael Robinson. Cambridge: Harvard University Press.

Shin, Gi-Wook, and Kyung Moon Hwang, eds. 2003. *Contentious Kwangju: The May 18 Uprising in Korea's Past and Present.* Oxford: Rowman and Littlefield.

Shin, Gi-Wook, and Michael Robinson, eds. 1999. *Colonial Modernity in Korea.* Cambridge: Harvard University Press.

Sievers, Sharon L. 1983. *Flowers in Salt: The Beginnings of Feminist Consciousness in Modern Japan.* Stanford: Stanford University Press.

Sin Illyŏng. 1988. *Yŏsŏng nodong pŏp* [Women, labor, and law]. Revised and expanded ed. Seoul: P'ulbit.

Sin Yong-su. 1991. *Yŏsŏng nodongsijangŭi chungjanggi chŏnmangkwa kwaje* [A mid- and long-term prospect on the women's labor market and its problems]. Seoul: Han'guk nodong yŏn'guwŏn (Korean Labor Studies Center).

Sin Yŏng-suk. 1995. Yŏsŏngundongŭi yŏksajŏk koch'al [A historical approach to the women's movement]. In *Yŏsŏngkwa han'guksahoe* [Women and Korean society], ed. Yŏsŏnghan'guksahoeyŏn'guhoe (Women's Korean Society Studies Association). Seoul: Sahoemunhwayŏn'guso.

———. 2000. Yŏsŏngundong [Women's movement]. In *Saerossŭnŭn yŏsŏngkwa han'guksahoe* [Rewriting women and Korean society], ed. Yŏsŏnghan'guksahoeyŏn'guhoe. Seoul: Sahoemunhwayŏn'guso.

Sŏ Chin-t'ae. 1998. Tasibonŭn migugŭi taehan kunsajŏngch'aek [Rethinking the U.S. military policy toward South Korea]. *Pangwisekye* [Defense world] 16 (February): 12–35.

Sŏ Hyo-il. 1995. *Kungaehyŏk irŏke haeyahanda, sang and ha* [Military reform should be done this way]. 2 vols. Seoul: Paek'am.

Solinger, Dorothy J. 1999. *Contesting Citizenship in Urban China: Peasant Migrants, the State, and the Logic of the Market*. Berkeley: University of California Press.

Somers, Margaret R. 1993. Citizenship and the Place of the Public Sphere: Law, Community, and Political Culture in the Transition to Democracy. *American Sociological Review* 58 (5): 587–620.

Song, Byung-nak. 1990. *The Rise of the Korean Economy*. Oxford: Oxford University Press.

Song Chae-bok. 1994. Kim Yong Samjŏngbuŭi kaehyŏkchŏngch'iwa nodongjŏngch'aeŭi kaehyŏkpanghyang [Politics of reform and the direction of labor policy reform in Kim Young Sam's government]. *Koryŏdae'nodongmunje'nonjip* [Korea University labor issues studies paper collection] 11 (September): 177–207.

Song Yu-jae. 1984. Telebijŏn tŭramŏe panyŏngdoen han'gungyŏsŏngŭi yŏkal mit imiji yŏn'gu [The role and image of women in Korean television drama programs]. *Yŏsŏnghaknonjip* [Women's studies papers collection] 1:56–91.

———. 1985. Yŏsŏngjapjie nat'anan han'gungyŏsŏngsang punsŏkyŏn'gu [Images of women in Korean women's magazines]. *Chujeyŏn'gu* [Thematic studies] 7:3–67.

Stiehm, Judith. 1989. *Arms and the Enlisted Woman*. Philadelphia: Temple University Press.

Sturdevant, Saundra P., and Brenda Stoltzfus. 1992. *Let the Good Times Roll: Prostitution and the U.S. Military in Asia*. New York: New Press.

Sung, Kyu-taik. 1978. Family Planning Education as an Integral Part of Day Care Services in Korea. *Studies in Family Planning* 9 (April): 71–74.

Takeshita, John Y. 1966. Lessons Learned in Taiwan and Korea. In *Family Planning and Population Programs: A Review of World Developments*. Proceedings of the International Conference on Family Planning Programs, Geneva, 1965. Chicago: University of Chicago Press.

Tangdaebip'yŏ ng [Contemporary critique]. 1999. Vol. 9 (winter) and Vol. 8 (fall). Seoul: Samin.

Theweleit, Klaus. 1987. *Male Fantasies*. Vol. 1, *Women Floods Bodies History*. Trans. Stephen Conway. Minneapolis: University of Minnesota Press.

Tilly, Charles. 1992. *Coercion, Capital and European States*. Oxford: Blackwell.

Tilly, Louise, and Joan W. Scott. 1978. *Women, Work, and Family*. New York: Holt, Rinehart and Winston.

Tolbege Editorial Division. 1983. *Wuridŭl kajingŏt pirok chŏgŏdo: Kŭllojadŭrŭi kŭlmoŭm* [Although we have only a little: The collection of workers' writings]. Seoul: Tolbege.

Tu, Wei-ming, ed. 1996. *Confucian Traditions in East Asian Modernity: Moral Education and Economic Culture in Japan and the Four Mini-Dragons*. Cambridge: Harvard Press.

Ueno, Chizuko. 2000. *Nationalism and Gender*. Korean translation. Seoul: Pakjongch'ŏl Publishers.

UNESCO. 1985. *Science Policy and Organization of Research in the Republic of Korea.* Paris.

Wade, Robert. 1990. *Governing the Market: Economic Theory and the Role of the Government in East Asian Industrialization.* Princeton: Princeton University Press.

Walby, Sylvia. 1994. Is Citizenship Gendered? *Sociology* 28 (2): 379–95.

Weiner, Myron, Samuel P. Huntington, and Gabriel Abraham Almond. 1994. *Understanding Political Development: An Analytic Study.* Prospect Heights, Ill.: Waveland Press.

Wells, Kenneth. 1995. The Cultural Construction of Korean History. In *South Korea's Minjung Movement: The Culture and Politics of Dissidence*, ed. Kenneth Wells. Honolulu: University of Hawaii Press.

Williams, Raymond. 1976. *Keywords: A Vocabulary of Culture and Society.* New York: Oxford University Press.

Workers Culture Correspondence [*Nodongja munhwa t'ongsin*] (Seoul), spring 1990.

———. July 1990.

World of Living Together [*Hamggesanŭn sesang*]. 1989. Nojoŏmnŭn Samsung'wang-guk, nojogyŏlsŏng panghaegongjagŭi silsang [The Samsung Kingdom without labor unions, the reality of its machination to obstruct the establishment of labor unions]. Vol. 1 (August): 178–86.

Yang Hŭi-wŏn. 1988. *Kundaemunhwaŭi ppuri: Kundaeŭi chŏnt'ongkwa kwansŭbŭl chungsimŭro* [The roots of military culture: Focusing on the military tradition and custom]. Seoul: Ŭljisŏjŏk.

Yang, Jae Mo. 1966. Planning the Program. In *Family Planning and Population Programs: A Review of World Developments.* Proceedings of the International Conference on Family Planning Programs, Geneva, 1965. Chicago: University of Chicago Press.

Yi Dal-sŏk, et al. 1985. *Nodongjaga toeŏ* [Becoming a worker]. Seoul: Hyŏngsŏngsa.

Yi Hyo-jae. 1996. *Han'gugŭi yŏsŏngundong: Ŏjewa onŭl* [Women's movement in Korea: Yesterday and today]. Seoul: Chŏng'usa.

———. 1997. Han'guksahoeŭi namsŏng ideologi [Masculine ideology in Korean society]. In *Namsŏngkwa han'guksahoe* [Men and Korean society], ed. Yŏsŏng-han'guksahoeyŏn'guhoe (Women's Korean Society Studies Association). Seoul: Sahoemunhwayŏn'guwŏn.

Yi Hyo-sŏng. 2003. "Yŏjŏnhan makkangkwŏllyŏk" ŏllonkwŏllŏk [Still mighty power the press power]. In *Kim Dae-jung chŏngbu 5nyŏn p'yŏnggawa No Mu-hyŏn chŏngbu kaehyŏkkwaje* [The assessment of the five years during Kim Dae Jung's government and the reform issues for Roh Moo Hyon's government], ed. Kyŏng-hyang Newspaper and People's Solidarity for Participatory Democracy (PSPD). Seoul: Han'ul.

Yi Jin-p'yŏng. 1990. Kongjangesŏ chiyŏkŭro, chiyŏkesŏ chŏngukŭro: Hyundai chung-kongŏp p'aŏpt'ujaeng ch'uijaebogosŏ [From the factory to the region, from the region to the entire nation: A report on Hyundai heavy industry strike]. *No-dongja'munhwa't'ongsin* 2 (July): 240–56.

Yi Mi-Kyŏng. 1989. Kukkaŭi ch'ulsan chŏngch'aek [A feminist analysis of the state's birth control policy]. *Yŏsŏnghaknonjip* [Women's studies papers collection] 6:49–76.

———. 1998. Yŏsŏng undongkwa minjuhwaundong: yŏyŏn simnyŏnsa [Women's movement and democratization movement: A ten-year history of the KWAU]. In *Yŏlin hŭimang: Han'guk yŏsŏngdanch'eyŏnhap simnyŏnsa* [Open hope: A ten-year history of the Korean Women's Associations United]. Seoul: Dongdŏk Women's University, Korean Women's Studies Center.

Yi Si-baek. 1990. 9onyŏndae ingujŏngch'aegŭi panghyangkwa t'adangsŏng [The direction and validity of the population policy in the 1990s]. In *Ingu'munje* [Population problems], ed. Yi Si-baek, Cho Nam-hun, and Yi Kyu-sik. Seoul: Kajok-kyehoekyŏn'guwŏn.

Yi Sŏng-ch'an. 1998. *Nŏhŭiga kundaerŭl anŭnya, sang; ha* [Do you know the military?]. 2 vols. Seoul: Tŭllyŏk.

Yi Suk-jong. 1995. Han'guginŭi anbokwan: 1995 Sejong kungminŭisik chosarŭl Chungsimŭro [Security perception among the Koreans: 1995 national survey by the Sejong Research Institute]. *Kuggajŏllyak* [State strategy] 1–2 (September): 53–80.

Yi, Sŭng-hŭi. 1991. Han'guk hyŏndae yŏsŏngundongsa [A history of the women's movement in contemporary Korea]. In *Yŏsŏnghakkang'ŭi* [Women's studies lectures], ed. Han'gukyŏsŏngyŏn'guhoe (Korean Women's Studies Association). Seoul: Tongnyŏk.

Yi T'ae-ho, ed. 1986a. *Nodonghyŏnjangŭi chinsil* [Truth of the labor place]. Seoul: Kŭmmundang.

———, ed. 1986b. *Choigŭn nodongundong kirok* [A record of recent labor movement]. Seoul: Ch'ŏngsa.

Yi T'ae-ho. 1996. Saenggye gollanja pyŏngyŏk kammyŏnjedoŭi pyŏnch'ŏn kwajŏng [A process of change in the system of reducing military service for the indigent]. *Pyŏngmu* 32 (winter): 63–67.

Yi Tal-hyŏk, et al. 1985. *Nodongjaga toe'ŏ* [Becoming workers]. Seoul: Hyŏngsŏngsa.

Yi Tong-hŭi. 1982. *Han'guk'kunsajedoron* [A study of Korean military institution]. Seoul: Iljogak.

Yi Uk-han. 1998. Kunkyŏngyŏk samjunghyet'aek, muŏsi munjeinga? [Triple benefits of military service, what is the problem?] *Yŏsŏngt'ŭkpyŏlwiwŏnhoesosik* [Presidential commission on women's affairs news] (Seoul) 2 (fall): 10–13.

Yi Yŏ-song. 1996. Pangwuisojip chedoŭi pyŏnch'ŏn [Change in the defense corps system]. *Pyŏngmu* 32 (winter): 77–79.

Yoon, Soon Young. 1977. The Role of Korean Women in National Development. In *Virtues in Conflict: Tradition and the Korean Woman Today*, ed. Sandra Mattielle. Seoul: Royal Asiatic Society.

Yŏsŏng. 1994. Chedae'gunine taehan kajŏmbuyŏjedo p'yejie kwanhan kak puch'ŏwa wiwŏnhoeŭi ipjang [Positions of each government ministry and council concerning the elimination of the extra-points system applied to veterans]. *Yŏsŏng*, October, 15–21.

———. 1996. T'ŭkchip 1: Yi Yang-ho kukbangbujangkwan ch'och'ŏng yŏsŏngjŏngch'aek kandamhoe [Special report 1: The Secretary of Defense, Yi Yang-ho, invited to discuss women's policy]. *Yŏsŏng*, November, 6–14.

Young, Iris. 1990. *Justice and the Politics of Difference*. Princeton: Princeton University Press.

Young, Louise. 1998. *Japan's Total Empire: Manchuria and the Culture of Wartime Imperialism*. Berkeley: University of California Press.

Yu, Chang-hee. 1993. Reform with No Caprice: Economic Performance of the Roh Administration. In *Korea under Roh Tae-Woo: Democratisation, Northern Policy, and Inter-Korea Relations*, ed. James Cotton. St. Leonards, Australia: Allen and Unwin.

Yu Mun-mu. 1999. Kungminŭi chŏngbu sahoejŏngch'aeŭi inyŏmjŏk kich'o'e taehan yŏn'gu: Sinjayujuŭi sajoe taehan pip'anjŏk taean [A study of the ideological foundation of the social policy of the people's government: A critical alternative to the trend of neoliberalism]. *Konggongjŏngch'aekyŏn'gu* [Public policy studies] 5 (February): 381–402.

Yu P'al-mu, and Kim Ho-gi, eds. 1995. *Siminsahoewa siminundong* [Civil society and citizens' movements]. Seoul: Han'ul.

Yu P'al-mu, and Kim Tong-ch'un. 1991. Pip'anŭisigŭi hyŏngsŏngkwa sahoebyŏnhyŏk undong [The formation of critical consciousness and radical social movements]. In *Han'guksahoewa chibaeideologi: Chisiksahoehakjŏk ihae* [Korean Society and ruling ideologies: A sociology of knowledge approach], ed. Han'guksanŏpsahoe yŏn'guhoe (Korean Industrial Society Research Association). Seoul: Nokdu.

Yu Yŏng-ju. 1982. Han'guk yŏsŏngŭi ch'uiŏpkujoe kwanhan yŏn'gu [A study of the employment structure among Korean women]. *Aseayŏsŏngyŏn'gu* 21: 151–77.

Yuval-Davis, Nira. 1997. *Gender and Nation*. Thousand Oaks, Calif.: Sage.

Yuval-Davis, Nira, and Flora Anthias, eds. 1989. *Women-Nation-State*. London: Macmillan.

Zeelend, Steven. 1996. *The Masculine Marine: Homoeroticism in the U.S. Marine Corps*. New York: Haworth Press.

Zürcher, Erik J., ed. 1999. *Arming the State: Military Conscription in the Middle East and Central Asia, 1775–1925*. New York: I. B. Taurus.